# Varieties of
# Residential Experience

Institutions are like fortresses. They must be well designed *and* properly manned.

Karl Popper

# Varieties of Residential Experience

Edited by
Jack Tizard, Ian Sinclair an    V. G. Clarke

Routledge & Kegan Paul
London and Boston

*First published in 1975*
*by Routledge & Kegan Paul Ltd*
*Broadway House, 68–74 Carter Lane,*
*London EC4V 5EL and*
*9 Park Street,*
*Boston, Mass. 02108, USA*
*Set in Monotype Times New Roman*
*and printed in Great Britain by*
*Unwin Brothers Limited,*
*The Gresham Press,*
*Old Woking, Surrey*
*A member of the Staples Printing Group*
*ISBN 0 7100 8165 0*

# Contents

**Figures**

# Preface

This book had its origins in a series of seminars held in the Department of Child Development of the University of London Institute of Education in 1971 and 1972. A good deal of the research going on in the Department at that time was concerned with factors associated with differences in the quality of care provided for children in residential establishments of different sorts—children's homes, mental subnormality units and residential nurseries. A national survey of all residential units for children was also being prepared; and we were in close touch with Professor Michael Rutter and Lawrence Bartak of the Institute of Psychiatry who were engaged in a comparative study of residential units for autistic children. We invited colleagues from the Home Office Research Unit interested in children's institutions to join us, and discovered that they too were making comparative studies of residential units for children and young persons—in their case, approved schools and probation hostels. The Home Office Research Unit were in touch with the Dartington group which had completed a series of studies of boarding schools and was using the conceptual framework they had developed to explore differences in the manner in which approved schools function.

At the time of the seminars very little of the work discussed in the seminar had been published. The various projects were mostly supported by the Department of Health and Social Security and the Home Office, but none of us was really aware of what others had been doing in the same field over the preceding few years. We were therefore pleased, but also surprised, to find that we had all more or less independently started from much the same point and at about the same time, made more or less the same false moves, and eventually adopted somewhat similar strategies to enable us to cope with the research questions we were interested in. It seemed likely that more contact at an earlier stage might have saved us all a good deal of time—though of course it might not have done.

Much of this work has now been reported in specialist publications. However Ron Clarke, Ian Sinclair and I thought that because of the scattered nature of the literature and the paucity of research in this area, it was worth approaching our colleagues to see if they would contribute papers describing their research which could be brought together in a single volume. This they generously agreed to do. We also approached Professor T. Grygier, now in Ottawa, since he had

had many discussions with the Home Office Research Unit team about his earlier work on the measurement of treatment potential.

A glance at the contents of this book will show that the coverage is very uneven. This unevenness arises out of the patchiness of comparative research on residential institutions for children. As far as we know, the papers included here are representative of current research, even if they do not include all of the ongoing comparative investigations in this area. The paucity of work on children 'in care' who are not themselves handicapped or delinquent is particularly striking. Moreover most of what *is* being done takes the form of single case studies. Valuable as such studies are, we believe that there are many problems that can only be answered by comparative studies which describe varieties of residential experience and attempt both to account for them and to measure their effects. In our editorial introduction we have drawn attention to some of the possibilities, as well as the modest accomplishments, of research in this area; and we comment on recent methodological advances which permit us to formulate many new questions in a manner which enables them to be tested.

There is, in the literature on institutional sociology, no standard terminology for many of the concepts which different authors use. In consequence different terms have at times been employed to describe essentially the same phenomena, and occasionally the same term is used in more than one sense. We have not attempted to standardise the terminology used by the different contributors to this book, but we have tried to help the reader by providing a very full index, with adequate cross-referencing. The editors are greatly indebted to Olwen Davies for undertaking this.

Chapters 4, 6 and 11 are Crown Copyright and are reproduced here by permission of the Controller of Her Majesty's Stationery Office. Material in Chapter 6 has appeared in *Hostels for Probationers* (HMSO, 1971) and material in Chapter 11 has appeared in *Absconding from Approved Schools* (HMSO, 1971).

JACK TIZARD

*Thomas Coram Research Unit*
*University of London Institute of Education*

# Contributors

| | |
|---|---|
| LAWRENCE BARTAK | Institute of Psychiatry, University of London. |
| ROGER BULLOCK | Dartington Research Unit into the Sociology of Education, Dartington Hall. |
| PAT CAWSON | Statistics and Research Division, Department of Health and Social Security. |
| PAUL CHERRETT | Dartington Research Unit into the Sociology of Education, Dartington Hall. |
| R. V. G. CLARKE | Home Office Research Unit. |
| TADEUSZ GRYGIER | Centre of Criminology, University of Ottawa. |
| KEVIN HEAL | Home Office Research Unit. |
| D. N. MARTIN | North Yorkshire Social Services Department. |
| SPENCER MILLHAM | Dartington Research Unit into the Sociology of Education, Dartington Hall. |
| PETER MOSS | Thomas Coram Research Unit, University of London Institute of Education. |
| MICHAEL RUTTER | Institute of Psychiatry, University of London. |
| IAN SINCLAIR | Institute of Marital Studies, Tavistock Institute of Human Relations. |
| BARBARA TIZARD | Dr Barnardo Senior Research Fellow, University of London Institute of Education. |
| JACK TIZARD | Thomas Coram Research Unit, University of London Institute of Education. |

# 1   Introduction

Jack Tizard, Ian Sinclair and R. V. G. Clarke

## The need for comparative institutional research

### The scope of the book

For the foreseeable future, large numbers of children will be placed in institutions, on whose quality their well-being must greatly depend. Despite this, there is little consensus about the principles which should govern institutional care and children are exposed to very varied patterns of upbringing based on equally varied theories of child development. These variations provide the starting point for the research described in this book.

The institutions with which we shall be concerned cater for children of different ages and with widely differing needs, and they differ both in the objectives they set themselves, and in their means of attaining them. They differ in size, in organisational structure, in staffing, and in the facilities they provide. Staff have more or less freedom to manage their affairs. Children have more or less contact with parents, social workers and the outside community, and they remain for longer or shorter periods in residence. Thus it may well be, as indeed some have argued, that the variations among residential institutions are such as to defy analysis, and that the best we can do is interpret rather than explain their diversity.

The research brought together in this book suggests that this is not the case. In any set of institutions a few factors appear to be of overriding importance, in that once they are defined and quantified they can account for a substantial proportion of the variance in other 'dependent' or outcome variables which are also operationally defined and numerically scored. Some of these factors are also significantly associated with the behaviour of children after they have left the institution.

Inasmuch as we can describe these determining features of institutional life and see how they influence behaviour and development, we can begin to make rational choices between different ways of running institutions. In the past, many institutions have been so badly run that they could be condemned out of hand by any humane and intelligent observer. But there remain real issues, the resolution of which is by no means easy. Common sense and good intentions alone cannot, for example, determine which of two competing philosophies should govern the treatment of autistic children, what are the immediate and long-term effects of different approved school regimes, or what is the influence of different types of staff training. Decisions on such matters should be based on evidence; and the evidence must be comparative.

## The comparative approach

The link between the studies included in this book lies in their comparative approach, in other words in their methodology. At first sight this seems a peculiar criterion to use, equivalent perhaps to bringing together studies on the ground that they employed statistical tests. We shall argue later that taken together the studies do have theoretical importance, but for the moment we should like to look at the advantages of a methodology which in essence involves comparing a number of institutions and measuring and inter-relating specific aspects of their structure and performance.

Every study in this book deals with at least three institutions and most of them with many more. This approach highlights the very great differences which exist between the institutions at the same time as it makes it possible to evaluate their effects. By contrast, early research into residential institutions relied heavily on the single case study, so that it could only be generalised on the untested assumption that any one institution is an adequate representative of its fellows. This book tests this assumption and shows it to be false.

The work to be reported generally involves measurement of the dimensions on which the institutions are compared and indeed an emphasis on measurement is one of its important features. As can be seen from the particularly careful and ingenious work of Bartak and Rutter and of Grygier, such measurement need not involve itself with trivial variables; and in research which may involve a large number of institutions, its employment is more or less inevitable. It is usually impracticable for a research worker to provide detailed qualitative descriptions of more than one or two institutions and even if he can do so he is likely to have great difficulty in collating and comparing the results. For example, there is currently considerable emphasis on trying to understand how the various actors in a social situation perceive and interpret it. This trend, desirable in itself, brings with it an attack on 'positivist' measurement which is believed to prevent rather than enhance understanding. However, institutions are not perceived in the same way by all their members. If one wishes to compare the way in which two or more institutions are perceived, some form of measurement and counting is needed to determine how many see them one way and how many another. These measurements can then be related to organisational and other factors of which the participants in the situation may not be directly aware.

The comparison of a large number of institutions within a single study enables a serious weakness of descriptive case studies to be overcome. This is the difficulty of linking the precise features of the care provided with its immediate and long-term effects. In small-scale studies too many variables are inevitably uncontrolled—thus even the random allocation or matched control experiments, in which two carefully described regimes are compared, cannot show which of a host of differences are responsible for any results, unless there is adequate replication. But if variables can be quantified and if a sufficient number of institutions can be compared, it becomes possible to use correlational techniques to rule out a great many variables and point with some confidence to the importance of others.

This comparative, analytical methodology has, of course, been foreshadowed by other work in the field. (We have recently reviewed some of this work—see Clarke and Sinclair (1973) for penal research and King, Raynes and Tizard (1971) for research on hospitals.) More commonly, however, institutional research has followed a very different tradition. The assumptions of this tradition have provided a starting point for much of the research reported here, at the same time as they have been called into question by it.

## *The steampress model*

Most previous research on residential establishments and their functioning, has started, not from the obvious fact of institutional variety, but from the equally obvious fact that the members of any class of institutions tend to resemble each other. An uncritical acceptance of this commonplace observation has led many investigators to undertake case studies of single institutions and to treat their results as though they apply to all members of a particular class of establishment (*the* mental hospital, *the* residential school, *the* children's home). Polsky (1963), for example, described a residential cottage in an American correctional school and deduced its functioning from the fact that it incarcerated youths with delinquent values. His argument suggests that these factors lead inevitably to the features he observed, and that they should therefore be found in other institutions with a similar function irrespective of their size, staff, organisation or theoretical orientation.

Starting from quite different premises, Goffman (1961) drew attention to features common to all institutions which encompass their residents' lives; from a general account of such places he constructed the stereotype of the 'total' institution—one which is dehumanising, and resistant to improvement or change. Goffman defined his concept of total institutions denotatively, including, for example, prisons, leprosaria, mental hospitals, barracks and orphanages. He was, of course, well aware of the manifest diversity of these places, and his writings abound in the rich detail of institutional life. Conceptually, however, he was concerned not with diversity but with what he perceived as an underlying unity, and although he intended to examine differences among institutions later, in fact he has never done so.

The features Goffman selected as common to all total institutions are likely to be found mainly in less enlightened institutions, indeed the evidence on which his ideal type is based mostly comes from studies of prisons, old-fashioned mental hospitals and other repressive institutions, rather than from modern children's homes, residential schools and other, more benign establishments. The model itself is a static one, largely incapable of accounting for differences or change. It is assumed that the specific characteristics of particular prisons or mental hospitals make little difference to the quality of life within them and can be safely ignored in any research.

This failure to analyse the specific features of institutions has equally characterised psychological research in the field. The neglect may be explained in part by a tendency to see institutions in terms of maternal deprivation, but whatever the reason, psychologists have expended much effort on describing the social and intellectual functioning of children in institutions and almost none on the institutions themselves (see Dinnage and Kellmer Pringle, 1967). Even the so-called enrichment experiments which have demonstrated the power of the environment on I.Q. have provided only qualitative accounts of the environment concerned. They are thus unable to show what aspects of the environment produced the good effects (King, Raynes and Tizard, 1971).

Both the psychological and sociological traditions we have been describing see institutions as having uniformly bad effects on their residents, and they adopt what we propose to call the 'steampress model' of the institution. According to this view the institution is a crude machine—one which is inflexible in its operation and which crushes the objects placed in it into a misshapen, uniform, mould. In other words, it destroys the resident's individuality by depriving him of the conditions necessary for this to develop, by crushing him, or by forcing him to react in rigidly determined ways.

*Reaction to the steampress model*

Among practitioners, reactions to the steampress model tend to involve either rejection of institutions altogether or the espousal of a new less 'institutional' model which has usually been heavily influenced by psycho-analytic theory. The main premise is that institutions should take the pressure off the children not put it on, and in more detail it is argued that:

(1) Some children need a 'primary experience' before they can be expected to develop skills or learn to deal adequately with other people.

(2) Training in skills and roles leads to conformist behaviour. The resident 'does his time', apparently learns more desirable behaviour, but is in fact a chameleon who returns at once to his former ways on release. It is better that he should 'act out' and show his true colours so that a genuine dialogue with him can take place before he leaves.

(3) It is possible to teach roles and habits that will endure, but these are in some sense false if they have not been adopted as a result of a genuine inner change. If this has not happened, a person loses touch with his feelings and becomes 'mechanical', capable only of 'pseudo-relationships' and incapable of finding a meaning for his own life.

Yet surprisingly, this radical alternative to the steampress model shares with it one basic assumption, which is that among existing institutions, variations in staff, organisation, buildings and the like have little importance. It is this assumption that the present book calls into question.

The book does not consider all sources of variation in residential institutions; it says little, for example, about co-education or resident self-government. It does, however, identify some of the major sources of variation and this is enough to destroy any belief that they are unimportant.

The factors discussed in the chapters which follow can be grouped under four main headings:

(1) *Ideological variation* There is not one 'ideal type' of institution: rather the field is characterised by a number of very different ideologies, embodied in very different types of institutions, and implemented in varying and conflicting ways by management, staff, and other bodies involved.

(2) *Organisational variation* Differences in ideology are often reflected in differences in organisation which are themselves associated with differences in staff and resident behaviour.

(3) *Staffing variation* There are important differences in staff behaviour and attitudes and these reflect variations at the levels of

ideology and organisation as well as differences in staff characteristics and in the behaviour of the residents.

(4) *Variation in resident response*    Differences at the three levels just mentioned would matter little if the residents responded only to the common characteristics of institutions. In fact there is evidence that this is not so, and this requires an account of learning and socialisation which allows for these variations in response.

In the following sections of the Introduction we pick out some of the book's main themes and discuss them under our four headings.

## Ideological variation

Residential institutions are commonly defined by some attribute of their populations and some popularly assumed objective. Thus hospitals are expected to cure the sick, children's homes to shelter the deprived, and maladjusted schools to educate and presumably 'adjust' the disturbed. It seems likely that these different aims enshrined in the names and public faces of institutions will result in differences in actual operations and achievements. The question is to what extent they do so.

In this respect Chapter 2 is of particular interest. In it Peter Moss describes the first comprehensive survey of residential institutions for children in this country and identifies three different models or types of residential institution, namely the child care institution, the school, and the hospital model. He shows how these differ in size, location, and staffing patterns as well as in the qualifications expected of those in charge. Each model tends to recruit its own type of professional staff, and as other chapters show, these professionals are likely to ensure that the institutions express in a great variety of ways the values held by staff to be important. This factor of shared values will therefore tend to increase the similarities within groups and the differences between groups of institutions.

The effects of these differences are often pervasive. In Chapter 3, Jack Tizard compares the treatment of subnormal children in hospital with that of similar children in hostels organised on a child care model. He found that the hospital children were brought up in a bleaker, altogether more impersonal environment, that they were faced by a confusing number of different staff whose assigned duties took little account of the children's needs, and that compared with children in small hostels the children in hospital were much less likely to meet acceptance from staff and more likely to find rejection.

These differences in regime were almost certainly reflected in differences in the children's happiness and behaviour.

There are, however, differences among hostels as well as between hostels and hospitals. This book provides ample documentation of sets of institutions that at first sight belong to one or other of Moss's types, but which nevertheless show many important differences among themselves. This situation is of course partly explained by the fact that, for many purposes, terms such as 'school model' are too broad. There is not just one school model but many, and these vary with the sections of society for which they cater and the functions they fulfil. Even institutions which draw on similar and highly selected populations, and which presumably have similar aims, may nevertheless have very different ideas about how these aims are to be achieved. In the schools for autistic children described by Bartak and Rutter, teacher behaviour differs very markedly between schools and in accordance with the particular theories on which the schools are based.

One reason for this variety must be the extraordinary variety of organisations that exist to promote and manage institutions. Moss estimates that, excluding independent schools, there are 'at least 620 bodies in the business'. These range in size from the large bureaucratic hospital board or local authority to the small independent boards of management and individual proprietors. Moss finds interesting differences within the policies of these bodies and these presumably reflect differences in tradition, resources, key personnel, commitment to religious, child care, and other ideas, and inheritance in terms of staff and physical plant.

Differences of the kind we have been discussing bring with them the possibility of conflict, a concept central to the analysis of institutions which Millham and his colleagues present in Chapter 9, and which is concretely exemplified in Chapter 4 where Heal and Cawson discuss recent changes in approved schools. As pointed out in these chapters, there are, apart from management, many other groups— for example, the neighbouring community, the police, and the referring agencies—which take a continuous or varying interest in the institution, and neither they nor those who run it are likely to be in complete agreement about the goals to be pursued. The existence of such vague and conflicting demands provides the staff with some latitude in deciding which elements to emphasise. Clearly they are not going to please all of the people all of the time and they need to erect a barrier between themselves and the outside world to hide some of their doings and to filter demands from the environment. Institutions differ in their permeability as in everything else, but their relative imperviousness permits their high level of diversity, resists supervision by the parent agency, and accounts for the persistence of potentially scandalous establishments alongside excellent ones. It enhances, in other words, their variability.

## Organisational variation

As pointed out in Chapters 2–4, differences in institutional ideology are almost always associated with differences in organisation and these need to be investigated in their turn if we are to understand how ideological variables achieve their effects. Moreover, differences between institutions of similar ideology often arise from differences in organisation, which are thus important in their own right.

In the chapters that follow there are discussions of a number of organisational variables, but in this section we shall concentrate particularly on unit autonomy and we do so for two reasons. In the first place, the findings on autonomy are important and provide relatively clear guides to policy makers. In the second place, they provide a paradigm through which the effects of other organisational variables can be understood.

The concept of autonomy is introduced in Chapter 3 and considered in Chapter 4 before it becomes the focus of Chapter 5. For the purposes of these chapters an autonomous unit is one in which a unit head has freedom to make decisions about matters which in other organisations are decided centrally. For example, the heads of subnormality hostels have a freedom to timetable the day which is denied to sisters in charge of hospital wards for the subnormal. Some, but not all, of the nurses in charge of family groups in residential nurseries, and some, but not all, of the housemasters in approved schools, have comparable freedoms.

Chapters 3 and 5 particularly underline the virtues of staff autonomy. In Chapter 5, Barbara Tizard finds that autonomous units tend to have a higher quality of verbal interaction between the staff and children, and in Chapter 3 Jack Tizard finds that staff in such units are more responsive to children's needs. However, autonomous units tend to have other characteristics; for example, they have older staff in Barbara Tizard's study and on average rather less handicapped children in Jack Tizard's one. This makes it difficult to be sure that the better results of these units arise from their great autonomy and not simply from their association with other factors. There is, therefore, particular interest in Barbara Tizard's finding that nurses behave more warmly towards children when they themselves are in charge (and hence relatively autonomous) than when they are under the control of somebody else.

As pointed out in the book, there are a number of possible

reasons for the superior performance of autonomous units. The heads of these units have greater flexibility and can arrange their day to meet the needs of the children rather than the demands of a central organisation. Children in the units are less likely to be faced with a rota of staff, with none of whom they can form strong relationships. Staff have a less restricted role and so are less likely to be bored and more likely to have something to talk to the children about. As they are not regimented from above, they have less need to regiment the children to meet the requirements of the organisation. Finally, because the staff have more power, children will be more likely to turn to them with their requests, knowing that these can be dealt with on the spot and not necessarily referred to a distant, central administrator.

The explanations just given for the good effects of autonomy suggest that it operates by freeing staff to make use of their own good qualities. It seems likely that other factors in the organisation can have the same restrictive effect as lack of autonomy. For example, staff flexibility is reduced when a very low staff/child ratio stretches staff to the limit; even in the most autonomous units, large or difficult groups of children turn staff minds to discipline; high staff turnover and frequent moves by staff or children from one cottage or ward to another discourage close staff/resident relationships; and certain jobs, for example that of instructor in an approved school, emphasise the task aspects of a staff role. Evidence for these assertions comes from several of the studies reported, notably from Grygier, who writes of the effects of staff ratio, unit size and type of intake on the 'treatment potential' of institutions, and from Heal and Cawson who deal with the effects of role on a staff member's supportiveness.

The effects on staff performance of rigid rules and routines are of particular importance. Centrally imposed routines necessarily restrict autonomy and, as the Tizards' researches show, regimentation of children and lack of autonomy for staff tend to go together. They are not, however, the same thing, for staff can presumably lack autonomy in unregimented establishments and staff in autonomous units can certainly impose regimentation. A number of the studies measure regimentation and allied variables (variously entitled 'institutional control', 'block handling', 'rule permissiveness', etc.) and the general conclusion is that it is very difficult to combine such institutional practices with close relationships between staff and children [although as Sinclair's study (Chapter 6) shows, in small establishments it may not be impossible].

Thus the significance of autonomy (and probably by implication of a number of other variables associated with it) lies in the fact that it is a necessary condition for the successful performance of certain staff roles. In relation to these aspects, the average level of staff performance in autonomous units is almost bound to be higher simply because staff in other institutions are virtually prevented from performing well. Indeed, since by definition autonomous staff have freedom in how they behave, it is perhaps more accurate to speak of autonomy as facilitating rather than leading directly to good results. Similarly, many other organisational variables determine the characteristics which a staff member requires in his job, but do not determine whether or not he has them.

It should not be forgotten, however, that staff perform within the constraints imposed by their organisational setting. In this respect Moss's survey of current institutional provision exposes a serious problem. He finds that the great majority of children in residential institutions are to be found in large, specialised institutions which are run on the hospital or school model and which are almost certainly centrally and hierarchically organised. What this can mean in concrete terms is shown by Jack Tizard's research reported in this book and by Oswin's (1971) sensitive account of institutions for the chronic sick. Good staff in such places can do little and may well leave (see Heal and Cawson, Chapter 4). Those that remain are often blamed for an institution they can do nothing to change.

## Staffing variation

The steampress model of the total institution allows little scope for good relationships between staff and residents; on this view their interactions are few, formal, and characterised by a deep distrust. Staff spend their time supervising residents, herding them in groups, blocking their access to higher, potentially more sympathetic, staff and withholding information about their future. Such staff/resident relationships as do exist carry an air of patronage or collusion, as where staff connive at the worst aspects of the inmate culture in order to procure a peaceful life. As for the inmate culture, it is seen as negative towards the staff, dominated by the tougher inmates and organised round such focal concerns as 'skiving', trafficking, and sexual exploitation.

As usual this picture of staff/resident relationships applies in some institutions but not others. The relationships between staff and children in mental subnormality hospitals seem distant and, with the exception of the official 'Auntie' system, close relationships were discouraged in all the residential nurseries described by Barbara Tizard and apparently in many approved schools as well. However, Heal and Cawson report that approved school staff have varied attitudes to social distance between staff and children and there are similar findings from probation and mental subnormality hostels. Moreover, the staff of Bartak and Rutter's unit A show an almost embarrassing amount of warmth.

Thus the evidence of the following chapters is of a great variety in the forms taken by the staff culture, the resident culture and the relationships between the two. The feel of this variety is perhaps best conveyed by Millham and his associates and they also describe and analyse some of its manifestations. In their account, inmate cultures differ in what they see as important, in their cohesiveness, in the ways in which their norms and values are enforced and in the functions which apparently similar pieces of behaviour perform. Previous research has tended to ignore these variations and the consequent need for theories by which they might be explained.

One reason for the previous neglect of these variations may lie in the fact that staff/resident relationships have been studied mainly by sociologists, whereas their full explanation must include not only sociological variables but also psychological ones, such as the personality and skills of the staff involved. As might be expected, sociologists following the steampress model have busied themselves with more general matters than the personality and skills of the staff, while psychologists have usually administered their tests to more docile and low-status populations. One of the more important results of the following chapters is the unanimity with which they underline the paramount influences of staff, particularly those in charge of units.

The first chapter to provide evidence on this topic is Chapter 3. In this Jack Tizard draws attention to the effects of training for unit heads, finding that hostels run by staff with child care training were superior in some respects to hostels run by staff with only nursing training or with none at all. In Chapter 6, Sinclair, also dealing with hostels, this time for probationers, demonstrates the enormous influence of the wardens and matrons on the delinquent behaviour of the residents. Sinclair's findings point to the importance of staff selection and in Chapter 7 Grygier provides evidence that correctional school houses whose staff have been particularly carefully selected tend to perform better on his measure of treatment potential.

Hostels and houses are, of course, small units in which the head has a great deal of contact with the residents and a direct influence upon them. The situation is quite different in large establishments, in which the head appears to be equally important but to exert his influence in rather a different way. Heal and Cawson in Chapter 4 and Barbara Tizard in Chapter 5 deal with approved schools and residential nurseries respectively and point out that unit heads have a very great indirect influence on the residents through their control over the amount of autonomy granted to junior staff. Chapters 8 and 9 suggest further ways in which the heads of complex institutions may exert their influence, for example through staff selection.

The distinction between the roles performed by the leader of large and small institutions may help to explain an apparent contradiction between Jack Tizard's finding that child oriented heads ran more child oriented institutions and Heal and Cawson's finding that approved schools whose senior staff expressed supportive attitudes were perceived as less supportive by the residents than were other schools. Obviously in a large institution the enabling, administrative aspects of a head's role are relatively more important, and if he tries to have much personal contact with children he may handicap his junior staff. This in turn exemplifies a theme developed by Sinclair in Chapter 6; namely, that the extent of a staff member's influence and the qualities he needs to exercise it properly depend on the organisational context in which he works.

Chapters 6–8 also illustrate a second factor which vitally affects the performance of unit heads, namely resident response. It is too easy to perceive influence as flowing only from staff who remain unmoved by resident reaction. Yet in fact, life in institutions is a continuous process of action and reaction in which staff and residents both have their part to play. Relationships between the two sides are fluid and dynamic and neither group is complete master of the other. Thus the book provides examples in which the residents reduce a key member of staff to immobility, where staff retrieve themselves from apparently hopeless positions, and where a sudden incident can make a previously fragmented inmate culture cohere.

This dynamic quality of institutions leads to variety not only between institutions but also within the same institution over time, and is the antithesis of the dead uniformity implied by the steampress model. Yet despite the dynamic and unique character of events in unique institutions, there are consistencies which emerge. Thus Sinclair found that although all probation hostels go through 'bad patches', under wardens of particular kinds these are more frequent and more serious than under others.

These findings should not result merely in a call for 'more training'. Training programmes will be wasted if they concentrate on the wrong staff and send them out equipped with the wrong skills to an inappropriate and unsupportive organisation. As we saw in the last section, trained staff in the wrong organisational context are largely impotent, and indeed as Heal and Cawson point out, they are likely to leave. Moreover, the question of *who* is trained is an important one. (Is it wise, for example, that training is concentrated on junior staff whose attitudes, according to Heal and Cawson's findings, would appear to be quite largely formed in post and whose influence compared with that of a unit head is minimal?) And one must also consider what type of training is needed; it is clear that different staff require different skills. Techniques such as those of Bartak and Rutter should enable these skills to be identified and taught with more precision rather than, as at present, picked up in a trial-and-error way on the job.

## Variations in resident response

We turn last to the question of whether the differences we have been discussing can have long-term effects on the residents. In doing so, we do not wish to imply that institutions should be wholly or even mainly justified in terms of their end results. Such places provide a way of life for their residents and this can be evaluated in its own right and without regard to its further effects. Thus Jack Tizard evaluates mental subnormality institutions in terms of whether or not they provide the sort of environment in which children should be expected to live. As many of these children will spend the greater part of their lives in institutions, evaluation in these terms is basic. Many institutions, however, do not keep their residents for this length of time and we need to know how, if at all, they affect these children's future lives.

Obviously views about the long-term effects of institutions are closely linked with theories of personality—a topic about which there is as yet little general agreement. Most personality theorists explain a person's actions in terms of an underlying pattern whose influence can be seen in a variety of social situations. Others attribute more importance to a person's environment, in coping with which he may learn specific pieces of behaviour which he does not exhibit elsewhere. On the first view, one would predict that an institution would find it difficult to modify underlying personality patterns but that changes which did take place would be lasting and generalised; on the second view, that changes would be lasting only when behaviour rewarded in the institution is similarly rewarded on release. Holders of the first view would be likely to explain the poor verbal facility and social functioning of institutionalised children on the grounds of a general defect of personality (perhaps a basic feeling of being unloveable), whereas holders of the second view would explain these deficiences on the grounds that children have less opportunity than others to talk at length with adults and to practise certain social roles.

Two chapters in the book provide relatively extended accounts of how institutions produce psychological change. In Chapter 11, Clarke and Martin put forward an 'environmental-learning theory' intended to account both for the great influence of the immediate environment on behaviour, and also for the fact that children differ in how they behave. They explain these facts without recourse to underlying personality differences and on the grounds that children in some environments are more likely to receive cues for certain sorts of behaviour, and that by responding to these they become more likely to behave similarly in future. Thus differences in behaviour occur because of differing environments and previous experience; consistencies in behaviour because of consistencies in environment and experience.

This account of behaviour makes little or no use of the concept of 'central mediating processes', and acts are said to occur because they have been performed before in a similar situation by the actors or by models who were rewarded for them. In distinction to this, Millham and his colleagues, in Chapter 10, are concerned with the learning of roles and styles of life, both of which involve complex sets of behaviour, and the perception of a variety of different behaviours as being in some way related. Consistent with this approach, they emphasise the importance of institutional symbols—for example, the Chapel or the School of Dance—which are most likely to affect the residents through a perceived association with a set of values or way of life.

Despite their differences the two chapters we have been discussing share two important similarities. In the first place they focus attention on behaviour and roles and in this they contrast with much of the theory of residential work which emphasises the need for change in underlying emotional dynamics. In the second place, neither account gives much grounds for hope that changes in individuals which occur in the institution will persist for long unless they are reinforced by the environment to which the residents return. (Millham and his colleagues almost go as far as to imply that some institutions, such as approved schools, which are apparently concerned with socialisation are in fact merely 'going through the motions'.) In these respects we can compare the position taken up by Chapters 10 and 11 with the evidence in the rest of the book.

It should be recognised that although the book produces abundant evidence on the differences in the emotional climates of institutions, there is very little evidence about the lasting emotional changes, if any, that these produce in their residents. Bartak and Rutter found that a classroom unit which looks as if it aimed to overcome a deep sense of unacceptability in the pupils, failed to improve family relationships more than did more traditional units—but perhaps one would hardly expect this sort of effect from a classroom unit in any case. There is certainly an urgent need for more studies of the long-term emotional effects of institutional regimes.

There is evidence that at least in the field of cognitive skills, improvement need not be preceded by a change in underlying dynamics. Bartak and Rutter, and Barbara Tizard both deal with cognitive problems (learning difficulties in autistic children and retarded speech development in institutionalised ones) which have been explained on grounds of deep emotional disturbance, and while both studies found that these problems could to some extent be overcome, improvement was not associated with the emotional climate of the units. There is, therefore, evidence that good emotional experience is not a necessary condition for cognitive change, although of course this could still be true with some children or with other problems. Interestingly, however, Grygier did not find that 'good' emotional climates as measured by his 'treatment potential' instrument were associated with the reduction of delinquency and there is a similar finding in Anne Dunlop's (1975) research carried out in approved schools in this country.

Turning to the problem of the persistence of changes which occur in institutions, the book provides both direct and indirect evidence. In the first place the differences in behaviour, and of emotional climates, between the various institutions are themselves evidence for the great power of the immediate environment and, hence, of the difficulty of enabling psychological change in a situation that will persist in other less favourable circumstances. It is true that in relation to deviant behaviour, Clarke and Martin, and Sinclair provide evidence that acting out in the form of absconding tends to be associated with an increase in delinquent behaviour on release. These authors, however, argue that institutions are unlikely to have a very marked long-term effect on delinquent behaviour, while Grygier, whose findings suggest a long-term institutional effect on maladjustment, speculates that this may be partly accounted for by good after-care facilities.

On the more positive side, the evidence just summarised does have implications for the way we should regard the effects of institutions. In the first place the evidence for the great power of the immediate environment on behaviour provides a strong case for working with the environment in which an individual first 'acts out' rather than for removing him from it. Yet paradoxically, experiments in intensive casework with offenders have generally proved more successful in reducing recidivism when carried out in an institution than when based in the community (Adams, 1962; Bernsen and Christiansen, 1965; Sinclair, *et al.*, 1974). It may be that children for whom effective intervention in the community cannot be attempted, benefit more from removal to an institution than from attempts to help them as individuals in situations where there is little room for change.

In the second place, the fact that behavioural and emotional change may to some extent be independent of each other raises questions for all the three models of institutions which have been identified. We have already argued that the school and hospital models tend to provide environments which, from an emotional point of view, are unsatisfactory. It should be recognised, however, that an exclusive concentration on emotional matters may leave children equally handicapped in relation to instrumental roles, which after all they will need when they leave. Unfortunately, in the past, institutions have tended to concentrate on one set of social roles to the exclusion of others. However, ordinary life is not lived entirely in schools or workshops, nor in therapeutic or supportive encounters. If institutions are to equip children for such a life they must provide them with a similar variety of experience.

# References

ADAMS, S. (1962) 'The PICO project', in Johnston, J., Savitz, L., and Wolfgang, M. E. (eds), *The Sociology of Punishment and Correction*, New York: Wiley.

BERNSEN, K., and CHRISTIANSEN, K. O. (1965) 'A resocialisation experiment with short-term offenders', in *Scandinavian Studies in Criminology I*, London: Tavistock.

CLARKE, R. V. G., and SINCLAIR, I. A. C. (1973) 'Towards more effective treatment evaluation', paper to *First Criminological Colloquium*, Council of Europe, Strasbourg.

DINNAGE, R., and KELLMER PRINGLE, M. L. (1967) *Residential Child Care: Facts and Fallacies*, London: Longman.

DUNLOP, A. B. (1975) *The Approved School Experience*, London: HMSO.

GOFFMAN, E. (1961) *Asylums: Essays on the Social Situation of Mental Patients and Other Inmates*, New York: Doubleday; Chicago: Aldine.

KING, R. D., RAYNES, N. V., and TIZARD, J. (1971) *Patterns of Residential Care: Sociological Studies in Institutions for Handicapped Children*, London: Routledge & Kegan Paul.

OSWIN, M. (1971) *The Empty Hours: A Study of the Weekend Life of Handicapped Children in Institutions*, Allen Lane, The Penguin Press.

POLSKY, H. W. (1963) *Cottage Six, the Social System of Delinquent Boys in Residential Treatment*, New York: Russell Sage Foundation.

SINCLAIR, I. A. C., SHAW, M. J., and TROOP, J. (1974) 'The relationship between introversion and response to casework in the prison setting', *British Journal of Social and Clinical Psychology*, 13, 51–66.

# 2  Residential care of children:
a general view

Peter Moss

## Introduction

Residential provision for children constitutes a complex system. It is made up of many, diverse components, and is provided by many organisations and individuals. These are guided by differing objectives, motivations and perceptions of the needs, nature and roles of children living away from home. Those who provide residential care also differ in their views of how this should be organised. The latter part of this chapter attempts to describe and compare some of the main features of the different types of residential provision and to determine a few of the underlying patterns and features of the total, rather diffuse system. The first part attempts to set the scene for this task with a brief look at the children for whom this provision is made.

At least 275,000 children from England and Wales are usually being cared for by statutory, voluntary or private agencies or individuals, away from the family network that would normally look after them. Or put another way, for every 1000 children under 18, about twenty will normally be living away from home and family.

A relatively small proportion of these children—about a sixth—live in private homes, with foster parents. But the great majority live in establishments providing full-time care for groups of children during most of the year, under the supervision of staff employed to provide this care, and of this majority (referred to below as being in 'residential care') over two-thirds live in schools of one kind or another with just over half in the independent school sector. Of the remainder, about one in six are in approved schools or children's homes (now mostly called 'community homes') and about one in ten are in subnormality, mental illness or non-psychiatric hospital units (see Table 2.1 for detailed breakdown.)

Two contrasting types of residential establishment for children can be broadly defined. Children's homes and foster homes, approved schools, borstals, schools for handicapped children and hospitals provide by and large for children who are severely deprived and impaired, whether socially (by reason of their home and family background) or personally (through mental, educational, psychiatric or physical handicap or poor health). In institutions which serve

TABLE 2.1    *Numbers of children in residential and foster care provision in 1970 in England and Wales*

| | No. | Age range | No. over 18 |
|---|---|---|---|
| **1 Children in homes provided by local authority and voluntary agencies for children in care or on remand** | | | |
| L.A. children's homes | 21,419 | 0–17 | |
| Voluntary children's homes | 10,946 | 0–17 | |
| Approved schools | 7,227 | 9–18 | 80 |
| Remand homes | (1,310) | 7–17 | |
| Total | 40,902 | 0–18 | 80 |
| **2 Children in special schools for handicapped** | 21,417 | 2–19 | (40) |
| **3 Children in other boarding schools** | | | |
| Maintained schools | 10,861 | 4–19 | (285) |
| Direct grant schools | 10,380 | 4–19 | (280) |
| Independent schools | 119,658 | 4–19 | (3,110) |
| Total | 140,899 | 4–19 | (3,675) |
| **4 Children in provision for mental handicap or mentally ill** | | | |
| L.A. hostels for mentally handicapped (England only) | 1,019 | 0–15 | |
| Voluntary and private homes for mentally handicapped children (England only)* | 636 | 0–15 | |
| Hospital beds + voluntary/ private provision used by Hospital Boards on contractual basis | 11,293 | 0–19 | (1,968) |
| Mental illness hospitals and units | 1,031 | 0–17 | |
| Total | 13,979 | 0–19 | (1,968) |
| **5 Children in non-psychiatric hospitals (*excluding mentally handicapped and ill*)** | 15,603 | 0–14 | |

| | No. | Age range | No. over 18 |
|---|---|---|---|
| 6 *Children in borstals/detention centres. Estimate assumes 45% of detention centre population and 25% of borstal population under 18* | (2,420) | 14–17 | |
| 7 *Children in mother-and-baby homes. Estimate assumes 33% of total mother-and-baby homes provision is occupied by girls under 18; no figure for babies included in estimated total* | (630) | 14–17 | |
| 8 Children in foster homes | | | |
| L.A. homes | 31,941 | 0–17 | |
| Voluntary agency homes | 2,018 | 0–17 | |
| Private foster homes | 10,811 | 0–17 | |
| Total | 44,770 | 0–17 | |
| Total 1–8 | 280,620 | 0–19 | 5,763 |
| Total 1–7 | 235,850 | 0–19 | 5,763 |

\* There are approximately 1450 places in voluntary and private provision for mentally handicapped children; the figure of 636 given here is only for children under local authority care and many of the other places in these types of provision are used by Regional Hospital Boards on a contractual basis, and are included under Hospital bed and voluntary/private provision.

N.B. Bracketed figures are estimates of children in care.

*Sources:* Department of Education 1971a; Department of Health 1970, 1971a, 1971b, 1971c; Home Office 1971a, 1971b, 1971c, 1972; National Council for the Unmarried Mother, 1968.

the needs of such children those from families in the lowest socio-economic classes are over-represented.

In marked contrast, the children in the other main grouping of residential provision, which includes independent and direct grant schools, might be described as privileged, at least in terms of the factors listed above, and come predominantly from families in the professional and managerial classes.[1] Thus in the mid-1960s, 84 per cent of boarders leaving public schools and 82 per cent of a sample of boarders leaving other independent schools had fathers in socio-economic classes I or II (Public Schools Commission, 1968b); for boarding pupils leaving direct grant schools in 1967–8 the figure was 85 per cent (Public Schools Commission, 1970).

In general terms, then, it becomes possible to identify certain groups of children as being at high risk of living away from homes; i.e. children from the extremes of the socio-economic class spectrum; handicapped children; sick children. And as a corollary, residential care is uncommon among children whose parents are in the middle of the class spectrum, or those whose children are neither handicapped nor ill.

However, at least one characteristic that different forms of care—both for deprived and privileged children—share in common is a marked tendency for them to include disproportionate numbers of boys. This can be seen clearly in Table 2.2 which shows the number of girls in different types of care per 100 boys, from which it can be calculated that if girls were found in residential and foster care in the same proportion as they are in the overall under-eighteen population, a further 71,000 foster home and residential care places would be needed.

TABLE 2.2    *Number of girls per 100 boys in main categories of residential provision*

| Categories of provision | Girls per 100 boys |
|---|---|
| Approved schools | 17 |
| Direct grant schools | 29 |
| Maintained boarding accommodation for non-handicapped pupils | 34 |
| Independent schools (recognised) | 50 |
| Special schools | 53 |
| Independent schools (non-recognised) | 54 |
| Hospital provision for mentally handicapped children | 66 |
| Children's homes (local authority) | 71 |
| Children's homes (voluntary) | 73 |
| Local authority hostels for mentally handicapped children | 74 |
| Non-psychiatric hospitals | 76 |
| Mental illness hospitals | 79 |
| Foster homes (voluntary) | 84 |
| Foster homes (local authority) | 96 |

*Sources:* Department of Education, 1971a; Department of Health, 1970, 1971a, 1971b, 1971c; Home Office, 1971a, 1971b.

This imbalance is especially marked for residential schools and only in local authority foster homes does a roughly normal sex ratio pertain. Whether the male bias in such facilities as subnormality hospitals, independent and special schools, local authority and direct grant schools and approved schools, reflects real differences in need or varying levels of discrimination and prejudice, rooted in tradition, this one factor alone must affect these institutions in numerous ways, especially since one consequence or cause is a high level of single-sex units.

Children in residential care can also be said to have in common a family context that has been judged inadequate to meet certain ends in the children's development and upbringing, which may include objectives concerned with health, behaviour, education or social adjustment. This inadequacy may be defined by society, through one of its agencies of control (e.g. courts, social service departments) or by families themselves; indeed one estimate—that the unmet demand among parents for boarding education covers some 12 per cent of school children (Public Schools Commission, 1968b)—suggests that a considerable proportion of parents are prepared to pass this sort of judgment on themselves, and middle-class families are more likely to pass it than working-class ones.

Residential institutions are means, at least in theory, to meet the objectives that families are judged to be inadequate to attain. Their greatest value is the facility they provide for children (or adults) to be removed from a diverse range of environments (normally family homes), and be placed and contained full-time in an environment which can be organised to exclude certain influences and introduce others so as to hopefully pursue certain goals effectively. The essence then of residential care is its potential for full-time control, and hence for containment and influence.

These essential qualities of residential care—control, containment, influence—have been applied to the achievement of numerous ends. Some of the most important are listed in Table 2.3, together with examples both current and past.

These functions range, in terms of contemporary ideas, from the malign to the benign, and it is a salutary exercise today to recall the number of philosophies and policies underlying past residential systems which were held to be right in their time, but which are now anathema.

Differences among children are paralleled by striking differences between the types of provision made on the one hand for privileged children and on the other hand for the deprived. These differences are by no means necessarily related to resources—indeed an irony of the present situation is that provision for deprived and handi-

TABLE 2.3    *Some functions of residential care—past and present*

| Function | Some examples of the function |
| --- | --- |
| Healing | Hospitals, convalescent homes, 'therapeutic communities' |
| Compensation for deprivation or disablement | Holiday homes, camp schools, special schools |
| Acquisition of certain common social skills/habits | Hostels and hospitals for the mentally handicapped; some other provision for the severely handicapped; detention centres; training homes for girls |
| To facilitate certain work or the acquisition of special roles or skills | Monasteries; military camps; military colleges; agricultural and other vocational schools and colleges; public schools; Adolf Hitler Schools |
| The acquisition of caste/class/ party values and habits | Public schools; institutions run by religious bodies for children of the religion; officer training colleges; Political Institutes of Education (Third Reich Germany) and other party and ideological training centres |
| Deterrence or punishment | Post-1834 workhouses; detention centres; prisons |
| Protection of the community from 'harmful' influences | Prisons; mental hospitals |
| Protection of inmates from corruption, exploitation | Monasteries and convents; subnormality hospitals; mother-and-baby homes |
| Elimination or neutralisation of inmates | Concentration camps; (?) workhouses in the 18th century |

capped children is quite often newer, better staffed and equipped, and more expensive to provide than that for the privileged. Despite this, in terms of performance and prognosis, the contrast between the populations of children's homes, approved schools, special schools, etc., and of independent and direct grant schools is marked. Children from the latter schools achieve high levels of academic attainment (e.g. in the mid-1960s 85 per cent of public school leavers and 66 per cent of a sample of leavers from other independent schools had four or more O levels; 52 per cent and 29 per cent respectively had one or more A levels); they are abundantly represented in further education and training for the professions (in 1965–6, 62 per cent of public school leavers and 45 per cent of other independent school leavers went on to universities, colleges or to professional apprenticeships); and many occupy controlling positions in politics, the economy, the law, universities and other major seats of power (for example, the proportion of former independent school pupils in the Conservative Cabinet (1963) was 91 per cent; in the Labour Cabinet (1966) it was 42 per cent; as directors of prominent firms (1967) it was 71 per cent; as judges and QCs (1967) it was 80 per cent; as vice-chancellors, heads of colleges, professors of all English and Welsh universities (1967) it was 33 per cent; and as governor and directors of the Bank of England (1967) it was 77 per cent) (Public Schools Commission, 1968b).

Children on the other hand who pass through provision for the handicapped and deprived, tend to show high levels of poor educational attainment, intellectual and especially verbal retardation, and behaviour problems (Moss, 1973). Few studies (perhaps significantly) trace their academic, further educational and career records and it seems likely that at best they are unimpressive.

This contrast in success needs to be set beside the long period of residential care that most children boarding in independent schools experience; about two-thirds of boarders leaving public schools and nearly a half leaving other independent schools will have been boarding for at least four years, and a significant proportion will have experienced up to ten years of residential care, starting at the age of seven or eight (Public Schools Commission, 1968b; Moss, 1973); indeed it may well be the case, though this cannot be known for certain from current data, that the longest periods in residential care are recorded on average by boarding pupils at independent schools. Comparisons between independent school children and children in other forms of residential care need interpreting with great caution, especially in view of the often inadequate or non-comparable data; but such evidence as there is has value to the extent that it suggests the danger of assuming too uncritically that residential provision has a necessarily deleterious effect and that the removal of a child from his home is to be avoided except in extreme circumstances. And it supports the view 'that a discussion of the effects of institutional upbringing on children has to take into account the age, handicaps and length of stay of the children in residence, the type and quality of the care provided in the institution, the alternatives actually or in principle available for children not able to be brought up in their own homes, and above all the consequences for the child and for the family of leaving the child at home' (Tizard and Tizard, 1974). To these factors might well be added many others, including the degree to which residential care is considered the norm in some families and so accepted and prepared for; family attitudes towards residential care; and the status and esteem attaching to different forms of care.

Indeed it is probably in terms of status that the most marked differences are to be noted between residential provision for the deprived and the privileged. Institutions serving the latter, despite high fees, enjoy long waiting lists, indicating strong long-term parental demands; a high level of public respect; and a certain pride in attendance which the 'old boy' ethos perpetuates and epitomises. But provision for the deprived traditionally carries a burden of stigma and suspicion, and attendance at such provision carries little prestige with it in adult life. The relationship between family and residential provision for the deprived and privileged also varies. Families with children at children's homes, approved schools, etc., are subject to the attention and efforts of social and other welfare workers, applying the mysteries of case-work and rehabilitation; families using independent schools are evidently considered very well adjusted and are left to their own devices—adequate wealth still secures the use of services without strings attached.

## The census

An attempt has been made up to now either to stress underlying common factors or to limit differences to a fairly simple dichotomy. But at a more detailed level, when it comes to describing residential units and some of the main features of the system which they compose, diversity and complexity become dominant features, and with some 4,278 residential units in England providing 217,951 beds, establishing some sort of order in this welter of provision is a major problem. To help with this, and provide the major source of information given in the remainder of this chapter, material has been drawn from a census of residential care carried out by the author, in October 1971 at the Child Development Research Unit of London University Institute of Education as part of a project financed by the Department of Health and Social Security.

The object of the census was to collect comparable information on certain basic items, across the whole range of residential provision. The existing information usually refers only to individual categories of provision, and information on one category tends not to be comparable with that gathered for another; while for each category, there are also extensive gaps in basic factual knowledge. An across-the-board study can highlight differing approaches and methods, act as a starting place for further comparative and evaluative studies, and hopefully enable the residential scene to be looked at as a whole. For despite recent moves to secure more co-ordinated planning,[2] residential care retains some important, divisions most notably between child care, special education, boarding schools, mental handicap and housing services. Coming from a child care background, it had sometimes seemed to me that there can be a danger of the child care segment forgetting that it forms only a relatively small part of the overall residential care picture and that other forms of care may have a more important role to play in the care of 'deprived' children than has up to now been considered[3]—and no doubt a similar potential for parochialism may occur in other branches of the residential system. We need to be moving to a situation where the full range of residential options is comprehended and evaluated, and a system developed for children living away from home which uses the best range of options to meet their needs, unhindered by administrative or professional insularity; and the beginning of this process requires a description of existing varieties of provision, their main features and significant differences of organisation and approach.

For the purposes of comparison and description in this chapter, the residential system has been divided into twelve main categories,[4] which are shown in Table 2.4, together with the number of units and beds provided in each.

The census was able to cover categories 1–6 and 10–11 in Table 2.4, which categories included 3,157 units with 85,506 beds, from which completed census returns giving the full range of census data were returned for 84 per cent of units with 79 per cent of beds. This response rate, however, varied between different types of units, ranging from 89 per cent of beds in children's homes to 53 per cent of beds in maintained boarding accommodation for non-handicapped children. However, information on geographical location, size, types of agency responsible for units and the sex groups of children resident, was collected for all the non-responding units, as well as for direct grant schools, independent schools for non-handicapped pupils and hospitals for mentally handicapped children (Department of Education. 1964, 1969, 1970a, 1970b, 1971b; Department of Health, 1971b; Home Office, 1965; NSMHC, 1971), which provide a further 132,445 beds in 1,121 units—and these units are included in some of the descriptions given below.[5]

Diversity in units is matched by, and in part arises from, organisational variety. A very approximate count of agencies or individuals providing residential care in England at the end of 1971 indicates something in the region of 620 or more 'bodies'[6] in the business, ranging from hospital boards and large local authority social service departments, responsible for hundreds of places, to the private proprietors of a school or home for a handful of handicapped children. This figure of 620 includes roughly 240 local authority social service and education departments; 14 regional hospital boards; 50 religious orders or diocesan/regional religious organisations; 20 national voluntary bodies; 160 regional or local voluntary

TABLE 2.4    *Number of units and beds in each of twelve main categories of residential provision*

|  | No. of units | No. of beds |
|---|---|---|
| 1 Approved schools* | 123 | 8,240 |
| 2 Children's homes—general (e.g. small group homes, large children's homes, cottage group homes) | 1,711 | 24,985 |
| 3 Children's homes—specialist (e.g. nurseries, remand homes, reception centres) | 577 | 11,094 |
| 4 Special schools and hostels for handicapped pupils | 403 | 23,634 |
| 5 Independent schools mainly or wholly for handicapped pupils (recognised and non-recognised) | 73 | 3,372 |
| 6 Maintained boarding schools and hostels for non-handicapped pupils | 131 | 11,235 |
| 7 Direct grant schools | 60 | 8,330 |
| 8 Independent schools for non-handicapped pupils—recognised | 854 | 110,550 |
| 9 Independent schools for non-handicapped pupils—non-recognised | 119 | 3,621 |
| 10 Local authority hostels for mentally handicapped children | 86 | 1,523 |
| 11 Voluntary/private homes/schools for mentally handicapped children | 53 | 1,423 |
| 12 Hospitals for mentally handicapped children (the figure under 'number of beds' is the number of mentally handicapped children aged 0–19 in hospital units caring for more than five mentally handicapped children) | 88 | 9,944 |

* Most of the information for this chapter was collected towards the end of 1971, when approved schools had not become community homes. Since even in their new guise, former approved schools will remain a very distinctive group of facilities (e.g. in terms of size, situation, staffing, etc.), a rather reactionary stance has been adopted in this chapter of categorising them separately under the heading of approved schools.

bodies and boards of management; 75 private proprietors of schools and homes for the handicapped; and 60 governing bodies of direct grant schools. Recent and future events, such as the effects of the 1969 Children and Young Persons Act on the status of voluntary homes and approved schools and the 1974 local government reorganisation will tend to reduce these numbers somewhat— though health service reform will work the other way by increasing the number of hospital authorities. Whatever the outcome of such organisational mathematics, the present system, although hopefully becoming increasingly co-ordinated, remains the consequence of diverse and numerous agencies and individuals who have contributed from the last century to the present day and who have been and are still working according to diverse motivations, objectives, standards and practices.

Excluding independent schools for non-handicapped pupils (but including direct grant schools, hospital provision for mentally handicapped children and non-responding census units), just over half the beds in residential provision are provided by local authorities; 25 per cent by voluntary bodies (7 per cent by national voluntary agencies; 6 per cent by religious orders or diocesan/regional religious bodies; and 12 per cent by other local or regional voluntary agencies); 10 per cent by hospital boards; 8 per cent by direct grant schools; and 3 per cent by private proprietors. The relative involvement of these different types of proprietor varies according to the type of provision involved—for instance whereas there is one voluntary or private place for every 1·5 local authority places in schools for handicapped children, the proportion rises to 2·3 for general children's homes and to 3·7 for specialist children's homes. The contribution of different types of voluntary bodies also varies. National voluntary agencies (e.g. Barnardo's, National Children's Homes, Salvation Army) contribute 12 per cent of all children's homes places, compared to 9 per cent by religious orders and regional religious bodies and 7 per cent by other local or regional voluntary agencies; the situation for schools for handicapped children (i.e. both special schools and independent schools) is markedly different, the proportions respectively being 8 per cent, 4 per cent and 20 per cent.

Even within categories of care, different types of agencies show different patterns of provision. Local education authorities provide over half the places in special schools for the educationally subnormal, the maladjusted and the delicate, while voluntary bodies provide over half for the blind and partially sighted, the epileptic and deaf; the physically handicapped fall in-between, with provision split roughly fifty-fifty. In child care, whereas 54 per cent of cottage group homes and 84 per cent of other general children's homes divided into separate sub-units are provided by voluntary bodies, they contribute only 7 per cent of small group homes (that is general units of twelve beds or less).

## Residential care as a community-based system

One aim of the enquiry was to examine to what extent residential care can be called 'community-based', in the sense that provision is planned and distributed to enable residential units to be situated in and serve individual catchment areas, which are small enough to be meaningfully referred to as communities.[7] The consequences for children going into residential care in a non-community-based system are fairly predictable—frequent placements far or at some distance from home; problems of maintaining contact and liaison between child, residential unit, family and other workers; the transfer of children into different and strange environments; and the child's inevitable break with his established contacts and roots in his home community—such as friends, school and relations.

The most conclusive way to judge the degree to which the residential system is community-based would be to examine the placement of children from each neighbourhood needing residential care. However as the residential care census and supplementary information were unit rather than child-oriented, conclusions have to rely on two other, less satisfactory sets of indicators—the geographical distribution of residential units and the size of units.

Size reduces the potential for community-based services, since if a unit has a specific catchment area, the size of that area will depend on the number of beds in the unit. Subnormality hospitals provide a good illustration of how this process works, for as a population of 100,000 will include about twenty-five mentally handicapped children (0–19 years) receiving hospital care, it can be easily calculated that the large average number of children per subnormality hospital (i.e. 113) would be drawn from a population area of around half a million people.

Most children in residential care live in large residential communities. Excluding independent schools for non-handicapped children where as many as 52 per cent of beds are in residential units of 200 or more, only 43 per cent of beds in residential provision (including direct grant schools, hospital provision for mentally handicapped children and non-responding census units) are in units of 50 or less and only 12 per cent are in units of 12 or less (though these units constitute respectively 83 per cent and 42 per cent of all units). These overall figures, however, are misleading in view of the wide extremes, shown in Table 2.5, between child care and local authority/voluntary mental handicap units on the one hand, and the remaining forms of care which are mainly schools on the other.

Within the child care category, local authority general provision is markedly smaller in size on average (12 places per unit) than voluntary general provision (28 places per unit), though the average size for specialist provision is about the same. This reflects the greater emphasis in local authority provision on small group homes, compared to that in voluntary provision on large units divided into sub-units.

TABLE 2.5   *Number of beds in different categories of residential provision*

| Category of provision | Average size | % of beds in unit sizes 0–12 | 0–49 | 50–99 | 100+ |
|---|---|---|---|---|---|
| Approved schools | 67 | + | 16 | 54 | 30 |
| Children's homes—general | 15 | 39 | 81 | 8 | 11 |
| —special | 19 | 16 | 93 | 5 | 2 |
| Special schools | 61 | 1 | 30 | 38 | 33 |
| Independent schools for handicapped children | 49 | 1 | 40 | 47 | 13 |
| Maintained boarding accommodation for non-handicapped children | 86 | + | 15 | 27 | 59 |
| Direct grant schools | 139 | Nil | 4 | 18 | 78 |
| Local authority hostels for mentally handicapped | 18 | 24 | 100 | Nil | Nil |
| Voluntary and private provision for mentally handicapped | 27 | 9 | 62 | 22 | 16 |
| Hospital provision for mentally handicapped* | 113 | 1 | 5 | 12 | 82 |
| All units above | 32 | 12 | 43 | 23 | 34 |
| Independent schools for non-handicapped children | 117 | + | 7 | 19 | 74 |

N.B. + = less than 1%.
\* These figures for provision for mentally handicapped children are based only on the number of mentally handicapped children in each hospital unit, and so underestimate the size of units that mentally handicapped children live in; many in fact share mental subnormality hospitals with adults (a unique arrangement for the long-term care of children, since the demise of the workhouse), while a small proportion are in non-psychiatric hospitals, where they constitute a small minority of total patients. This hospital figure also excludes the hospital units with less than five mentally handicapped children in them, which in fact contribute few places to the overall total.

If the need for residential provision were constant throughout the country, a community-based system of services would imply an even distribution of residential provision, each unit situated in and serving its community catchment area and each area served by approximately the same level of provision in relation to its child population. Since need, whatever that might be defined as, is unlikely to be at the same level of prevalence in all areas, some geographical variation of rates of provision would be expected, even in a community-based system. In England, the geographical distribution of residential provision varies markedly between different areas, at regional, county or borough and district levels, the differences between areas getting progressively more marked the smaller the unit of administration considered. These variations raise problems of interpretation. Such variations may mean large differences in the level of need between different areas, or that residential provision has been established with little or no regard to relating it to catchment areas and their need for services, with consequent bunching of services is some areas and gaps in others. But even if need and provision both vary markedly, their geographical distribution may not coincide— there may be heavy need paralleled by a dearth of provision in one area, but similarly heavy needs coupled with high levels of provision somewhere else. Without more detailed data analysis, conclusive answers to these problems of interpretation cannot be given— however, the data given below may suggest some general patterns and answers, which seem on the whole not to be compatible with a community-based system.

Table 2.6 shows the number of beds per 1,000 population under 15 in eleven regions of England in different categories of provision and overall.[8] There is a concentration of provision in the Home Counties and the southern regions, especially the South East and South West, which contrasts with the low number of places in London, due to the dearth of approved schools and other residential schools and places for the mentally handicapped in the GLC area and despite the fact that the London region has the highest level of children's home places in the country. East Anglia also shows a high level of provision, though this is largely due to the many maintained and direct grant school places in the region, without which it would be more in line with the lower rates of the six Midland and Northern regions. Residential school places, and to a lesser extent accommodation for the mentally handicapped, are less in these six regions but the provision of approved schools and children's home places in these regions, and especially in the North and Yorkshire regions, is generally in line with, or even higher than, in the Southern regions, apart from the South East which is far ahead of all other regions in all forms of provision.

Differences between local authority rates are even more marked. In Table 2.7 local authorities have been divided into four groups: counties; London boroughs; county boroughs in other conurbations; and non-conurbation county boroughs. For each of these groupings the mean and standard deviation for the number of beds per 1,000 child population for the constituent local authorities has been given for a number of broad categories of residential provision. This classification of local authorities shows up the heavy concentration of residential provision in county council areas, with the exception of children's homes; county areas have two to three times the level of provision of the three borough groups for schools and mental handicap provision, many times the boroughs' level of approved schools, and twice the level for provision overall. Between the three groups of borough authorities, although there is little difference for children's homes provision or accommodation for the mentally handicapped, non-conurbation county boroughs show higher average levels for residential schools and total provision, largely due to the effect of a relatively small number of boroughs which have exceptionally high levels of provision for one or more types of residential unit, e.g. Doncaster, Southport, Worcester, Great Yarmouth, Brighton, Hastings, Bournemouth and Torbay.

By dividing local authorities into four groups and by limiting the study of local authority variations to contrasts between authorities in each of these groups, the overall level of inter-authority variation is considerably underplayed. But the wide variations that do occur between individual local authorities can be illustrated with a few examples.

In a region such as London, the highest levels of provision[9] (i.e. beds per 1,000 population under 15) are in the outer boroughs of Croydon and Redbridge, which are three to five times as high as those in the inner London boroughs of Westminster, Lambeth, Tower Hamlets and Southwark. In the North West, Southport has ten times the level of provision of Wigan, Burnley or Barrow; while in the conurbations of this region, Liverpool has thirty times the level of provision of neighbouring Bootle, three times as much as Salford and two and a half times as much as Manchester. On the South coast, Hastings has proportionately nearly four times as much provision as Southampton, Bournemouth has twice the level of Portsmouth, and Exeter five times as much as Plymouth. As a final example, on a county council basis, Surrey has nearly four times the level of provision of Lancashire; Devon has three times the level of neighbouring Cornwall; East Sussex twice as much as West Sussex; and both East and West Sussex have substantially more than such industrial counties as West Riding and Durham.

Up to this point, geographical variation has been treated as involving comparisons of regions or county councils and county boroughs. But these are areas that are far larger than the neighbourhoods that people live in and identify with. To get a more precise view of distribution therefore, the distribution of residential units in county council areas, (most county authorities being large in terms of population or size or both) was plotted according to the urban or rural districts that units were sited in. These district areas get nearer to the realities of community, even though many are still far too large to equate with neighbourhoods. This exercise also,

TABLE 2.6  *Beds in different types of residential provision for children per 1,000 population under 15 by region*

| Region | Approved schools | Children's homes | | Schools for handicapped* | Mentally handicapped prov.† | Maint./DG schools‡ | Total | Ind. schools§ |
|---|---|---|---|---|---|---|---|---|
| | | Local authority | Voluntary | | | | | |
| North | 1·2 | 2·3 | 0·7 | 1·8 | 1·3 | 2·0 | 9·3 | 3·4 |
| Yorkshire | 1·0 | 2·4 | 0·6 | 1·9 | 1·0 | 1·3 | 8·2 | 6·2 |
| North West | 0·8 | 2·0 | 0·8 | 2·0 | 1·1 | 0·9 | 7·6 | 1·9 |
| W. Midlands | 0·7 | 2·5 | 0·7 | 2·8 | 1·3 | 1·1 | 9·0 | 8·0 |
| E. Midlands | 0·6 | 2·0 | 0·5 | 1·7 | 0·8 | 1·5 | 7·1 | 7·0 |
| E. Anglia | 0·7 | 1·9 | 0·6 | 2·4 | 1·5 | 4·4 | 11·5 | 9·1 |
| Home Counties (North) | 0·6 | 2·3 | 0·9 | 2·8 | 1·7 | 2·1 | 10·3 | 25·0 |
| London | 0·1 | 3·1 | 1·2 | 0·6 | 0·4 | 0·3 | 5·7 | 2·8 |
| South East | 1·5 | 2·9 | 2·1 | 6·5 | 2·2 | 3·6 | 18·8 | 30·9 |
| Wessex | 0·6 | 2·1 | 0·8 | 3·0 | 1·3 | 2·5 | 10·2 | 19·3 |
| South West | 1·1 | 1·6 | 1·1 | 3·9 | 1·5 | 3·5 | 12·8 | 21·2 |

* *Schools for handicapped*         = Special schools and independent schools wholly or mainly for handicapped children.
† *Mentally handicapped prov.*    = Local authority hostels, voluntary and private homes/schools, and hospital provision for mentally handicapped children.
‡ *Maint./DG schools*               = Maintained boarding schools for non-handicapped children and direct grant schools.
§ *Ind. schools*                        = Independent schools except those wholly or mainly for handicapped children.

TABLE 2.7 Beds in different types of residential provision for children per 1,000 population under 15: means and standard deviations of individual local authorities by type of local authority

| Type of provision | County councils | | London boroughs | | Conurbation county boroughs | | Other county boroughs | |
|---|---|---|---|---|---|---|---|---|
| | Mean | S.D. | Mean | S.D. | Mean | S.D. | Mean | S.D. |
| Approved schools | 1·1 | 1·1 | 0·1 | 0·3 | 0·2 | 0·6 | 0·3 | 1·0 |
| Children's homes (local authority) | 2·5 | 1·3 | 4·2 | 2·3 | 3·3 | 1·7 | 4·0 | 2·1 |
| Children's homes (voluntary) | 0·8 | 0·8 | 1·1 | 1·5 | 0·6 | 0·7 | 1·1 | 2·0 |
| Schools for handicapped* | 3·8 | 2·6 | 0·5 | 0·9 | 0·9 | 1·5 | 2·5 | 4·6 |
| Mentally handicapped prov.† | 1·6 | 1·4 | 0·5 | 1·7 | 0·4 | 1·0 | 0·4 | 1·0 |
| Maint. and direct grant schools | 3·9 | 4·0 | 0·3 | 0·9 | 0·3 | 0·7 | 2·1 | 6·5 |
| Total of above | 12·9 | 6·1 | 5·5 | 3·4 | 5·1 | 3·4 | 9·0 | 9·2 |
| Independent schools for non-handicapped | 20·0 | 22·7 | 2·6 | 4·2 | 0·4 | 0·9 | 10·7 | 4·2 |

* *Schools for handicapped* = Special schools and independent schools wholly or mainly for handicapped children.
† *Mentally handicapped prov.* = Local authority hostels, voluntary and private homes/schools, and hospital provision for mentally handicapped children.

of course, does nothing to break county or London boroughs into their constituent districts or neighbourhoods.

Disparities of distribution and the concentration of provision in relatively few areas is at its most noticeable at district level. A study was made of districts with populations of over 15,000 in the five most populous English counties (Lancashire, West Riding, Cheshire, Kent and Essex), from which three main points emerge clearly.[10] First, as in the studies at regional, county and borough levels, children's homes are relatively the least unevenly distributed form of care (though voluntary children's home provision is more unevenly distributed than local authority provision). Second, substantial areas of these five counties have no residential accommodation, either for certain categories of provision or for all types of provision. In the most extreme case, the West Riding, a third of the child population of these larger districts lies in districts with no residential provision of any sort sited in them; while for a particular category of provision, children's homes, which are the most evenly distributed form of provision, the number of larger districts in each of the five counties with no children's home provision in them, ranged from 5 out of 23 for Kent, to 29 out of 52 for West Riding and 19 out of 30 for Cheshire.

Third, and as a consequence of the situation described above, residential provision in these counties tends to be concentrated in a relatively few districts. The most extreme example of this is Cheshire, with 61 per cent of the residential provision in the largest districts in five districts containing only 16 per cent of the child population; and even for the least extreme example, the proportions—56 per cent of beds and 27 per cent of the child population—are still markedly disparate.

Another example, taken from the largest county, Lancashire, illustrates how these extremes in the level of residential provision apply in practice and suggests again that variations in need are not necessarily related to the variations in supply. In this county, 2,827 beds—nearly three-quarters of the county total—are concentrated in eleven of the 103 urban and rural districts, which have only one in six of the county population. This leads to the situation where the county's three major overspill districts for Liverpool, with a combined population of over 210,000 and which are faced with major social problems due to the rapid decanting of population from the city, have 86 residential places between them; while the five districts to the west, also on the periphery of Liverpool, with a strong rural and suburban character, have 887 places in an area of similar population size.

Many more illustrations of variations at regional, county and borough and district levels could be given (and inclusion of independent schools would produce even more marked extremes); but as has already been suggested, the interpretation of these variations, especially in relation to their implications for the degree to which provision is community-based, is difficult. In particular, such variations in provision would only be compatible with a community-based system, with units serving and sited in specific limited catchment areas, if they reflected and coincided with, area for area, equally marked variations in need. Unfortunately the degree to which this is or is not the case cannot be categorically answered at present, given a lack of serious thought and hard data on need, which tends to be equated in practice with the actual numbers of children from different authorities in different types of care, a definition which is unsatisfactory on many counts.

But even if the concept of need as being equivalent to present numbers of children in residential care is accepted, 'need' shows a poor fit with 'supply'. Thus, when the thirty local authorities with the highest number of beds in relation to population were compared with the thirty authorities with the highest rates of children in residential care in approved schools, children's homes, schools for the handicapped and mental handicap provision[11] (for sources of rates of children in residential care see Home Office, 1971a, 1971b; Department of Education, 1970; Department of Health, 1971), there was little correspondence. The number of local authorities in the top thirty positions both for provision of beds and rates of children in residential care were:

| | |
|---|---|
| approved schools | 2 |
| children's homes | 13 |
| schools for handicapped | 8 |
| mental handicap provision | 4 |

The match of beds and children is particularly bad for approved schools and mental handicap provision, not just at an individual local authority level but also in terms of types of local authority. Most beds are in county areas but the high need in terms of children is in urban areas. Thus although there are no counties among the thirty local authorities with the highest need (in terms of children currently in care) for approved school provision and only one for mental handicap provision, in both cases twenty out of the thirty local authorities with the highest provision are counties. The fit improves somewhat for schools for the handicapped (eighteen counties in the top thirty for provision against ten in the top thirty for need), since counties are heavier users of these facilities, possibly in part because of long travelling distances involved in attending day

schools, but also possibly because boarding education is in general a
more common and accepted mode of care in county areas. The fit
for these schools is, however, particularly bad for London, which
has eleven boroughs in the high need group of local authorities,
but none in the high provision group. This reflects the capital's
general shortage of residential school places. The best fit is for
children's homes, where counties play little part in either supply or
demand, the only marked discrepancy being the over-representation
in supply of non-conurbation and outer London boroughs (e.g.
Southport, Hastings, York, Bromley, Croydon and Redbridge),
compared to the under-representation of inner London and other
conurbation boroughs. This better fit of child care units reflects the
relatively lower variation in their distribution, which in turn is partly
due to the comparatively small size per unit.

In conclusion, while we are left without any clear indication of levels
of actual need, the large size of many residential units, the high
levels of variation in the distribution of provision at all levels,
especially at district level, and the poor fit between local authority
areas of high supply and areas of high need, suggests that the overall
residential system is not community-based. However, the degree to
which this is true varies according to type of provision and between
different areas.

A study of geographical distribution and size serves only to show
how the residential system may be incompatible with a community-
based provision, but gives little indication of why the system is like
this. It would however have been surprising to find that a community-
based system had developed, without the consistent application of a
concerted policy to this end by agencies involved in providing care—
and with so many varied agencies involved in providing services,
such a policy has neither been adopted or applied. Moreover apprecia-
tion of the value of home, family and community roots is a relatively
recent concept, and much of today's provision was built at a time
when protection of the community or removal of children from
'harmful' family and home ties were important influences.

## Specialisation in residential care

The most powerful factor, however, making for the continuation of
the current situation, is that the system is based on a high degree of
specialist or segregated provision for children, so that children are
allocated to units on the basis of some personal or familial attribute,
rather than according to the neighbourhood in which they live. As a
corollary, many units in the system serve children with one of the
particular attributes involved, and draw their intake from a wide

area as a consequence. Of course to the extent that all children needing residential care in an area are not put in the same unit, a residential care system will always be partly specialist or segregated, but the degree of this varies and can be best gauged by examining the range of attributes which may determine placement. Six attributes commonly determine placements in the present residential system:

*Sex*—about two in every five children in residential care live in single-sex groups (this includes non-responding units but excludes mental handicap hospitals and direct grant and independent schools for non-handicapped pupils; at least in the case of schools the proportion of children in single-sex residential units is much higher than two in five).

*Age*—about one in three children in residential care are in units which only take children for part or all of the age range 0–11 or 10 plus.

*Handicap*—extensive separate systems of care, especially in special and other boarding schools and in hospitals, homes and hostels for the mentally handicapped, have developed to provide separate care for handicapped children and indeed separate care for different types of handicap.

*Behaviour*—separate provision for maladjusted and severely disturbed children (including delinquents) is provided by social service and education departments, voluntary bodies, hospitals and private proprietors.

*Religion*—different denominations and religious orders still make their own provision in various areas of residential care, and though doubtless the degree of sectarian exclusiveness is declining, the existence of such provision must have some implications for the placement of some children.

*Parental wealth*—this is especially relevant for independent schools—in 1970 the median fee (for both tuition and boarding) at recognised independent schools was £455 (Department of Education and Science, 1970a) or about 29 per cent of the median earnings (before deductions) for all full-time male workers, manual and non-manual, which was £1,550 (Central Statistical Office, 1972): since 1970 fees have increased considerably.

It seems likely that specialisation, or segregation, is increasing. For instance a recent development has been the increasing provision by child care agencies of special units for 'severely disturbed' children. Or, as an example of an opportunity to reduce segregation not being taken when presented, local authorities have and are continuing to meet their responsibility to provide residential care for mentally handicapped children by building up a separate system of hostels, rather than integrating the children into the existing or planned child care residential and foster care system. In this way, not only will mentally handicapped children continue in existing highly segregated hospital care, but those who are less disabled will fill a new segregated non-hospital set of provision.

This pattern of segregated residential care is partly a response to the inadequacies of the generalised approach to the care of children and adults practised by the nineteenth- and twentieth-century Poor Law, where all-inclusive provision too often meant neglect of many children with particular disabilities; and partly also the consequences of earlier educational neglect of many children with handicaps. However if we set specialisation alongside size as common features in much residential provision, the two can also be seen as the products of the industrial, technical society in which they have developed, and which has itself created extra need and demand for services, as well as the resources to meet these and the climate which has shaped the form services have taken.

The most striking features of the Industrial Revolution (which began the generation of this climate), in relation to the organisation of work and production was its development through the factory system of a very high degree of specialisation of work (via breaking down jobs into individual components, many of which could then be mechanised), and a concentration of labour in previously unknown numbers onto individual work-sites, to enable the most profitable exploitation of power, human resources and machinery. These dual features have been further emphasised by industrial societies to a point where size and specialisation are perhaps the most essential features of modern day life.

Given the extra demands of the Industrial Revolution, and the factory model to draw on, it is not surprising that large scale and increasingly specialist residential care was a product of the nineteenth century. The grim and large workhouse was perhaps the most typical residential monument to that century and the Industrial Revolution, and though in practice workhouses usually produced poorly segregated care for all ages and conditions, the proponents of the system constantly urged the need for separate care for different groups within the workhouse. By the latter half of the century, Poor Law care for many children had transferred from the workhouse to separate provision, including cottage group homes. The residential care of poor, orphaned and deprived children was also altered by the end of the century with the rapid growth of voluntary child care agencies, who provided much new provision, again often using the cottage group home model which involved large-scale provision. The public schools responding to the need to 'civilise' the progeny of *nouveau riche* industrialists and businessmen and of 'rude and ignorant baronets from the hinterland' were busily constructed from the 1840s onwards and were based on the strict specialisation of wealth and caste. Publicly run asylums, for both the mentally ill and subnormal, also began to flourish at the same time. Industrial and reformatory schools, precursors of the approved school system, began their development in the mid-nineteenth century, and the involvement of the state in special education for the handicapped largely dates from the end of the century.

Even though the size of units may have been decreasing over past years, it has been mainly a movement from the very large to the plain large or sizeable, and many very large units are still in use; specialisation on the other hand, as already noted, has if anything become more marked and this situation is likely to continue.

## Residential care in the 'total institution'

Another feature of the residential situation, which is so obvious that its significance may be in danger of being overlooked, is that many, if not most children in residential care live in 'total institutions', where they live, work and play on one site. The large contribution of boarding schools to residential provision has been referred to several times so it is not perhaps surprising that almost half the beds of units included in the census were in units where all children received education in the unit or in a school, class or playgroup attached to the unit;[12] a further 13 per cent of beds were in units where some children were so educated. On-site education was not the monopoly of school units and all forms of provision included some units with this type of provision. Thus two-thirds of voluntary mental handicap unit beds (which included a number of residential schools for the mentally handicapped); just over half of the specialist child care beds; and a third of local authority mental handicap hostel beds, were in units which had provision for the education of all or some children, on site.

This situation inherently reduces opportunities for contact with people, places and experiences outside the institutional setting and, given the high level of resident staff in boarding schools, similar limitations must apply to many staff. A situation has developed in which the need of a child for both special schooling and care away from home often means living in a residential school. And attendance at such a school often means that a child must live some distance from home, limiting his opportunities for regular home visits, which could otherwise be a counter to some of the effects of life in a total institution.

## Staffing

To this point, the emphasis has been on the residential provision itself and the children living in it. This overlooks an essential part of residential provision, the question of staffing. Here once again we enter a field of enormous variety and differing approaches. That we know so little about these exemplifies the extent to which residential care has developed, both in isolation between its separate parts and in an environment uncluttered by too much empirical study or substantiated knowledge.

Table 2.8 gives some indication of the level of staffing in different types of unit—or rather the 'ideal' level of staffing as it relates the staff establishment to the number of beds in each unit. Taking the

TABLE 2.8    *Proportion of units, for different categories of provision with different staff establishment: bed ratios*

| Category of provision | | Child care staff establishment (full-time equivalent) as proportion of permanent beds* | | | | | |
|---|---|---|---|---|---|---|---|
| | | 0–12% | 13–24% | 25–37% | 38–50% | 51%+ | No Information |
| Approved schools (N = 99) | % | 15 | *60* | 18 | 4 | 3 | Nil |
| Children's homes: | | | | | | | |
| general (N = 1,522) | % | 1 | 23 | *63* | 11 | 2 | 1 |
| specialist (N = 509) | % | 1 | 9 | 37 | *33* | 20 | 1 |
| Special schools (N = 329) | % | 31 | *48* | 15 | 3 | 2 | 1 |
| Independent schools for handicapped (N = 41) | % | 24 | *42* | 22 | 10 | Nil | 2 |
| Maintained boarding accommodation for non-handicapped children (N = 65) | % | *100* | Nil | Nil | Nil | Nil | Nil |
| Local authority hostels for mentally handicapped (N = 53) | % | 2 | 21 | *51* | 17 | 10 | Nil |
| Voluntary/private homes for mentally handicapped (N = 28) | % | Nil | 18 | *36* | 1 | 32 | 4 |
| Total (N = 2,646) | % | 8 | 25 | *48* | 14 | 6 | 1 |

N.B. The median staffing ratio for each type of provision is in italic type.

* The proportions, expressed as percentages, imply approximate staff/bed ratios as follows: 0–12% = 1 full-time staff or less to 8 beds; 13–24% = 1·1–2 full-time staff to 8 beds; 25–37% = 2·1–3 full-time staff to 8 beds; 38–50% = 3·1–4 full-time staff to 8 beds. Thus for example, a unit with 20 beds and an establishment of 3 full-time child-care staff would be placed in the column headed 13–24%, since 3 as a proportion of 20 is 15%.

median level for each type of unit, the highest levels are found in the child care and mental handicap provision, and particularly in the specialist child care units (residential nurseries are the most highly staffed units of all), while the lowest levels are for local authority boarding schools (though similar levels may have pertained to direct grant and independent schools, if they had been included for this measure). In between, but still at a level below the median for all units, come approved schools and schools for handicapped children.

Within individual categories, the level of staffing varies widely—some approved schools (including special care and assessment units) and some special schools (especially those for the physically handicapped) have very high ratios and some child care units have very low staffing levels.

A striking example of differences in staff/child ratios between units making up one type of child care provision is provided in Table 2.9 which sets out the numbers of child care staff in 261 small group children's homes, all of which had twelve or fewer children in residence. Do the 7 nine- and ten-bedded units with less than two staff each lead to a greater deprivation for their children than the 18 units of similar size with four or more staff? And if so, how does this deprivation manifest itself? Or do the better staffed units lead to over-protection and wasteful use of staff? What hours do the staff in the two contrasting extremes of small group homes work and how does their actual work vary? How do varying staff levels affect the organisation and daily running of the units? Clearly, given the problem of recruiting staff of high quality for such demanding and lower paid work, more knowledge is needed about the consequences of different staff levels.

TABLE 2.9   *Staffing and size of 261 small group homes in two regions*

| No. of child care staff | Number of beds | | | |
|---|---|---|---|---|
| (*full-time equivalent*) | ⩽6 | 7–8 | 9–10 | 11–12 |
| <2 | 2 | 4 | 7 | Nil |
| 2–2·9 | 14 | 56 | 47 | 8 |
| 3–3·9 | 3 | 20 | 41 | 12 |
| ⩾4 | 1 | 7 | 18 | 21 |

Of similar importance in determining the supply and sources of future staff is the need for more knowledge about the desirability and feasibility of recruiting full-time and resident workers, and the potential for using part-time and non-resident staff. Differences already appear to exist in agencies' practices in these two areas, local authority child care units having higher proportions of part-time staff than voluntary child care units, and local authority mental handicap hostels having even higher levels. Indeed over a half of these hostels have one or more part-time workers, and over a quarter have three or more. Similar patterns occur for proportions of staff resident; local authority child care provision and mental handicap hostels have fewer than half their staff resident, while voluntary child care units have 78 per cent resident. Most staff in schools are also resident, the highest proportion for any category of provision (82 per cent) being in local authority boarding accommodation for non-handicapped children.

These trends for resident staff partly reflect the smaller size of local authority (as opposed to voluntary) child care units, there being possibly less room for resident staff. Also the greater use of part-time staff in local authority child care provision and mental handicap hostels would mean that they have fewer resident staff, since part-timers are usually non-resident. Finally, there may also be a tendency for local authority non-school provision to be more often situated in built-up residential areas, where non-resident and part-time work is more popular and feasible, and provides one solution to the problem of recruiting staff.

Schools of all types show a significant difference in staffing 'mix' when compared to other forms of care, in their use of teachers to do 'extraneous' duties which supplement the work of the child care staff. These duties can vary from running an evening hobby class to full-scale supervision and care of children, and most schools have one or more teachers helping in this capacity. In some schools (notably some approved schools and special schools run by national child care voluntary bodies) there has been a recent move to clearly differentiate the teaching and child care role, so that teachers do no extraneous duties and child care duties are the sole responsibility of child care staff. However, this is a minority situation at present, and in over half of the approved schools and two-fifths of special schools covered in the census, teachers doing extraneous duties constitute, in number, between a quarter and a half of the total child care personnel.

In nearly a fifth of all units, providing 44 per cent of beds, teachers also play an important role in residential care services, as the senior staff members. This happens mostly in schools, but is also found in specialist child care provision, where teacher-trained staff are responsible for 16 per cent of beds. Over half the senior staff in child care units and 44 per cent of all seniors have a child care qualification,[13] about 30 per cent of senior staff in child care units holding the one year certificate in residential child care. Eight per cent of senior staff but over half of those in local authority and voluntary mental handicap units and over a third of senior staff in residential nurseries, have nursing qualifications; the nursing/medical proportion would also have been higher if subnormality hospitals had been included in this section. Overall, a quarter of senior staff, responsible for 18 per cent of beds, have no relevant qualification, the highest level of unqualified seniors being in general child care units (34 per cent of all seniors), local authority boarding accommodation for non-handicapped children (37 per cent) and local authority mental handicap hostels (25 per cent).

Forty-four per cent of senior staff have been at their present posts for 5 years or more, compared to 25 per cent with less than 2 years' tenure. The highest level of senior staff stability is in local authority boarding schools—where nearly three out of four seniors had been in post for 5 years or more—and special schools—where the figure was nearly three out of five. The least stable units (excluding local authority mental handicap hostels, which, being recent developments, have offered little chance of long tenure) are local authority child care provision, where just under two in five senior staff have been in post for 5 years or more, while 35 per cent of seniors in local authority specialist provision and 27 per cent from general units have been there for under 2 years.

There is also evidence for greater stability in senior staff of voluntary, as opposed to local authority, child care units, which may reflect a greater sense of vocation and agency loyalty of staff of voluntary agencies. And in an age of often frequent job movement by staff in the social and education services, it was salutary to note that 579 senior staff had been in their posts for ten years or more and to find such individual examples of commitment as the children's home superintendent with forty-one years' service.

## Inertia and inflexibility in the system

Before concluding this examination of some of the main features of residential provision in England, some other important, underlying features need to be stressed, such as its inherent tendency towards inertia and inflexibility, interrelated characteristics which achieve their effects in a number of ways. Any generation is heavily dependent on individual residential establishments, and also on the overall systems of which they form part. These are the product of past generations and may go back for up to or even over a 100 years. Individual units and systems survive, even when the original *raison d'être* for them has passed, due to the inertia caused by the high cost of replacement and the well-established and influential patterns of staffing and management, with the sectional interests to which they give rise. All of these may be reinforced by an intricate network of tradition, philosophy, values and sentiment. Inflexibility comes in because old buildings, outmoded in design, scale, location and overall concept, are impossible to convert into provision in line with contemporary thinking, and are probably unsaleable or unusable as anything else but residential provision. In this way, the residential scene of any period is marked by a struggle to convert, use, exploit (and finish paying for) past structures and organisations, so that they can be made to meet current needs and thinking and sustain a viable justification for their continued existence.

Inertia and inflexibility are present in all organisations and services, but the combination of brick, ethos and a total way of life (which can make institutions highly symbolic and give them monumental qualities) makes inertia and inflexibility particularly inert and inflexible—even potent—in the case of residential care. Thus, provision for mental and physical illness and mental handicap remains dominated by vast, unsuitable nineteenth-century hospital buildings—and with the current heavy investment in hospital building programmes, this situation will probably be repeating itself in the next century with today's hospital buildings. Child care agencies are still having to use cottage group homes and other manifestations of the nineteenth and early twentieth centuries, when so much of child care was a responsibility of the Poor Law (which left another legacy with the workhouse). And to give a final example, it will require considerable ingenuity to establish a rationale for some approved schools, within the new community homes system. This is of course an on-going process and the problem of coming to terms with rapid changes and producing flexible and, if necessary, disposable residential care, which will not be a liability in twenty years' time, is still with us.

The need for flexibility in residential provision is caused by the relative speed with which needs and perceptions of needs change, philosophies go in and out of fashion and knowledge is acquired. Orphans and foundlings have given place to deprived children and the view that delinquent and other children in public care need removing as far as possible from the influence of home and family, has been overtaken by the present emphasis on the value of home and family contact and the need to do everything possible to maintain these. Delinquency increasingly is seen as a form of disturbance requiring treatment rather than punishment, and the age of criminal responsibility has become increasingly higher. Infectious diseases, including tuberculosis, and other illnesses have almost been eradicated as major causes of hospitalisation, as have a number of handicapping conditions, to be replaced by new causes and an increase in others already established (e.g. thalidomide, road accidents, spina bifida). Camp schools and work camps for hungry or workless city children have given way to adventure centres, holiday schools and outward bound courses. The demand for mother-and-baby homes has fallen rapidly in recent years, even though illegitimate births have not, and the number of children in residential nurseries has also declined steadily. In special schooling, a marked decline in numbers of 'delicate' children and a drop in the proportion of children who are blind or deaf has been more than matched by a striking rise in special provision for the educationally subnormal and the maladjusted. The workhouse policies of deterrence, cottage group homes, even the Poor Law itself have lost favour after being seemingly well established in the nineteenth and early twentieth centuries. While the philosophies and practices which led to the great mental asylums of the last century have, hopefully, also receded, the objective of current services, in theory at least, having changed from keeping mentally handicapped people away from the rest of society, in case they contaminate others, to offering a proportion of these people community care and 'normalisation'.

## The expressive nature of residential provision

Services of any kind are very expressive. If we look at them closely, they tell us a lot about the ways in which their founders perceived the nature and status of those who were to receive the services, as well as the founders' conceptions of the responsibilities and relationships of the service providers to the service receivers. Such expressiveness is most marked when services are manifested as bricks and mortar—the site, general design and architecture, the interior layout and decor of a residential unit are all highly symbolic. This symbolic significance of services, and especially residential services, has been vividly described by Wolfensberger (1969) in his analysis of the origins and nature of institutions for mentally handicapped people, in which he relates various institutional models and features to the different role perceptions of the mentally handicapped which have been held at different times. Among the common and influential roles that Wolfensberger identifies are perceptions of mentally handicapped people as—sick; subhuman organisms; menaces to society; objects of pity; burdens of charity; holy innocents; and developing persons. Each perception carries its own clear-cut implications for the way in which services influenced by the perception are run and the general type of residential service provided for mentally handicapped people. As a corollary, different institutions from different periods and societies, tell us how their mentally handicapped inmates were perceived by the population at large.

Because institutions are so expressive in the ways they reflect different role perceptions of their inmate populations, they have a profound influence on the way in which the community at large views the residents inside them. Unfortunately because of the inertia and inflexibility of residential provision referred to earlier, outmoded perceptions and attitudes, incorporated in older institutions, may continue to influence the public, even when professional opinions are beginning to change to new perceptions of the inmate populations. This situation is exemplified again in the field of mental handicap, where a system of mental hospitals, based on a former generation's perceptions of mentally handicapped people as sub-human and threats to society, still exists and makes it harder to sell the concept of community care, based on a view of mentally handicapped people as developing persons. This places a heavy responsibility on planners and management of residential services, to question the meaning of the provision they develop, to look at its symbolic significance and seek for its effect not just on the inmates' behaviour, education, etc., but on their social status and situation within society as a whole.

## Conclusion: towards a genuine community-based system

If in conclusion we make an attempt to encompass the whole residential system, three main models of care can be discerned, which perhaps help to focus attention on some of the different approaches which exist. These three might be labelled 'child care', 'educational' and 'medical/nursing', and some of their main contrasting features are given in Table 2.10, though as the census did not cover hospitals the 'medical/nursing' model has to be more speculative.

A fourth model which is largely missing in present provision (at least for deprived or handicapped children), but which might be developed in future, is a housing model; a good example of this in practice from the further education field is halls of residence or blocks of self-catering student flats and bedsitters. As applied to the residential care field it might involve similar if smaller blocks of provision with varying degrees of limited supervision or none at all, and which might provide for a range of young people, including students, young workers and others living away from home, handicapped youngsters and adolescents in care. The emphasis in such a model would be on the function of providing accommodation, with varying degrees of supervision and 'built-in' companionship, and on

TABLE 2.10

| | Type of model | | |
| | Child care | Educational | Medical/nursing |
| --- | --- | --- | --- |
| Size of unit | Small | Medium/large | Large |
| Siting of unit | Urban | Mainly rural/ county areas | Mainly rural/ county areas |
| Distribution of units | Fairly even | Uneven | Uneven |
| Staff/child ratios | High | Low | High |
| Type of staff | Child care trained; considerable proportion non-resident | Proportion of teachers; high proportion resident | Nursing trained |
| Head of unit | Child care trained; or no training | Teacher trained | Medical or nursing trained |
| Education provision | Children go out to school | Children educated on site | Children educated on site or no education |
| Children | Mixed sex; wide age range; minority handicapped | Single sex; limited age range; all handicapped in some provision | Mixed sex; wide age range; all handicapped or 'sick' |
| Emphasis in unit | Children's emotional development/relations | Children's educational/ behaviour development | Medical/Nursing needs and care of children* |
| Time in care | Medium/long with eventual discharge; all-year | Medium/long term with eventual discharge; term-time only and some week days only | As child care but no eventual discharge |

* These days, the emotional, social and educational development of handicapped children in hospital is being increasingly stressed. However since the *raison d'être* for maintaining this highly abnormal form of long-term care, especially for mentally handicapped children, hinges on the argument that the children have special medical and/or nursing needs, it seems reasonable to assume that these are the major concern of hospital units.

the housing needs of young people (and their need to develop independence), rather than on any educational, emotional or social problems they might have.

Such a range of models can be brought together to develop an overall model for a future community-based system. In this model, the aim of the system would be community provision, that is provision for and sited in a well defined small area. Segregation would be kept to a minimum, the main attribute for determining placement being a child's needs for adult help and support or his or her 'dependency level'. Children with high dependency levels (e.g. the severely physically handicapped, severely disturbed or emotionally insecure children or children in long-term care with no family ties), might be cared for in one or two small group units serving each catchment area; trained and experienced staff would be concentrated on these units, which would have high staff ratios (though as they would be small, high ratios would not involve large numbers of adults per unit). Children with low dependency levels might live in a boarding annexe attached to a local secondary school for the area; many if not most of these children would go home at weekends and holidays, and the annexe would include a wide mix, including some handicapped and some from socially disadvantaged backgrounds, children in care, as well as children whose parents wanted them to have some experience of boarding education or else had some other need for this form of care. The annexes would be larger than the small group homes, and staff ratios would be low, with a combination of child care staff and teacher/housemasters being used. Children in both types of accommodation would attend local schools.

These two types of accommodation (based in part on certain features of the child care and education models described above), might be supplemented by a housing model as described above. A few children (and it should be only a few) might need other provision, but the criteria for admission to such provision would have to be clear and well justified, and the case for an individual child's admission would need to be well argued. Apart from children needing active medical treatment or examination, and only when such treatment or examination could only be administered by hospitalisation, the hospital model of care should prove superfluous and should certainly not be required for long-term care.

Of course in practice there would be major—though not insuperable—obstacles to planning such a genuinely community-based system, not least its basic incompatibility with the existing system already described above. Such is the investment in that system, and such is its inflexibility, that any change to a real community-based system would take scores of years. The model described above also assumes co-operation and joint development between social service, education and housing authorities in planning residential provision, and there is little tradition of this to draw on. And as there is similarly little tradition of community-based boarding provision in local schools, this form of care would need careful introduction and development.

The model also poses a dilemma. Real community care is not compatible with a high degree of specialisation (and as a corollary it might be argued that a high degree of specialisation and segregation is also incompatible with the development of an integrated community, which can accept and absorb its handicapped and other deviant members). At present community care and specialisation are both principles that are generally approved of, but in practice their incompatibility has resulted in the dominance of specialisation. Community care, with consequent greater integration, would therefore not only oppose current trends, but would also run against the belief and commitment to specialisation held by many individuals and organisations; and since a more integrated and community-based system, with a strong educational component, would have implications for the future of special schools and schooling, this could be another area of potential conflict. Finally, it would also raise problems of determining the future role and work of major national and religious voluntary bodies; if such agencies started providing for and in very specific areas, the question of whether they were merely subsidising local government, relieving it of its responsibilities, would become increasingly difficult to decide and a basis for co-operation with statutory bodies would also be hard to define.

On a more practical level, there would be a number of specific problems to overcome in establishing a community-based system on a more integrated basis. For instance, if a more integrated system means a greater mix of children with special needs, there are certain logistical problems to be overcome to ensure that such needs get any necessary special help. Staff preparation and training would need overhauling, and anxieties and misconceptions about various types of children would need to be tackled; new groups of workers—for example, teacher/houseparents—would need to be established, or at least be used more extensively than at present. Then there would be the need to ensure adequate sites or existing buildings to provide the residential accommodation in and for each community area; responding to the different levels or 'mixes' of provision needed in different areas.

That these sort of obstacles and problems would arise is partly because, as already suggested, residential care, like Topsy, has just grown and even despite recent developments to secure more co-ordinated planning, the whole residential care scene retains important divisions between various sectors. Also the system has grown without adequate attempts being made to examine, question or evaluate it, either in terms of specific features, such as staffing, or as an overall system—each component in the system has been unable to look at other components. There have been few, if any, attempts to develop overall models, using child care, education and housing approaches together, and no attempt to evaluate different overall patterns of care. What seems needed urgently now are both specific evaluation projects, looking for instance at aspects of staffing and the different effects of different approaches, and large-scale evaluation of different service models, such as the one outlined briefly above. Until such evaluations are undertaken, while we can all ascribe the most benign of motives to the providers of care and to the society which encourages and pays them, we will be left to speculate whether benign intent converts in practice to benign effect.

# References

CENTRAL STATISTICAL OFFICE (1972) *Social Trends, No. 3*, London: HMSO,
DEPARTMENT OF EDUCATION AND SCIENCE (1964, with amendments to 1971), *List of Direct Grant Grammar Schools in England and Wales (List 73)* London: HMSO.
DEPARTMENT OF EDUCATION AND SCIENCE (1969, with amendments to 1971) *List of Special Schools for Handicapped Pupils in England and Wales (List 42)*, London: HMSO.
DEPARTMENT OF EDUCATION AND SCIENCE (1970a with amendments to 1971) *List of Independent Schools in England and Wales Recognised as Efficient (List 70)*, London: HMSO.
DEPARTMENT OF EDUCATION AND SCIENCE (1970b) 'List of 182 schools with boarders in maintained schools, January 1970: England and Wales', unpublished.
DEPARTMENT OF EDUCATION AND SCIENCE (1970c) 'Local authority returns to D.E.S. for 1970 concerning handicapped pupils receiving education in special schools, independent schools and special classes, under Section 56 of Education Act, 1964', unpublished.
DEPARTMENT OF EDUCATION AND SCIENCE (1971a) *Statistics of Education for 1970. Vol. 1*, London: HMSO.
DEPARTMENT OF EDUCATION AND SCIENCE (1971b) 'List of independent schools in England and Wales not recognised as efficient', unpublished.
DEPARTMENT OF HEALTH AND SOCIAL SECURITY (1970) 'In-patients under 20 years of age resident in or on short-term leave from mental illness hospitals on 7/1/70', unpublished.
DEPARTMENT OF HEALTH AND SOCIAL SECURITY (1971a) 'Mental health statistics for 1970 (England)', unpublished.
DEPARTMENT OF HEALTH AND SOCIAL SECURITY (1971b) 'Census of mentally handicapped patients in National Health Service hospitals and contractual beds on 31/12/70', unpublished material from census.
DEPARTMENT OF HEALTH AND SOCIAL SECURITY (1971c) 'Census of children

in non-psychiatric hospitals in England and Wales on 7/10/70', unpublished.

HOME OFFICE (1965 with amendments to 1971) *Directory of Approved Schools, Remand Homes and Special Reception Centres in England and Wales*, London: HMSO.

HOME OFFICE (1971a) 'Summary of local authority returns of children in care at 31/3/70', London: Home Office Statistical Division.

HOME OFFICE (1971b) 'Summary of returns of children in care for voluntary organisations in England and Wales at 31/3/70', London: Home Office Statistical Division.

HOME OFFICE (1971c) *Annual Report of Prison Department for 1970*, London: HMSO.

HOME OFFICE (1972) *Statistics Relating to Approved Schools, Remand Homes, and Attendance Centres in England and Wales for Year ending 1970*, London: HMSO.

MOSS, P. G. (1973) 'Characteristics of children in residential care', unpublished paper.

NATIONAL COUNCIL FOR THE UNMARRIED MOTHER AND HER CHILD (1968 with amendments to 1970) *Directory of Homes and Hostels for the Care of Unmarried Mothers and Their Children*, London: NCUMC.

NATIONAL SOCIETY FOR MENTALLY HANDICAPPED CHILDREN (1971) *Directory of Residential Accommodation in England, Wales and N. Ireland*, London: NSMHC.

PUBLIC SCHOOLS COMMISSION (1968a) *First Report. Volume I*, London: HMSO.

PUBLIC SCHOOLS COMMISSION (1968b) *First Report. Volume II*, London: HMSO.

PUBLIC SCHOOLS COMMISSION (1970) *Second Report. Volume II*, London: HMSO.

TIZARD, B., and TIZARD, J. (1974) 'The Institution as an environment for development', in Richards, M.P. (ed.), *The Integration of a Child into a Social World*, Cambridge University Press.

WOLFENSBERGER, W. (1969) 'The origin and nature of our institutional models', in Kugel, R. M., and Wolfensberger, W. (eds), *Changing Patterns in Residential Services for the Mentally Retarded*, Washington DC: President's Panel on Mental Retardation.

WOOLFE, R. (1968) 'A role for boarding education in the context of the social services', *Social and Economic Administration*, 2, 116–30.

# 3    Quality of residential care for retarded children

Jack Tizard

Most severely retarded children in residential care live in conditions which compare very unfavourably with those which govern the lives of ordinary children brought up away from parents in long stay residential nurseries and children's homes. It is usually said that two factors account for the difference: the severe problems of nursing and managing mentally retarded children, and the gross inadequacy in staff numbers and in resources available in mental subnormality hospitals. Such factors are of course of very great importance—but they are not all-important in that even among institutions caring for the same type of child, and having much the same resources, there are marked differences in child upbringing patterns. My colleagues and I (King, Raynes and Tizard, 1971) carried out a series of studies to explore the reasons for such differences. Our general beliefs were, first, that the organisational structure of a residential unit in large part determines staff roles and role performances—that is, the manner in which staff act towards each other and towards the children over whom they have control. Second, we believed, *staff behaviour* influences the manner in which children behave, and the competencies which they acquire.

This chapter describes the kind of children with whom we were concerned in our studies, the manner in which we set about the inquiries, and the general conclusions we drew from them.

## *Severely retarded children*

Severe mental retardation (I.Q. under 50) is a chronic handicapping condition, sometimes diagnosable at birth and usually during the preschool years. In almost all cases the handicap persists throughout life. Severely retarded children do of course grow and develop and acquire competencies, just as normal children do, though development is slower and often differs qualitatively from the development of normal children. Unlike normal children, however, and unlike mildly retarded, educationally subnormal, or slow learning children, few of the severely retarded grow up into socially independent adults. The great majority become independent in the physical and social skills of eating, dressing, washing, walking, and managing their toilet and most learn to talk, but few severely retarded adults are able to live and work independently of others. Without parental or other support therefore, most of them eventually go into some kind of residential care.

Many severely retarded children have additional mental and physical handicaps. In a study of ninety such children living at home and of sixty in institutional care, it was found (Tizard and Grad,1961) that only 47 per cent enjoyed good physical health and a further 26 per cent fair health. There were 11 per cent with stable health but 'total physical incapacity', while 16 per cent had poor health or very severe health problems. About half the sample had *special* health problems (epilepsy, a sensory or motor handicap, or a disabling heart condition) and for about half of these the handicap was severe. There was little difference between the sample living at home and that in institutional care in these respects.

Many children also had behavioural problems. Fewer than half (41 per cent) were rated as being normal in temperament; 9 per cent were sluggish or under-active; 25 per cent were over-active; 9 per cent were uncontrollable; while the remaining 16 per cent were too low grade to rate. Of those at home 31 per cent presented no special problems of management, but 38 per cent gave some problems and the remaining 31 per cent presented severe problems. Only a quarter of the institutional sample presented no problems of management, while 42 per cent presented severe problems.

As measured on the Vineland Scale the 'social age' of about a third (34 per cent) of the children living at home was less than three years, and a further 29 per cent had social ages of less than six years. Among the institutional children 77 per cent had social ages of less than three years, and a further 13 per cent of less than six years.

Children such as these present very difficult problems of upbringing, and it is easy to see that they are at risk of being placed in institutional care.[1] Today in England and Wales about one-fifth (9,200 out of an estimated 45,000) of all severely subnormal children are in institutional care; 7,400 in mental subnormality hospitals and 1800 in local authority, voluntary or privately run hostels. Some children are admitted to 'short-stay' care in paediatric and mental subnormality hospitals for medical or social reasons, but most severely retarded children once they go into residential care remain there for years if not for life. The institution thus serves as a second home, of if they are admitted when young, as the only home they know or will ever know.

## The quality of residential care for retarded children

A succinct and remarkably self-critical description of residential care for the mentally handicapped has been offered in the recent

White Paper *Better Services for the Mentally Handicapped* (HMSO, 1971). This report points out that until the end of the Second World War it was thought best that those who could not be cared for at home should be segregated from the rest of society in institutions—or 'colonies' as they were often called. Most of these were run as self-sufficient and closed communities. The institutions provided a sheltered environment in which comprehensive care throughout life was available for the mildly as well as the seriously handicapped, segregated from the rest of society. The institutions served a social as well as a medical need.

Despite other changes brought about by the establishment of the National Health Service, it was not until the *Report of the Royal Commission on the Law Relating to Mental Illness and Mental Deficiency* (1957), and the new Mental Health Act of 1959, that changes were proposed in the pattern of residential services for the subnormal. The Royal Commission recommended that hospitals should be responsible only for those requiring specialist medical treatment or training or continual nursing provision, while local authorities should provide small residential homes or hostels for adults and children who could not remain at home but who did not need to be in hospital. These, it was said, should not be isolated but be in centres of population where the residents could take part in the life of the community.

During the 1960s slow progress was made in the implementation of these proposals. At the end of 1969 there were only 1,800 children in residential homes run by local authorities or voluntary bodies, and partly as a consequence of the lack of alternative forms of care most mentally subnormal persons (both adults and children) who were not living in their own homes were still in mental subnormality hospitals. As the White Paper (1971) pointed out many of these are isolated, difficult to get to, large in size, overcrowded and housed in unsuitable buildings which allow little privacy. Most hospitals are also seriously under-staffed: shortage of finance has limited the total numbers employed; the size and location of many hospitals has made it difficult to find sufficient staff locally; and poor working conditions have made it hard to attract new recruits (*ibid.*, para. 107).

The criticisms of mental subnormality hospitals made in the White Paper and by others (Morris, 1969; Martin, *et al.*, 1970) rightly drew attention to the poor material conditions in mental subnormality hospitals, to the shortage of staff, and to the substantial proportion of residents who present mental and physical problems which require a level of care which cannot at present be provided. However the White Paper also noted that 'many hospitals fail to plan the therapeutic resources at their disposal so as to use them to best effect for the population concerned . . . (poor living and working conditions) are the fault of management at all levels, not of ward staff, and the latter are understandably resentful of criticisms they have sometimes received'.

## The child welfare project

Despite the recognition, in the White Paper and by other critics, of the importance of 'management' factors, few analyses of these have been undertaken, and our own studies were concerned with such matters. We did not of course deny the importance of the shortages and inadequacies in material resources and in personnel to which the White Paper drew attention: their influence in depressing standards of care may be compared to the influence of poverty in causing malnutrition among children in developing countries. But just as not all children living in similar circumstances in developing countries suffer from *kwashiorkor*, so, we argued, not all institutional upbringing need be so bad as much of it is. In particular we were not convinced that conditions in mental subnormality hospitals would necessarily be raised to a level comparable with that achieved in good residential units serving the needs of ordinary children in long-stay care if improvements were made simply in staff ratios, in the reduction in size of living units and establishments, and in the material environment of such places. Organisational factors seem to be at least of equal importance; and our own studies explored and analysed these, by comparing institutions which catered for the same type of child and which had much the same range of resources available to them but which were differently organised and which used their resources in different ways. We first carried out an extensive series of *field studies* in 2 large homes for children, with twenty-two and thirty-six units respectively, in 5 long-stay wards in a children's hospital, in 16 wards in a mental subnormality hospital for children, and in a local authority hostel and a voluntary home both of which cared for severely subnormal children. After further pilot work we then carried out a *survey* of 16 institutions for mentally retarded children, in each of which one living unit was selected for study.

The field studies indicated that there were remarkable differences in the manner in which children's lives were organised in different types of unit. In the long-stay hospitals (both the hospital for physically handicapped children of normal intelligence and the hospital for mentally handicapped children) child management tended to be rigid and inflexible in routine, children were regimented in groups and made to queue and wait around without anything to do for lengthy periods, and in general had few possessions or opportunities for self-expression or initiative. There was a 'social distance' between the staff and children which was manifested by the formality of staff/child contact and in the discontinuities between staff and inmate 'worlds'. These features, which Goffman (1961) singled out as being characteristic of *total institutions*, were scarcely to be found in either the children's homes or the mental subnormality hostels. Here child management practices were on the whole child oriented: management practices were flexible, being adapted to take into account individual differences among the children of different circumstances; activities were organised in such a way that residents were allowed to participate or not in them as they pleased and were allowed to do things at their own pace; there were opportunities for residents to show initiative, to have personal possessions, to be alone if they so desired; and the social distance between staff and children was diminished through the sharing of living space and the opportunities that were made available for staff and children to interact in functionally diffuse and informal situations.

We argued that the differences could not plausibly be attributed to differences in the characteristics of the children. Children in both the long-stay wards of the hospital for sick children and in the wards of the mental subnormality hospital were brought up in an institutionally oriented manner, whereas severely retarded children in the local authority hostels and the voluntary home were brought up in a child oriented manner which resembled that found in the units studied in the all-age children's homes for normal children deprived of normal home life. Moreover there were no systematic differences in patterns of care between wards in the mental subnormality hospital having patients who were more, or less, severely handicapped; and there was ample evidence in the literature to suggest that non-handicapped but deprived children had been brought up in an institutionally oriented manner in the past.

Our second study was a survey of practices in sixteen institutions. Differences among units and between types of institutional care were further explored, and attempts were made to account for them. We argued that different patterns of organisational structure in different units would tend to result in different patterns of staff activity and interaction; these in turn would tend to bring out different patterns of child care; and differences in child care patterns would be responsible for differences in patterns of child behaviour and attainment.

Since our central objective was to account for differences in child management patterns, our first task was to devise a measure of child management practices which would permit units to be compared one with another. After much pilot work, we devised an objective and highly reliable, thirty-item, child management scale to enable us to measure certain commonly occurring child management practices and so permit comparisons among units to be made. Later, other scales were devised to measure the autonomy or responsibility given to staff, to obtain details of the unit organisation, and to get from staff information about activities that were a regular part of their job or, on the other hand, only done occasionally or never. A simple interview with the head of each establishment provided us with information about the number and size of the constituent units and the general administration of the establishment; more detailed interviews with the head of each unit studied gave us information about numbers and deployment of staff, responsibilities given to particular staff members, how decisions regarding purchases of toys and clothes for the children were made, how birthday presents were obtained, and the arrangements made for the children's holidays. We also found out whether the head of the unit had a petty cash allowance, and asked how decisions affecting the children and staff were made. In addition, in each unit, observations which in aggregate amounted to nearly two full days of observing and recording were made on a time sampling basis. They provided us with detailed information on the activities of the staff and the way in which they interacted with the children in their care.

The units selected were alike in the age range of the children they cared for, and were comparable in other ways including assigned staff ratios. However they differed in size, as well as in patterns of organisation, and we were not wholly successful in matching hospital and hostel units according to the proportion of children in them who presented severe problems.

A week was spent in each of the sixteen units studied. At the end of the period all staff members were asked to fill in and return a questionnaire concerning themselves and their role in the unit. A full account of both studies is given in King, Raynes and Tizard (1971).

# Findings

These can be discussed under four main headings: (1) Differences in child management practices; (2) Factors regarding staff ratios and staff deployment; (3) Staff roles and role performance; (4) Relationships among the findings concerning the amount of responsibility or autonomy given to staff, the manner in which staff were trained, and child management practices.

## Differences in child management practices

Findings relating to differences in child management practices can be summarised briefly. There were indeed large and characteristic differences in child management practices, as these were measured by the child management scale, between the two main types of unit— hostels, and mental subnormality hospital wards. (Of the three voluntary homes, one was for practical purposes indistinguishable from a local authority hostel, one functioned as a small hospital, and the third displayed idiosyncratic factors which made it impossible to classify. These units can therefore, be omitted from this summary of findings.) All the hostels had child oriented patterns of care, while *all* the hospitals were institutionally oriented. Children in the hospitals were generally rather more handicapped than the children in the hostels. However it was possible to find units of different types—hostels and hospitals—caring for very similar groups of children but with very different patterns of care. The data thus again suggested that differences in management practices were not related to the level of handicap of the residents.

Neither the size of the institutions nor the size of the living units could be definitely related to differences in child management practices. The hospitals were, of course, larger than the hostels, and in general hospital wards had more children than did the living units in the hostels. However, considering hostels and hospitals separately, the differences relating to the size of the institution and to the size of the unit, were not systematically associated with differences in child management scores. In short, differences in child management scores were found between hospitals and hostels (with no overlap in scale scores between one group and another) but we did not think that these were related to the size of the establishments, the size of the units, or the handicaps of the children.

## Factors regarding staff ratios and staff deployment

Findings about staff ratios and staff deployment also appeared to us to be clear cut.[2] All of the units we studied had staff *assigned* to them in reasonable numbers by today's standards. (To that extent they were *not* typical of mental subnormality hospitals in their staffing ratios.) There was no relationship between assigned staff ratios and scores on the child management scale. However staff in the different institutions were used very differently, and when we calculated *effective* staff ratios for different periods of the day we found that child oriented units had most staff on duty at 'peak' periods of the daily routine when they were most needed. In institutionally oriented units this did not happen and there were no differences in staffing when peak and slack periods were compared. Child oriented units also enjoyed greater continuity of staffing than institutionally oriented units, not simply because their turnover was lower, but also because staff were not moved around from one unit to another. We concluded that the differences in child management practices were not due to staff numbers, though they were related to staff deployment.

## Staff roles and role performance

A third, and more significant, series of findings concerning factors affecting staff roles and staff role performance differentiated institutionally oriented from child oriented units. The heads of child oriented units spent a significantly greater proportion of their time in activities which necessarily involved them with children, while heads of institutionally oriented units spent significantly more of their time in tasks which did not necessarily involve them with the children, namely domestic and administrative activities rather than social, physical and supervisory child care. In child oriented units the staff also interacted more frequently and more warmly with the children, whatever else they were doing at the time, than did the heads of institutionally oriented units. They spoke to the children one-and-a-half times as often, were twice as likely to *accept* and three times less likely to *reject* the children than the heads of institutionally oriented units.[3] When they were engaged in domestic or administrative activities the heads of child oriented units tended to undertake them in the presence of children rather than in isolation from them. To some extent the same associations were found when these variables were examined within institutional types.

There was also more division of labour in institutionally oriented units, tasks being allotted to staff according to their status, whereas child oriented units were characterised by greater role diffusion and by greater participation by senior staff in menial or dirty jobs.

Junior staff were required to do much the same tasks in different establishments: but they carried them out very differently. In child oriented units, as measured by the scores on the child management scale, junior staff interacted with the children more frequently and more warmly than their counterparts in institutionally oriented units, just as their seniors did. They talked to children to a significantly greater degree, and rejected children significantly less often than junior staff in hospitals. In other words, both staff roles and staff role performances differed as between types of institution.

*The relationships among the findings*

How can we account for these three sets of findings summarised above? The data from the survey reinforced the views which we had formed during the course of the earlier field studies concerning the determining influence of the head of the unit on establishing and maintaining different patterns of child care. The more that unit heads were involved in the everyday care and supervision of the children, and the more they talked to them, the more likely were junior staff to behave warmly towards their charges, and the more child oriented were the patterns of care in the unit.

But why should some unit heads be more involved in child care than others? Why should the differences between types of institution be much greater than the differences among institutions of the same type? Psychological factors relating to staff are no doubt in part responsible for differences in staff behaviour in institutions of the same type. But unless we postulate that mental subnormality hospitals recruit, or selectively retain, staff who prefer administration and domestic work to actually caring for handicapped children, whereas hostels recruit and retain staff who 'naturally' spend as much time as possible in child care and as little as possible in administration, we cannot account for the absolute differences in child management practices which we found. An explanation of differences in terms of selection and retention of staff of different personality types has a certain plausibility—but there is little evidence in support of it. It is difficult, for example, to account for the behaviour of junior staff in these terms. Nor can psychological explanations explain changes in institutional style which have occurred both in residential institutions in the child care services (Heywood, 1959; Flint, 1967) and in some mental hospitals (Jones and Sidebotham, 1962; Wing and Brown, 1970). Many well documented transformations in patterns of care have occurred in institutions in which few significant changes in personnel have taken place.

We concluded therefore that differences in management style could not be accounted for in terms of unit size, staff ratios, the handicaps of the children, the facilities available or the personal qualities of the staff. Nor could we explain the differences in terms of the sheer amount of administrative and domestic work requiring to be done in the different types of unit. Though they are short staffed, hospitals do after all have domestics; food is ordered and meals are prepared off the ward; clothing and laundry are centrally organised; nurses are expected to nurse, not to do administrative and domestic duties. In the hostels the unit head was responsible not only for child care but for almost all aspects of the day-to-day management of the unit as well. In short, she ran the place, as a parent runs a household. Thus she had more, not fewer calls upon her time than a charge nurse in a ward, who was largely relieved of many 'non-nursing' responsibilities. It was clear, therefore, that other explanations of differences in child care practices, and more generally in unit style, were required to account for our findings.

We examined two such factors: first the relation between the amount of responsibility given to unit heads, and second the influence of the kind of professional training they had had.

## Responsibility and child management

The autonomy of the unit heads was assessed by a scale containing items relating to the degree of freedom from inspection and supervision by supervisors which she enjoyed; by the degree of control she had over policy decisions affecting the children, and the buying of goods for the children in the unit; staffing decisions; and matters relating to unit management, particularly the organisation of the children's regime. We asked questions of the head of each unit about each of these areas of responsibility, and made up a scale of eighteen items. Each item was scored on a three point basis ranging from 0 when the unit head claimed to have little or no say in the decision, through a score of 1 for cases where her advice was sought, to 2 where she had full power to decide the issue.

Each item in the scale discriminated statistically between institutionally oriented and child oriented units, and when scores were summed there was no overlap between types of institution and total scores. The summed scores for the five hospitals ranged from 6 to 12, indicating a uniformly low level of unit autonomy; those for the hostels ranged from 22 to 30, all very much higher.

The data thus indicated that the term 'unit head' takes on a quite different significance in different organisational settings. In the hostels, the position of the head of the unit does not merely carry status, but also effective control over a wide range of unit matters. In each unit there is only one person in charge, and although her authority is limited to some extent by budgeting and other constraints, the limitations are relatively small. The position of the head of the unit (ward) in the hospital is very different. In all wards many of the responsibilities which fell to the head of a hostel unit were entrusted to departments or staff members who were not attached to any particular living unit. The position thus carried status but little effective control. The findings suggested to us that much of the activity recorded as administrative within the hospitals was administration of an intermediary kind required by the wider organisation—filling in requisitions, writing daily reports, maintaining records—so that others whose responsibility this was could check them. The delegation of more responsibility to hostel heads, allowing them to negotiate direct with outsiders for goods and services, actually appears to have released more of their time for the daily care of children.

## Staff training

The second factor we examined in seeking an explanation for differences in the patterns of staff activities, and more particularly the way in which those activities were performed, was staff training. For purposes of the analysis we divided type of training into three categories: nurse training, child care training (with or without nurse training as well) and no relevant training.

All but one of the heads of units had received a relevant course of professional training. All of the nursing sisters or charge nurses were trained in mental subnormality nursing. Three of the heads of hostel units were nurse trained and five had received child care training. In all types of establishment a high proportion of junior staff were untrained and because so many junior staff were not trained we restricted further analysis to heads of units—a status group which in any case seemed to be of overriding importance in determining events in the living units.

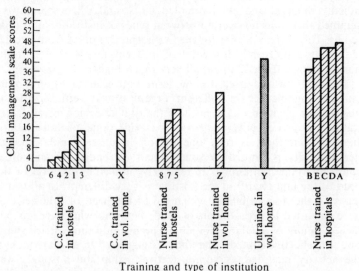

FIGURE 3.1    *Training of unit heads and child management scale scores*

We had predicted that the role performance of unit heads would be related to the type of training they had received. We expected that unit heads who had high rates of interaction with the children would have received a training in 'child care' in which such matters are given some emphasis; and that unit heads with low rates of interaction would have been trained as nurses, their training stressing physical aspects of health and disease.

There was considerable support for this hypothesis. Figure 3.1 presents the child management scores for all 8 hostels, the 5 hospitals, and the 3 voluntary homes according to the type of training which the head of each unit had received. The data show no overlap between hostels and hospitals in child management scores, the range in scores for hostels being from 3 to 22 and for hospitals from 37 to 47. The three voluntary homes differ widely in child management scores.

Moreover, as Figure 3.1 shows, the type of training that unit heads in hostels and in voluntary homes had had was also related to child management scores. The five hostels in which the head was child care trained had an average child management score of 7·4 whereas the three units in which the head was nurse trained had a mean score of 17. Despite the small size of the sample this difference is statistically significant.

Further analyses indicated that child care heads were more likely to talk to children, less likely to reject them, and more likely to be interacting with children while engaged in domestic or administrative duties than were heads of units who were nurse trained. They were also more involved with the physical care of children. There was also some evidence that hostel wardens who had had a nurse training were more likely to assign tasks to junior staff according to their status (as was done in the hospitals) than were the wardens of hostels who had had a child care training.

The scores of the three voluntary homes were in accord with these findings. Voluntary home X, with a child care trained head, had a lower score on the child management scale than voluntary home Z with a nurse trained head. The head of unit X, moreover, talked more to children, rejected them less often, accepted them more frequently and had a higher rate of interaction during domestic and administrative work than the head of unit Z. Voluntary home Y, with a head of unit who had received no relevant training, resembled the hospital units in a great many respects, including the pattern of role performance of the person in charge. The findings suggested that the type of training received by staff exercises a powerful influence—not only on the way in which they carry out their duties, but also on the patterns of care maintained in the units. Within the broad constraints imposed by the organisational structure of establishments of different types, the training of unit heads seems to be a most important variable in determining what happens within the units.

## Effects on the children

A problem which is as yet almost unexplored is to describe and account for differences in the behaviour of mentally handicapped children in institutional care and mentally handicapped children living at home. There are of course many descriptions of 'typical' institutional behaviour, both of deprived children of normal intelligence in children's homes, and of mentally retarded children in hospital. There are however very few reports of the prevalence of such behaviour, and virtually no attempts have been made to relate it to specific features of the institutional regime. The design of our own study did not permit us to relate patterns of care to behavioural differences in the children—and the fact that the hospitals had more seriously handicapped children than did most of the hostels would in any case have made this difficult. We did, however, collect some data. In the field studies we had found that children in hostels were more skilled at feeding and in speech than otherwise comparable children in the hospitals. In the survey, it was possible to compare groups of children of similar diagnosis, physical handicaps, age and intelligence in different types of institution. Those in child oriented units were significantly more advanced in speech and feeding than those in institutionally oriented units. We could not rule out the possibility that such differences resulted from selective factors. However, we thought it likely that the greater frequency of conversation to the children by staff, more of whom were available at peak times when the children were in the units, and the fact that the staff ate with the children thus providing an adult model for them to copy, accounted for the higher levels of skill on the part of the children in the child oriented units.

This matter deserves much more study; and only investigations in which detailed observations are made of child behaviour as well as staff behaviour are likely to be illuminating (see Chapter 8). A sympathetic, qualitative study of 'the empty hours' spent by children in long-stay hospitals has been carried out by Oswin (1971).

## Implications

The studies summarised above grew out of earlier work in the Child Development Research Unit which had, in different and less explicit ways, explored qualitative differences among institutions and attempted to account for them (*Portfolio for Health*, DHSS, 1973). For us in the Unit, the child welfare project provided guidelines which we have attempted to use in subsequent inquiries. The chief ones are: (1) institutional studies must, if they are to produce findings which can be generalised, be comparative. Single case studies can at best only be interpretive (though they may, and often do, provide the insights which make subsequent comparative studies possible). Given the richness and variety of everyday life it is as easy to devise interpretations of why things are this way rather than that, as it is difficult to decide among conflicting speculations. Replication, an essential element in all scientific endeavour, is particularly important when one is studying complex phenomena.

(2) Comparative studies must, almost of necessity, use quantitative techniques through which to measure differences between one unit and another. The reasons are twofold. First, complex organisations usually differ quantitatively rather than qualitatively: discontinuities in function are uncommon. Hence questions of the sort: 'Is A more like B than B is like C?', 'Do A, B and C form a group which is different from X, Y and Z? ,'What influence do P and Q have upon R, S and T, and which is greater?, are essentially statistical questions rather than categorical ones implied in a theory of ideal types. And inasmuch as this is so they require quantitative data to answer them. Second, the complexity of complex organisations suggests that no explanation which makes use of only a limited number of variables can account for all the differences between one institution and another. We can in other words only account for part of the variance. But how much? And of what variance? And with what predictors? Such questions can only be answered by 'hard' data rather than 'soft'. Moreover it is only through the use of hard data that we are likely to be able to throw light on the unsolved and still badly formulated questions of the extent to which particular institutions can depart from a modal type. As yet we know little about how to introduce institutional change, or about the factors (size? autonomy? isolation? organisational structure?) which make for institutional stability, ultrastability or instability in how institutions function; nor do we know whether institutional reform has a natural history, or indeed how to monitor the progress of such reform. To study such problems we require to analyse their elements and to see how these interact in different combinations and conditions. The analyses are bound to be complex, and if they are to be replicated by others the elements must be specified in a manner which makes data collection replicable.

(3) In our studies we have relied largely upon observational rather than interview data, and have used behavioural rather than

attitudinal material where possible. Sometimes the data were judgments made by the observers of the *quality* of the behaviour being observed. The reliability of all data, but especially judgmental data, must of course be established in advance, and checked at intervals during the field work. Thus in the present inquiries concepts such as *rejecting* and *accepting* were given an operational definition in terms of specific types of staff behaviour; the reliability of the observers' judgments was known before we started—and known to be high; and reliabilities were checked at intervals during the fieldwork.

(4)  Basic to the method of approach is the examination of phenomena at different *levels*. In our own studies we looked at the organisational structures of the institutions we were studying; at the behaviour of staff; and to a limited extent at the competencies of the children. Clearly the analysis could and should go beyond this. What determines the organisational structure of a ward? What happens when only some elements of a particular type of organisational structure are present, or when the 'strength' of different elements differs? How are children's competencies affected by the length of exposure to different treatments? What is the modal range in staff behaviour in differently organised units? Questions like these arise naturally from a dimensional approach, and an analysis at different levels seems to us essential if one is to answer them. At each 'level' it is true many questions can be answered in a sort of way without studying phenomena at other levels. But the answers will be incomplete and will probably be eked out by generalisations drawn from other levels which apparently fit the explanation. Too often, however, what passes for knowledge here is, rather, surmise—social cliches which explain and could explain everything or nothing. And the fewer and more unstandardised the data, the more confined to one 'level', the easier the 'explanation' and the greater the likelihood that it will turn out to be mere anecdote.

(5)  Our final conclusion was that it was valuable to attempt to specify hypotheses in advance, and to lay out the criteria of falsification before undertaking the field work. We were able to do this partly because we went round the course twice so to speak—the first time during the field studies, and the second during the survey. The field studies gave us the landmarks while the survey enabled us to chart them properly. Again, it must be stressed, we were fortunate in that our generous grant from the Association for the Aid of Crippled Children enabled us to do this.

*A final word*  Having said all this the unsatisfactory nature of inquiries of the type described above must be pointed out. They are immensely laborious to carry out. The number of replications required to test hypotheses is almost always very much larger than the number of institutions able to be studied. Institutional characteristics have a tendency to 'clump' so that sometimes one cannot find a single instance which would enable one to get at least *some* evidence about the effect of a discrepant variable (e.g. we did not find any hospital wards in which the sister in charge had had a child care training in addition to a nurse training. No doubt there are such nurses: we just did not meet them, though we did meet hostel wardens who were doubly trained in nursing and child care). All of this means that 'explanation' must, as far as we can see, remain at present a mixture of theory and tested inference on the one hand, and of assertion and illustration on the other. The best hope for the future may be that replication and validation may be possible through the study of different types of institution (e.g. boarding schools, old people's homes, children's homes, mental hospitals). Inasmuch as we can predict from studies of one type of institution what the characteristics of members of other types of institution are likely to be, organisational theory will have some power.

# References

DEPARTMENT OF HEALTH AND SOCIAL SECURITY (1971) *Better Services for the Mentally Handicapped*, Cmnd, 4683, London: HMSO.

FLINT, B. M. (1967) *The Child and the Institution*, Hodder & Stoughton.

GOFFMAN, E. (1961) *Asylums: Essays on the Social Situation of Mental Patients and other Inmates*, New York: Doubleday; Chicago: Aldine.

HEYWOOD, J. S. (1959) *Children in Care*, London: Routledge & Kegan Paul.

JONES, K., and SIDEBOTHAM, R. (1962) *Mental Hospitals at Work*, London: Routledge & Kegan Paul.

KING, R. D. (1973) 'Alternatives to the hospital for the residential care of the mentally retarded', in Wing, J. K., and Haffner, H. (eds), *Roots of Evaluation: The Epidemiological Basis for Planning Psychiatric Services*, proceedings of the International Symposium held at Mannheim 26–9 July 1972. London: Oxford University Press for the Nuffield Provincial Hospitals Trust.

KING, R. D., RAYNES, N. V., and TIZARD, J. (1971) *Patterns of Residential Care: Sociological Studies in Institutions for Handicapped Children*, London: Routledge & Kegan Paul.

MARTIN, F., BONE, M., and SPAIN, B. (1970) *Services for the Subnormal*, Oxford: Pergamon.

MORRIS, P. (1969) *Put Away: A Sociological Study of Institutions for the Mentally Retarded*, London: Routledge & Kegan Paul.

OSWIN, M. (1971) *The Empty Hours: A Study of the Weekend Life of Handicapped Children in Institutions*, Allen Lane: The Penguin Press.

*Portfolio for Health 2* (1973) 'The developing programme of the DHSS in health services research', London: Oxford University Press, for the Nuffield Provincial Hospitals Trust.

ROYAL COMMISSION (1957) *Report of Royal Commission on the Law Relating to Mental Illness and Mental Deficiency*, London: HMSO, Cmnd 169.

TIZARD, J., and GRAD, J. (1961) *The Mentally Handicapped and Their Families: A Social Survey*, Maudsley Monograph no. 7, London: Oxford University Press.

WING, J., and BROWN, G. (1970) *Institutionalism and Schizophrenia*, Cambridge University Press.

# 4 Organisation and change in children's institutions

Kevin Heal and Pat Cawson

## Antecedents of change

Conflicts between new and traditional ideas can be seen in many types of residential care, and in one area, the care of delinquents, these have recently led to the passing of a major piece of legislation, the Children and Young Persons Act 1969. This Act changed the whole conceptual framework for the residential treatment of delinquents by integrating it with community services for deprived children. This chapter discusses findings based on recent research which it is hoped will eventually be published in full. The results suggest some organisational characteristics of approved schools which could hinder the expression of this change in outlook.

Established in the mid-nineteenth century as a means of rescuing delinquents from the prison system, the reformatory and industrial schools were founded in the belief that delinquency was caused by poverty, neglect and faulty training. The solution was therefore to remove the children from their bad environments and provide them with the trade training and moral example which would enable them to become good citizens. Eventually these schools were incorporated into the approved school system by the Children and Young Persons Act 1933. This Act consolidated the original pattern of provision and management of the schools under the supervision of the Home Office, which has responsibility for law enforcement and the control of crime. Although internally the approved schools of today are very different places from their nineteenth-century counterparts, the administrative structure within which they operated prior to 1970 had therefore been substantially the same for more than a century (Carlebach, 1970).

Concern at the rise in delinquency and at the increasing failure of existing attempts at prevention and cure, led during the 1960s to two Government White Papers outlining new approaches to the problem. The second of these, *Children in Trouble* (Home Office, 1968) formed the basis of the 1969 Act and summarises the arguments and plans on which legislation was based. Its text reflects changes in attitude to the causes and cures of delinquency:

> It is probably a minority of children who grow up without ever misbehaving in ways which may be contrary to the law.

Frequently such behaviour is no more than an incident in the pattern of a child's normal development. But sometimes it is a response to unsatisfactory family or social circumstances, a result of boredom in and out of school, an indictation of maladjustment or immaturity, or a symptom of a deviant, damaged or abnormal personality. . . . The aim of the changes . . . is to increase the effectiveness of the measures available to deal with juvenile delinquency. Effectiveness means helping children whose behaviour is unacceptable to grow up, to develop personal relationships and to accept their responsibilities towards their fellows, so that they become mature members of society; in some cases it also means firm control of anti-social behaviour.

Here the ingredients of the problem are outlined: unsatisfactory homes, boredom, maladjustment and abnormality. The solutions are the provision of good substitute care and control, with treatment where necessary. The Act, which came into force at the beginning of 1970, provided for the progressive disbandment of the existing centrally controlled approved school system, and its integration with the locally controlled system of care for children who are in need. The legal changes were accompanied by a transfer of responsibility for children's services in general from the Home Office to the Department of Health and Social Security, and their amalgamation with local authority social service provision. The redesignation of approved schools from being special schools to being 'community homes with education on the premises', reflects the major change in the emphasis behind the legislation. The focus for treatment now is on the social rather than the educational and training needs of the child.

For both schools and local authorities, the legal changes required a major reappraisal of working relationships and co-operation. Awareness of the possible problems led to the establishment of a co-operative venture between central and local government which aimed at charting the progress of change and monitoring its problems. Three local authorities planning to develop new community homes on the basis of existing approved schools mounted an experimental project with the Children's Department Development Group, formerly in the Home Office and now the Development Group of the Social Work Service in the Department of Health and Social Security. A report was produced (The Community Homes Report, *Care and Treatment in a Planned Environment*, Home Office, 1970) which discussed issues seen as crucial to the 'Community Homes' ideal. The research programme associated with the project was intended to describe and analyse the difficulties in adaptation which the schools experienced, in a way which would help other schools in a similar situation.

In planning the research it was decided to attempt a cross-institutional study, rather than a case study. While case studies of institutions have been valuable in generating understanding of problems, they are limited by the difficulties of deciding when problems are the results of idiosyncratic features of one institution. However it was felt that the study should aim at knowledge in depth, as well as general comparison, and the project therefore developed two parts: an intensive study of the three project schools, and the development of reliable instruments for cross-institutional comparison. For the second part of the study six other schools were asked for help. Most of the data on which this paper is based come from the cross-institutional comparison of the nine schools, but some material from the project schools is used to illustrate the findings.

Many of the more important recommendations of the Community Homes Report were concerned with the manner in which the schools were organised, and two in particular were seen by its authors as crucial for the fulfilment of the ideals behind the legislation. One was that the pattern of staffing and staff relationships should change (p. 28):

> In our view a situation in which the leader exercises his authority
> from a central co-ordinating position, rather than as the head
> of a hierarchy, is most likely to provide a setting in which
> supportive relationships can grow, and in which all staff are
> encouraged to take their full responsibility as adult members of
> the community.

The second is that the new community homes are expected to provide much greater help for the development of interpersonal relations between individual staff and children, of a kind which can begin to compensate for the impoverished relationships which many children have previously experienced. This is not to say that such relationships could not or did not develop under the old system, but rather that improved conditions, such as small groups, better material facilities, higher staffing ratios and a different conception of role, can make such relationships easier to form and maintain (pp. 26–7):

> The staff of a community home needs to create and maintain
> an environment where children, including those who are very
> disturbed and difficult, can feel welcome, comfortable and safe.
> Such an environment can encourage the growth of personal

relationships between children and adults, enabling the staff to provide support to the children while helping them to cope with their individual problems and to face the implication of disturbing behaviour. . . . In such a situation adults and children are able to respond to and respect one another as persons and relationships can be formed without regard to any staff structure or specific function of individual adults.

The emphasis on the importance of the organisation reflects a growing awareness that organisational characteristics have an important part to play in creating the patterns of behaviour and relationships which prevail between individuals. In looking at the approved schools' attempts to adapt to the new legislation, and the change of emphasis from training to treatment, we felt that many of their problems could best be understood in terms of the conflict between two models of organisation, the school model and what we shall call the child care model.

Although never integrated with other provision for state education, approved schools have nevertheless developed as educational institutions, headed and staffed mainly by teachers. Their organisational structure reflects that described by educational sociologists as characteristic of the traditional day school. Experiments with staff democracy and therapeutic communities take place in some areas of both normal and special education, but in general the school organisational structure is hierarchical, with the headmaster in a uniquely powerful position. Comparative educational research has emphasised the power of the headmaster as a characteristic of British schools which distinguishes them from those of other western countries, and this is often traced back to the development of the headmaster role by the great Victorian headmasters, such as Arnold (Baron, 1956).

In the school model the headmaster's power extends to all areas of school life, and he normally makes rules to govern the most trivial details of behaviour (King, 1968, pp. 94–5):

> The extent of his authority not only enables him to possess a high degree of personal autonomy but also to define the degree of autonomy of those subordinates. . . . He may control (pupils') actions in most spheres of their activities at any time within the school and anywhere within the school. He may use his power to regulate the length of their hair, where they may whistle or walk, even the colour of their underwear.

It is necessary to distinguish between two concepts, the power structure and the style of management. The power structure defines the rights of the individuals at various levels, and the scope of their authority. The style of management is a question of the personal approach which a manager takes towards his staff. The power structure in itself does not enforce or prohibit authoritarian or democratic styles of management, but can make them harder or easier to maintain. In practice the power structure is modified by professional norms, and in the school these create the expectation that teachers will be conceded autonomy in the classroom settings (Hargreaves, 1972). One distinction which has been made with reference to professional roles is that between 'programmed' and 'unprogrammed' decision-making (March and Simon, 1958). A programmed decision is one made in accordance with instructions from above, or existing precedents. An unprogrammed decision is made to meet a new situation with reference to professional goals or ideals. In the educational setting it is usual for decisions on teaching style and classroom management to be unprogrammed and left to the skill and judgment of the teacher. Decisions on outside classroom matters, such as corridor and dining room management and general school rules, are programmed by the headmaster.

In the day school these rules governing behaviour operate in only a limited part of the child's day, but in the residential school they extend throughout the twenty-four hours and to all the pupils' activities. The headmaster therefore has the power to regulate areas of the child's life which would normally be the prerogative of parents. In the approved schools, since normal school holidays are not followed, and the children's natural parents have been divested of parental rights by the care order, the power of the headmaster is even greater than in other school systems.

The day school organisation also sets patterns of expectations about interaction between teacher and pupil. The teacher's role requires him to interact with a large group of children simultaneously. For this to be successful, it has traditionally been considered necessary for him not to become too involved with a particular child or group of children, since this may result in loss of control or alienation of the unattended group. Advice given to teachers still commonly follows this pattern. Although teachers are expected to have good relationships with their children, and to be concerned about them, this must not go too far (Hoyle 1969, pp. 42–3):

Before any of the broader social roles can be adequately performed, the teacher must be able to control his class. . . . This fundamental preoccupation with control generates a wide range of norms through which teachers hope to minimize the spread of indiscipline. These norms include the maintenance of 'social distance' from the pupils, and in public at least, a ceremoniousness in interaction with colleagues.

It has been suggested that the formality of relationships has developed because the school social order is a means by which it carries out its task of educating. 'Formality is the basis of the order that is necessary for education to go on' (Shipman, 1968). This is consistent with the findings of research on task performing groups, which has shown that under certain conditions efficiency is dependent on the leader maintaining sufficient distance (Fiedler, 1967). The norms of impartiality and good discipline have become integral to the teacher's role, accepted alike by teachers and pupils (Musgrove and Taylor, 1969). These constraints upon the teacher's role have implications for their functioning in the residential school setting, which will be explored later.

There has been little research on the organisation of children's homes, but the material that is available suggests that a fundamentally different organisational model from that of the school, that of the 'quasi-household', is now usually adopted (King *et al.*, 1971). In this model, houseparents operate as substitute parents, making the detailed decisions about the children's day-to-day life and the running of the home which would normally be controlled by the family, and staff duties are arranged to facilitate a high degree of personal involvement with particular children. Superintendents, matrons and other senior staff are likely to adopt a managerial role. Unlike the headmasters, they would not usually expect to control the day-to-day routines and domestic matters, since these are seen as a basis for parent/child involvement, and the expression of care. In terms of decision-making, the children's short-term upbringing is largely subject to unprogrammed decision-making by the child care staff in immediate contact with the children. Although policy decisions are made by the top levels of management, 'the usual practice in the homes was for these matters to be discussed with unit heads first, often at their instigation' (King *et al.*, 1971). (Unit heads in children's homes are houseparents.)

The recommendations in the Community Homes Report are in fact concerned not with the organisation of teaching in community homes, but with the style of substitute care to be offered. They deal not with the traditional areas of school responsibility, but with the extended roles which a residential establishment has, of being 'a good parent' and of providing treatment for the disturbance from which the child is thought to be suffering. They recommend that this extension of function should be reflected through individual role extension of all staff, so that all staff can fulfil the functions of treatment and what we shall call 'parenting'. The Report appears to advocate a substitution of something resembling the child care model for that of the traditional school, with the intention of changing the emphasis from education and training to that of substitute care and treatment.

It is apparent from the two models we have described that there is some organisational incompatibility between the 'school' and 'home' models. Therefore, existing within the legislation there is an unstated organisational conflict which is distinct from the legal and administrative implications of the Act. It seemed important to see how closely approved schools adhered to the ideal 'school' model, since this would provide some indication of the difficulties confronting any school trying to incorporate a 'community home' model.

### The survival of the school model

The schools in which the research took place were in many respects diverse in character. All were approved schools for adolescent boys, but there were marked differences in regime. Ages ranged between 10–18 years, but each school covered a span of four or five years within this range. Three of the schools were 'house' schools with all boys living in self-contained house buildings designed to approximate to the family home. In such schools 'house' staff usually live on the premises with the boys, with most remaining staff occupying 'tied' houses on the school site or in the local community. Five were 'block' schools with all boys living in shared common rooms and dormitories as in a traditional boarding school. In only one of these schools did houseparents live on the premises. The remaining school was at an intermediate stage with some boys in the main block building and some in a separate house building. The size of the schools varied from 18 to 80 boys, and of the staff group from 8 to 25. In all, more than 500 boys and 150 staff took part in the research. In common with many other studies of institutions we found that our results were not accounted for by size of institution, by staff/boy ratio, nor by the age range of boys in the schools, and these variables will not be discussed further in this paper.

All nine of our schools had some level of organisational division into small groups. All were organised into class or trade training groups for the purposes of education, and all but one had some form of house system. Although allocation to class, trade group or house is not necessarily fixed or permanent, most boys would normally remain members of the group for a large part of their stay at the school. Only one of our schools allowed boys to change working group or house more or less at will, and groups could therefore be regarded overall as having a reasonably stable membership. Allowing for problems of staff shortage and staff turnover, the schools also tried to maintain stable links between the small groups and a particular member or members of staff, although the extent to which this was successful varied between schools.

The meaning of house membership was clearly not the same in all schools. In some it entailed residence in separate buildings, in others shared house common rooms and dormitories, in others it appeared to be merely a name. The main organisational effects of an operative rather than nominal house system which could be observed lay in the extent to which staff/boy contacts were channelled. Particular members of staff would be responsible for supervising the free time and personal concerns of the boys in a particular house. In the school with a nominal house system, staff supervised the entire school on a rota basis, and links were limited to being responsible for administrative matters such as the files. Houses usually consisted of from 15 to 25 boys. They had one housemaster or house warden with official responsibility for the house, and might have assistant housemasters, housemothers, teachers or instructors attached to a house team. This practice seemed to reflect a greater commitment to house organisation than did the use of other staff entirely as a central pool.

Approved schools have two kinds of work group, the usual school class for boys below school leaving age and the trade training group for those above school leaving age. Originally the trade groups were intended to emulate the apprenticeship setting, and were staffed by craftsmen instructors. Recent developments, such as the raising of the school leaving age, have led to a tendency for trained teachers to replace the craft instructors, and shortly after our field work ended several of the schools which we knew began a process of amalgamating trade groups into their ordinary teaching timetables. Work groups were generally smaller than house groups, containing between seven and ten boys as a rule, and at the time when we were studying the schools, the boys' contacts were primarily with one teacher or instructor rather than with a team or group of staff.

## School organisation and perceived environment

The work began with periods of participant observation and informal discussions with staff and boys. This enabled ideas derived from previous research to be interpreted in terms applicable to the approved school situation, and gave valuable guidelines for the development of questionnaires. The differences between the two organisational models previously described lies in the power distribution and role definition among the staff, and in the patterns of relationship between staff and children. In the school model, power lies with the chief administrator, who delegates less to his subordinates than in the child care model; relationships between teachers and pupils tend to be more formal than the quasi-parental style aimed at in children's homes. A number of techniques were developed to examine these aspects of the approved schools more systematically than was possible by observation. These focused on the staff perception of their role, and patterns of problem solving in the school; staff attitudes to children; and the children's perception of behaviour and relationships in their school.

From the data collected we concluded that there had been very little departure from the school model of organisation in the schools which we examined. Results were consistent in pointing to the retention of a centralised school model in which the senior staff were the effective people.

The children's perception was examined by use of a scale developed to measure the 'social climate' of their schools (Heal *et al.*, 1973). By this was meant the pattern of work, behaviour and relationships perceived by the boys as normal or usual. The questionnaire took the form of a number of statements in each of the areas examined, boys being asked to say whether these statements were true or false of their school. The two areas of particular relevance to this paper were those defined as 'Work' and 'Staff Support'. Examples of the statements which boys were asked to consider are: 'It is easy to skive here when you should be working' (Work subscale) and: 'Staff encourage boys to talk about their feelings' (Staff Support subscale). Other sections of the questionnaire dealt with perception of staff strictness, the friendliness of other boys, the behaviour patterns common in the schools, and general satisfaction with school experience. Results made it possible to select areas in which the schools differed significantly from each other. The boys in any one school showed a high level of consensus in the way in which people behaved and got on together in their schools, and the crude background variables which we were able to examine (the age of the boys and the length of time which they had been in a school) did not significantly affect their assessment of it. The fragmentation into small groups for living and working also appeared to have relatively little effect: the small group climates were rarely strong enough to override the school homogeneity, and in some schools were not found at all. Subsequently a closer examination of answers in the schools where differences were found proved revealing, and will be discussed later, but in general the results indicated that small group climates were a reflection of that of the whole unit, rather than existing in their own right.

Staff attitudes were measured using a scale developed from previous work on organisational and attitude change in mental hospitals and 'correctional' schools. Staff were asked to state their agreement or disagreement with a number of statements concerning the treatment of the children in their care. The dimensions measured could be divided into two areas, that of control and that of relationships. Schools proved also to have individual attitude climates which were not accounted for by the training, background or experience of staff, or by personal qualities such as age and sex. Results from both scales therefore suggested that the schools were operating very much as a single unit rather than as a collection of small groups.

When the relationships between staff attitudes and social climate as perceived by the boys, was examined in detail, very little relationship was found with the attitudes of lower level staff.[1] This was so even when it was possible to relate the answers of individual teachers or housemasters to those of boys in their own house or work group. However, a significant relationship was found between attitudes of senior staff, and the boys' perception of the support, strictness and work orientation of their schools. The direction of the results was opposite to that expected, in that the schools which were seen as most supportive, and least strict and work orientated, were those in which senior staff favoured more formal relationships with the children. As suggested later, we came to feel that the results can best be explained in terms of the effect which the senior staff have on the actions of other staff. The unexpected results and the small number of schools involved mean that the analysis needs to be treated with caution but the overall picture is one of schools functioning very much in the traditional school way, with a charismatic and powerful central leadership setting the 'tone' of the establishment.

## Staff roles

It is not difficult to understand the processes by which this situation could arise, in a system whereby most effective decisions are made at the top. The examination of staff role perception showed clearly the areas in which this centralised decision-making pattern was most influential. Decision-making in schools is required in a number of areas: the educational curricula, the timetable and routine, the system of rewards and sanctions, are but a few of the possible areas. We were interested in the way in which the school dealt with its non-school functions, the parental and therapeutic roles. Staff were asked to complete a role definition questionnaire, giving them a list of tasks which fall into five role areas: the education/training role; the parental role; the organisational; custodial and treatment roles. They were asked to rank these tasks in the order of priority which they felt the school required of them in their role. This is their assessment of what Levinson calls the 'perceived role demands' of the organisation (Levinson, 1959). It does not necessarily reflect what staff are in fact expected by seniors to do, but is an estimate of the goal priorities which have filtered through to staff.

In contrast to the other questionnaires, there were here only very slight differences between schools, and results suggested that roles were defined and perceived similarly in all schools. There was thus a strong consensus of opinion among teachers, for example, as to what a teacher in an approved school does, and a similar consensus among house mothers as to the role of a housemother. This similarity suggests that the organisational structure within which roles are determined was similar for all schools which were studied.

Table 4.1 gives the answers from 99 staff in nine schools. It can be seen that all categories of lower level staff feel that they have high involvement in the custodial function of 'keeping order', and that they are more involved in this than in the treatment areas of 'treatment planning' and 'contact with the boys' families'. Educational staff, teachers and instructors, report that their education and training functions assume priority over their treatment and parenting functions, while house staff see their organisational functions as being important. This is particularly so for housemothers, who rate domestic work as the most prominent part of their job.

In the area defined as 'parenting', one item was entitled 'showing concern for boys'. This was described by such activities as 'taking an interest in the everyday pursuits of the boys, and discussing their personal problems with them, as a parent would with his own children'. Although all staff see this as important, only housemasters appear to feel that they are able to treat it as the primary characteristic of their role. For all other lower staff it becomes secondary to an educational or organisational task. Trade instructors and teacher/instructors both record that their custodial task of keeping order assumes prominence over the tasks associated with their parental role.

The category of 'treatment planning', as defined to the staff, covered areas of decision-making such as attendance at case conferences, writing reports on boys, and making decisions about treatment and discipline. Again, only housemasters give this a rank which suggests that they see it as an important part of their present

TABLE 4.1  *Perceived role demands—rank order judgment by 99 staff*

| | | Teachers | Craft* trained instructors | Teacher* trained instructors | House-masters | House-mothers | Senior staff |
|---|---|---|---|---|---|---|---|
| Education | { Education | 1 | 5 | 5 | 7 | 6 | 6 |
| | Work training | 5 | 1 | 1 | 10 | 9 | 9 |
| Parenting | { Showing concern | 2 | 3 | 3 | 1 | 2 | 1 |
| | Social training | 4 | 4 | 4 | 4 | 3 | 5 |
| Organisation | { Domestic | 10 | 10 | 9 | 9 | 1 | 10 |
| | Administration | 8 | 7·5 | 7 | 5 | 10 | 3 |
| Custody | { Protecting society | 6 | 6 | 8 | 8 | 8 | 8 |
| | Keeping order | 3 | 2 | 2 | 2 | 4 | 7 |
| Treatment | { Treatment planning | 7 | 7·5 | 6 | 3 | 7 | 2 |
| | Contact with boys' families | 9 | 9 | 10 | 6 | 5 | 4 |
| Number of staff | | 25 | 14 | 13 | 25 | 13 | 9 |
| Kendall's coefficient of concordance   W | | 0·48 | 0·47 | 0·56 | 0·37 | 0·53 | 0·62 |

* Answers from trade instructors were examined separately according to whether they had a teacher's or a skilled craftsman's background.

All W values significant at $P < 0.001$, i.e. within each category of staff, the agreement on ranking the 10 items was extremely high, the probability of this occuring by chance being less than 1 in 1,000.

TABLE 4.2 *Perceived role expectation—rank order judgment by 99 staff*

| | | Teachers | Craft* trained instructors | Teacher* trained instructors | House-masters | House-mothers | Senior staff |
|---|---|---|---|---|---|---|---|
| Education | Education | 2 | 5 | 3 | 5 | 6 | 6 |
| | Work training | 5 | 1 | 2 | 8 | 8 | 9 |
| Parenting | Showing concern | 1 | 2 | 1 | 1 | 1 | 1 |
| | Social training | 4 | 4 | 4 | 4 | 4 | 5 |
| Organisation | Domestic | 10 | 10 | 10 | 10 | 3 | 10 |
| | Administration | 8 | 9 | 8 | 7 | 9 | 4 |
| Custody | Protecting society | 9 | 8 | 9 | 9 | 10 | 8 |
| | Keeping order | 7 | 3 | 7 | 6 | 7 | 7 |
| Treatment | Treatment planning | 3 | 7 | 6 | 2 | 5 | 2 |
| | Contact with boys' families | 6 | 6 | 5 | 3 | 2 | 3 |
| Number of staff | | 25 | 14 | 13 | 25 | 13 | 9 |
| Kendall's coefficient of concordance W | | 0·55 | 0·45 | 0·61 | 0·62 | 0·51 | 0·57 |

* Answers from trade instructors were examined separately according to whether they had a teacher's or a skilled craftsman's background.

All W values significant at $P < 0.001$, i.e. within each category of staff, the agreement on ranking the 10 items was extremely high, the probability of this occurring by chance being less than 1 in 1,000.

role, and here it is seen as less prominent than their responsibility for supervision. All other lower level staff give ranks to 'treatment planning' which suggest that they see it as a very minor part of their role performance. For senior staff the position is reversed, and they see themselves as very much involved in the treatment and parenting areas and very little involved in the others except for the task of administration. In general therefore lower level staff see themselves as having higher involvement in the traditional areas of school, and lower involvement in the 'extended' parental and therapeutic areas. Senior staff see themselves as the agents of the schools' therapeutic and parental functions.

Second, staff were asked to rank the items in the questionnaire in the order of their own ideal role conception; the priority which they expected to be able to give to the different tasks. Table 4.2 gives the answers from the same 99 staff. By comparison between tables 4.1 and 4.2 it can be seen that senior staff rank treatment and parenting variables similarly on both, and thus were apparently content with their existing role definitions in these areas. They aspire to greater involvement with boys' home background, rather than delegation of this area, and to lesser involvement with routine administration. Although there are some individual differences, lower level staff on the whole aspire to greater involvement in parenting and treatment areas and less involvement in custodial and organisational matters. The biggest single difference is on the task of 'keeping order', in which four of the five categories of lower staff clearly feel that they are too frequently used merely to keep the school running, rather than as members of a professional team.

The findings present a consistent picture, in that the areas in which the senior staff feel highly involved are those from which others feel relatively excluded, and vice versa. The tables suggest a centralised decision-making structure, particularly in the area of treatment. This is in accordance with the suggestion that senior staff are largely influential in setting the school social climate. Some indication of potential conflict is also given in that the only area which senior staff wish to delegate further, administration of routine school matters, is one in which lower level staff feel themselves already overburdened, while the areas which senior staff see as their prerogative are those which other staff aspire to take over.

Some evidence from the three project schools both helped to complete the picture of centralised power in the parental and treatment areas, and to pinpoint one of the possible effects of centralisation. Part of the intensive research project included a sociometric questionnaire to measure patterns of relationships in the project schools. One question from this examined the patterns of approach to the staff for help. Boys were asked: 'If you were worried about a problem at home, which member of staff would you talk to about it?' Their answers gave a neat picture of their perception of power in this area. Table 4.3 shows that boys are considerably more likely to name a senior member of staff than any category of lower level staff.

TABLE 4.3    *Staff who would be consulted about a problem*

|  | School 1 | School 2 | School 3 | Total |
|---|---|---|---|---|
|  | % | % | % | % |
| Senior staff | 71 | 56 | 65 | 62 |
| Other | 21 | 37 | 17·5 | 29 |
| No one | 8 | 7 | 17·5 | 9 |
| Total | 100 | 100 | 100 | 100 |

Total number of boys = 138. School figures are given in percentages to conceal the identities of the schools.

Evidence from all sources was therefore consistent in suggesting that attempts to introduce change towards the child care model through building, staffing and training had not seriously affected the organisational structure.

The degree to which all schools participating in the study adhered to the traditional school model was most immediately apparent in relation to the possession and exercise of power by the headmaster and deputy, and the way in which they 'defined the autonomy' of their subordinates. Preliminary observation showed that many of the daily routines and rules governing the 'home' life of the boys were made centrally by the headmaster. Where lower staff did have power to make decisions in such matters as boys' haircuts, clothes or bedtimes, for example, they were not exercising power as a right, but on the understanding that it could be withdrawn at any time if the headmaster felt that individuality was getting out of hand, or if he wished to impose sanctions of his own for misbehaviour unconnected with lower staff.

The scope of centralised rules did of course vary to some extent between schools. Some headmasters seemed more prone than others to withdrawing or checking on delegated power, while in some there seemed little to withdraw. For example, in one school which appeared to have a relatively high commitment to house organisation, housemasters were allowed complete discretion to plan the evening and weekend programmes for the boys in their house. After some incidents of vandalism, the headmaster decided that during free time boys were to be kept in their house rooms, and not allowed to wander freely about the premises. This was a severe curtailment of the housemaster's decision-making power, made without prior discussion with the staff concerned. Yet the power to make un-programmed decisions about the boys' evenings was still greater in this school than in the three schools where two or more hours of organised activities were compulsory every evening for all boys.

Of particular importance is the possibility that the schools, when faced with the extended roles of substitute parents and therapists, appear to respond, not by adapting their organisation to fulfil these roles, but fitting them into the framework within which they have previously tackled educational, organisational and custodial objectives. This does not imply that the existing organisational structure is innately deficient, but that it was designed for one set of objectives and is now being required to meet a different set. How far the existing structure succeeds in meeting the 'care and treatment' objectives is a  matter of crucial importance to the future develop-ment of 'Community Homes'.

## Central decision-making, care and treatment

The suggestion that the senior staff regard themselves and are regarded by others as the chief pastoral agents in the school, has a number of implications. Senior staff are extremely busy men, often with matters outside the school, and are not the people with whom the boys have close day-to-day contact. Although this may some-times give them a detachment and calmness that staff in closer contact could lack, it will not enable problems to be dealt with in the context of a close personal relationship. It also has the dis-advantage that senior staff may simply not be there at the time when the help is needed. The ability of staff to give support with problems as they arise must clearly depend in part upon the extent to which lower level staff are able to make 'unprogrammed' decisions rather than referring difficulties to seniors.

To examine the problem of staff autonomy and the provision of emotional support of a parental and therapeutic nature to the boys, we looked more closely at the level of differentiation between the small groups in the school. As suggested earlier, although overall their effects did not seem large, they appeared to have more effect in some schools than in others, and to affect some areas of school life more than others. To the casual observer, even the most decentra-lised schools showed relatively little difference between the units. In only one of the schools did boys reply to a question during interview by saying 'well, it depends which house you're in'. The more usual answer was 'well, it depends whether the Head or the Deputy is on duty'. However, one area of the boys' questionnaire which did show differences between houses in some schools was that of perceived staff support, the extent to which staff were seen as interested in and helpful with boys' personal problems. The range of differences between schools was also high. For example in one school the statement 'Staff encourage boys to talk about their feelings' was said to be true by 96 per cent of the boys, while in another only 53 per cent felt that it was true of their staff. Differences within the school were associated only with the house membership, and work group membership had no significant relationship with levels of support. In some schools houses seemed to have very different patterns of support, while in others, answers from different houses were indistinguishable. Interestingly this was not particularly related to the existence of separate buildings or premises. Some schools which had physically independent buildings showed no difference between houses, some in which all houses shared common accommodation showed wide differences in perceived support.

This seemed to bear out our observation that commitment to house organisation could affect the degree and nature of contact between staff and boys, but did not explain why work groups, which are smaller and with longer hours in contact, did not have the same effect on staff support in the schools. This, and the apparent unimportance of the separate buildings to the school climate, indicated that some other factor than outward structure influences the behaviour and relationships which develop in the house setting. In schools where no differences were found between groups, it seemed unlikely that this resulted from identical personalities or abilities of a number of staff, and we therefore concluded that diversity between houses reflected the amount of autonomy allowed them. In some schools, the organisation may be so planned that the personalities of the housemasters can have little impact on house social climate. In others, we suggest those where staff may have greatest power to make 'unprogrammed' decisions, the level of support is much more influenced by the individual staff in charge of the houses. The finding that the more 'formal' senior staff appeared to run more supportive schools can be seen in this context. In such schools the seniors are perhaps less likely to perceive themselves as 'chief therapist' and more likely to allow their staff to deal with boys' personal problems.

The 'staff support' scores are not, of course, a measure of how much the staff do in fact care about boys' problems, but reflect whether they have succeeded in conveying this interest to the boys. The existence of differences between house scores on staff support was closely associated with the overall school level of support: the schools which had a high perception of support were those which had more house diversity, whereas the schools where differences between houses were small or non-existent had lower overall levels of support.

These findings were particularly important in the light of recent work on staff roles in children's institutions, which has suggested that a hierarchical and bureaucratic style of organisation is associated with a poorer quality of staff/child interaction, what has been called the 'quality of care' (see Chapter 3; also King *et al.*, 1971). The authors suggest that the explanation for this is that in a centrally controlled system, staff are treated as replaceable units in the system, rather than as having a contribution in their own right. To do this is to deny the professional skills of the staff, and make it impossible for them to operate in the 'particularist' manner which most professional groups regard as essential for good performance of their roles.

In the approved schools there was evidence from observation that this could happen. 'Well, it's no good asking me, you'll have to see the headmaster' is a commonly heard answer to boys' requests. Some staff noted this reaction in themselves, and analysed its causes. A housemaster in one of our most *decentralised* schools described his own job in the following words:

'What it actually consists of is referring things. I am in no position to make decisions. . . . If ever a boy feels that he needs to go home, and you think there are good reasons for it, you can't say 'yes, you can go'. It's up to the headmaster. . . . Your knowledge and judgment counts for nothing at all. If a boy came to me and said he had found a job and did I think he would be allowed to go home, I really couldn't say. I would have to tell him to go and see the headmaster, and if it were at the week-end when the headmaster was off duty, the boy would have to wait till Monday. I couldn't give any indication.'

Further evidence that bureaucracy could make it difficult for staff at a lower level to use their personal skills to help the children was found in re-administration of the social climate scale in three of the larger schools after a period of eight months. All three schools had staff changes during this period but only in the school which had earlier shown the highest level of house independence in 'staff support' scores were there any significant changes in social climate. These changes were those which would be expected to result from the departure of familiar and trusted staff, and their replacement by newcomers: lower levels of support, friendliness and satisfaction, greater emphasis on strictness, and a rise in bad behaviour. In the schools which had relatively little 'small group' differentiation, substantial staff changes appeared to have had little impact on the boys.

Among the staff interviewed as part of the intensive project, there was certainly a considerable body of opinion that the lack of autonomy affected boys' perception of staff.

'Because staff aren't involved [in planning treatment] it means that boys have less respect for you. They don't see us as a team, who are working together, they see us as the Headmaster and his staff.'

'If the boy asks you what happened at the case review, I have to say that I don't know. This is the time when you feel absolutely useless and redundant.'

Clear also from these comments are the underlying feelings that staff themselves object to their lack of autonomy. It was not un-common in some schools for them to speak of themselves as merely childminders, policemen, domestics, or clerks.

It was possible to use the answers on the role definition question-naire to examine more systematically staff satisfaction with what they saw as the order of priorities in their existing roles. This was done by using Kendall's rank correlation to compare the perceived 'performance' ranking of each individual member of staff with his ideal 'expectation' ranking. If staff rank the two similarly, they may be presumed satisfied with the way in which their role is defined in the school. We found that senior staff and craft-trained instructors were the most satisfied with their role definition. House staff and teacher-trained trade instructors were least satisfied, and the average scores suggested that for most staff in these categories there was very little relationship between what they saw themselves as doing, and what they felt they ought to do. Low satisfaction scores seemed to relate to having no area in which the individual is able to define his role in accordance with his wishes. In particular the house staff, with peripheral status in the school model, have no area of autonomy unless senior staff choose to allow them one.

When training was related to role satisfaction throughout the staff group, it became clear that it was the staff with the most appropriate training for treatment and 'parenting' who were least likely to be satisfied. Those with either their major training or with supplementary or in-service training in child care, youth or social work, record the lowest levels of satisfaction. Those with teacher-training only, those with craft or technical training, or with no training, were much more likely to accept their assessment of the *status quo* as satisfactory. Examination of staff turnover figures in the intensive project showed that lower level staff with training in residential child care or social work were significantly more likely to leave their schools than others. The loss could not be accounted for by upward mobility of well-trained staff, since only two of the nineteen leavers left for promotion, and only three of the group remained in the approved school service, most of the remainder moving to other areas of child care, special education or social work.

Overall, the relationship between role satisfaction and staff turnover did not reach the 5 per cent significance level. Turnover will obviously be affected by other factors such as staff relationships, tied accommodation, or family matters. Nevertheless the results suggested that approved schools have difficulty in retaining those staff whose training is most appropriate to their developing treatment and parenting functions, and that role dissatisfaction may contribute to the unwillingness of such staff to remain in the approved school service. This has implications for the success of the community home ideals, and for the processes by which change can be implemented within such an apparently self-perpetuating system.

### Resistance to change

If the problems outlined above are to be successfully tackled by the embryo community homes, it is important that their constituents are understood. In a residential establishment, possessing some or all of the characteristics of the total institution (Goffman, 1961) conflict between stability and change acquires a perspective which is in many ways unique. Residential care of all kinds has, for a variety of social, economic and historical reasons, tended to develop in a context of social isolation. This reflects the ambivalent attitude towards the deviant and can take a visible form, with hospitals, homes and prisons often being situated some distance from residential areas. It also frequently involves a distinct organisational and professional culture, with staff experience, promotion and training taking place separate from the professional mainstream. Residential social work has not so far followed the example of the social service field professions in developing a common training and professional structure. Differences in salaries and working hours, and the frequent provision of tied accommodation all contribute to the pressures on staff to stay within a particular system (though not necessarily in a particular institution) and to build their personal and professional lives around it to a greater extent than would perhaps be common today in non-residential employment. In the approved schools the staff who stay within the system are those who were found to be most likely to have traditional attitudes, the trade instructors. In our complete staff sample, trade instructors had been in their present posts significantly longer than other categories of staff, and similar results have been found in a study of approved schools in the South West Region (Millham *et al.*, 1972). As the people who stay seem to be those least likely to demand change, the balance is in many ways more in favour of stability than change.

The problems of incorporating new ideas on the treatment of delinquency have been exacerbated by certain features of the schools' development and history. Particularly important is the separate administrative and legal framework within which the schools operated from the founding of the system until 1970. The fact that they were distinct from locally provided facilities for the care of destitute children, the education of handicapped children and the treatment of disturbed children, has been a major contributor to their relative isolation at local level from other types of children's institution. One consequence of this separation was that it became possible for social workers and approved schools to develop misconceptions about each other, which in turn aroused mutual anxieties over the proposed integration. Examination of the respective staff journals of the approved schools and the child care service provides much material on the tensions and hostilities which were expressed in the years between publication of the plans for Community Homes and the enactment of the legislation.

The refusal of the two staff associations to adopt the officially provided new title of 'community home', and their self-appointed title of 'community school' reflected the direction of feeling in many approved schools. They had pride in their school tradition and function, and wished to retain this.

Practical expression of this conflict first became possible when links with child care were established through the development in the 1950s and 1960s of a comprehensive local authority service for deprived children, also under the supervision of the Home Office. This laid the foundations for a period of transition which was to prove crucial to the approved schools. The growth of child care as a profession has been associated with many changes in the standard of care offered to children in institutions, and the Children's Department and Children's Inspectorate of the Home Office took an increasingly positive role in feeding new knowledge and ideas from the field of child care to the approved schools system. Changes such as the establishment of separate house buildings to replace large dormitories, dining rooms and other living accommodation; and the introduction of child care staff in the form of housemasters and housemothers, to complement the existing teaching and training staff, were moves initiated by central government, and were preliminaries to the major legal changes implemented by the 1969 Act. The fact that changes were to a large extent imposed on the approved schools resulting from pressures by the child care professions and central government, rather than from within the system, is critical when considering the problems of stability and change in the schools. However the conflict is not only an external one but finds expression within the schools themselves, because the staff are not members of one profession with common training and promotion structure, but fall into three groups, the teachers, the trade instructors and the house staff, each reflecting a different ideology and different strand in the approved school tradition.

The hostility towards approved schools often expressed by the child care profession, and the tendency for the public to over-react to any disturbances which occur, seem likely in the short run at least to lower morale and discourage more adventurous policies. Nevertheless it did seem to the research workers that there were other contributors to the static nature of approved school organisation, which were not transient features of the current political climate in relation to approved schools but were rooted in their inheritance from the education system as firmly as is their present organisational structure. The evidence suggests three areas in particular which may lead to misunderstanding and problems in communication and management in the schools.

## The pastoral role of the senior staff

The results of the role definition questionnaire, suggesting the high value which senior staff place on their pastoral role, are similar to findings of research on headmasters and deputies in other types of school. It is common for headmasters and deputies to feel that they are in a position to exercise a more lenient and understanding manner towards pupils when necessary than are their subordinates, who are in constant daily contact and trying to maintain authority. The attitude scale showed that senior staff were indeed more likely than lower staff to express liberal and permissive attitudes. Their position as seniors has also enabled them to operate as an ultimate deterrent to wrongdoers.

It has often been pointed out that it is not by chance that the most senior position in a British school is called the Head Teacher, rather than the Principal, as is the case in Europe or America. The role is traditionally seen as one which involves personal contact with the children, rather than a purely administrative function. If headmasters and deputies in approved schools were to delegate many of the decisions on the treatment and discipline of the boys and the daily running of the school, which they currently regard as their prerogative, this would imply a fundamental alteration of their role. No longer could they operate as head teachers in the traditional sense, but rather as co-ordinators and administrators dealing with staff, as outlined in the Community Homes Report. Their reluctance to accept this change is no doubt related to their desire to retain some of the personal contact with the children which provided the enjoyment of their teaching days, and to remain within the area of their professional expertise.

This dilemma is not unique to the approved school situation, and the development of larger schools is having a radical effect on the headmaster role in education generally. In the personal service professions, where promotion necessarily involves a level of isolation from the client, similar conflicts are found. Some senior staff were well aware of this problem:

'My philosophy used to be—it isn't now!—that if I had the same staff ratio as a fragmented school, in a block school building, I could run a better school. I have now grown up, and realised I am not God. I can't expect to have all the say: other staff want the chance to exert their own influence on a group of children, not be under my thumb all the time.'

A different approach was outlined in another school:

'I try to make all routine things so routine that we don't need to worry about them. I lay down the policy for each boy when he comes. [House staff] will usually come for final decisions but I expect them to deal with day-to-day routines.'

This summarises two characteristics of a centralised system: the making of decisions at senior level, and the handing down of routines to be implemented at lower level.

It is important to realise that this attitude does not result from individual headmasters' wishes for absolute control, but from a genuine belief that it is helpful to staff to have such clear-cut policies. It is seen as reducing the stress accompanying a very difficult job. In the traditional school setting this belief is probably justified, because outside-classroom matters are peripheral to the teachers' major task. In the residential special school, however, the outside-classroom problems and 'domestic' routines take on a new importance, as intrinsic to the staff's development of a parental role.

The development of the 'houseparent' role is dependent on the senior staff's willingness to withdraw to some extent from the 'programming' of all such decisions. This does not mean that they should abdicate responsibility, since they share with the heads of all institutions for children the ultimate responsibility for the safety and behaviour of the children. Furthermore, research on professional workers in a variety of settings has shown that they value leaders who adopt a positive and interested approach to the work of subordinates (e.g. Gross and Herriott, 1965; Halpin, 1966). But it is suggested that the traditional 'headmaster' role may need reinterpretation to deal effectively with the wider aims of the residential school.

Any alteration to the existing pattern of responsibility is made more difficult for the approved school head because the very much wider scope of approved school power, particularly before 1970, meant that miscalculation could have a devastating effect on the future and happiness of children already 'at risk'. Because the head has control over the child's total environment, in a way rarely equalled in other institutions for older children, he also has very wide responsibilities. Because his pupils are by definition difficult and anti-social, the community demands their control. This situation places enormous pressures on the head, and this same situation makes it both possible and tempting to relieve those pressures by centralising control over his areas of responsibility.

But the differences in the extent and areas of control found within this group of schools, and in other research on approved schools (Jones, 1968; Millham *et al.*, 1972) suggest that their special population cannot fully account for the existing patterns of control. While permission to leave school grounds could be seen as a response to the population, restrictions on, for example, the children's appearance or television viewing, or staff attendance at case conferences, cannot. The proportion of staff who are untrained is also often argued as a factor affecting delegation, but the lower role satisfaction scores of staff with appropriate training suggest that this too cannot be the whole answer. In terms of staff training, approved schools in general are rather better off than most institutions for children (Department of Health and Social Security staffing returns, 1970). Research on other forms of children's institution has shown that detailed programming of duties, domestic routines and involvement in treatment plans is not innate to the residential situation, but related to the professional traditions of staff and the management structure of the institution (Street *et al.*, 1966; King *et al.*, 1971). The centralised pattern of control in approved schools is in keeping with an acceptance of the traditional 'headmaster' role found in other types of school. Because this is not simply a question of individual inclination, but of a powerful professional tradition, still supported extensively by colleagues within the profession, it is far harder for individuals to reject or modify the role.

## The pastoral role of teachers

The role expectation rankings also showed that staff with a teaching background consider that their parental task of showing concern for the children should be a more important aspect of their role than teaching or work-training. This too is not unique to approved school teachers, although it seems likely that the feeling would be particularly strong among people attracted to work with disturbed children. Studies of the role conceptions of teachers in primary and secondary modern schools (the teaching background from which most approved school teachers come) have shown that they commonly consider their social and moral functions as more important than their instructional function (Morrison and McIntyre, 1969). It seems possible that the belief that their role as teachers should enable them to perform a pastoral function of this kind, contributes to the resistance of schools to organisational change. If teachers feel that the emotional needs of the individual child can be adequately met in the classroom, it is unlikely that they would see the necessity for organisational change, and the introduction of an alien professional group. This is particularly true since such developments are an implied criticism of the teacher's ability to provide pastoral care, and one being made by the newer and less well-established profession of child care.

Observation suggested that in the approved schools such an assumption was deep-rooted. Some staff stated this explicitly:

'Where small groups' relationships are concerned it's the teachers who play a more important part at the moment—they are the people who really talk to the boys.'

'I would like to see [evening supervison] done by housemasters. It's different for teachers, you can build up good relationships in the workshops and when you take activities, because you have small groups . . . [in the evenings] you're just walking round looking for things going wrong . . . you're just walking round counting heads. You're not working together.'

While not all teaching staff would support this extreme point of view, the use of staffing and other resources seemed often to be planned in accordance with a belief in the supportive value of classroom and workgroups. Much of the day in most schools is spent in group activities. The approach to staffing ratios is similar to that taken in a day school, and the higher ratios are allocated to the organised groups. During the unstructured time, staff resources are normally cut back to a minimum, as they would be in the playground or dining hall at the day school. Often there seemed considerable evidence of a failure to clarify the ways in which the skills of a parent and the parent/child relationship differ from those of the teaching situation, and the feeling that child care staff were not really necessary to the functioning of the school was made apparent through inadvertent comments. On a visit to one of our schools, for example, the question of staff shortages was discussed. Following the drop in numbers of children in approved schools, which occurred after the implementation of the 1969 Act, schools with particularly low numbers were asked not to fill staff vacancies. The headmaster in one school told one of the research workers that this restriction had caused very little problem for him. 'The only staff we have lost have been housemasters, none of my teachers or instructors has gone.'

Evidence from this study certainly does not support the assumption that work or activity groups can provide adequately for the boys' emotional needs. There was a negative correlation between boys' perception of the emphasis placed on work in their school and the supportiveness of the staff, indicating that there is some level of conflict between the two, since schools only seemed to provide a strong emphasis on one at the expense of the other. Furthermore in the schools in which levels of staff support were associated more closely with work group membership than with house group membership, the overall levels both of work and support were lower than in those schools which appeared to provide support through the house system. This has important implications, not only for the 'care' provision, but also for the educational needs of children who are often serious under-achievers. The implications for 'support' are clear: work groups were not efficient providers of support, and small groups were no more supportive than large groups. In the conflict between support and education within a work group, the latter usually seemed to predominate. Individual teachers were aware of this, and would talk about the difficulty of paying attention to individual boys' problems when there was a task to be completed, or a group using expensive or dangerous equipment to be supervised. Of the boys who completed the sociometric questionnaire, only ten (7 per cent) named teachers or instructors as the person to whom they would talk if worried about problems. This is not a reflection in any sense on the personal qualities or kindness of the staff involved, but does seem to indicate that the boys do not see the teacher/instructor role as one concerned with the solution of personal problems.

It is not meant to suggest that teachers show less concern for the pupils than do child care staff, which would be manifestly untrue to anyone who knows the schools. However, the teachers' background and training focuses their attention on the child's educational needs as distinct from his social or emotional needs. The resistance within the approved school system to becoming 'homes' rather than 'schools' has already been mentioned. This resistance, however, reflects a concern at what was seen as the devaluing of the schools' education and training contributions, rather than antagonism to either greater decision-making at lower levels, or closer involvement with children.

## Staff cohesion and co-operation

Many headmasters, of course, were aware of the misunderstandings which could exist between their teaching and child care staff, and of the different approaches which the two groups often took towards the boys. Part of the impulse towards central control seemed to be fear that the staff could fall into professional camps, with a state of cold war or lack of co-operation.

Observation suggested that the seeds of this situation could exist in some schools. Child care trained staff were heard to refer to 'teacher dominated' schools and 'the typical schoolmaster attitude', while teachers not infrequently made verbal distinctions between 'professional' and 'child care' staff, and commented on the inability of child care staff to cope with discipline and maintaining order. Examination of the staff attitude scale results showed that polarisation of attitudes between the educational and house staff did seem to occur in some schools, but not in others. Using the difference in scores between the two groups as a measure of this polarisation, we related it to the boys' perception of social climate. We found that the 'satisfaction' dimension of the social climate scale, which recorded boys' perception of the pleasantness and value of their training, had a strong negative link with the difference in attitudes between the two professional groups. In other words the greater the degree of difference in attitudes between the two groups, the less boys feel that they benefit from their training. This finding was interesting in that it did not occur in connection with overall differences among the entire lower staff group. Boys did not seem to need all of their staff to think the same way, but they did seem to dislike schools in which the two sides of the school had totally different ideas about the way in which they should be treated.

However, our findings on role definition, together with informal discussions and observation in the project schools, suggested that over-centralisation, by increasing the staff dissatisfaction and frustration, could in fact make the problems of co-operation greater, rather than lessening them. We therefore predicted that there would be a negative relationship between the school decentralisation, as measured by 'between house' variance, and staff polarisation, as measured by the difference between educational and child care staff attitudes. Although not reaching the 5 per cent level of significance, the correlation of $-0.58$ was in the expected direction. It offers little support for the fears that decentralisation will undermine staff cohesion, and suggests that on the contrary it tends to be associated with greater agreement, and is therefore more likely to promote good professional co-operation.

Nevertheless, observation and results indicated that delegation may require a structured federal system within which the rights and duties of individual sections of the school are clearly defined, rather than a general devolution of power with overlapping areas of responsibility. The absence of such clear definition could result in confusion, with staff disputing among themselves as to the right to make a particular decision, and having contradictory expectations of the boys. Problems of staff co-operation then become difficult to resolve, and only add to the pressures towards centralisation. In this situation seniors may come to believe that their staff cannot cope with decision-making responsibilities, and retract the delegated power for this reason.

## Summary and discussion

In examining the movement of these schools towards the concepts and methods implicit in the 'community home' ideal, it was concluded that one major obstacle to change lay in the incompatibility of features of the 'school' model of organisation with features of the 'child care' model. The traditional school pattern of centralised bureaucratic power had been vary largely maintained, and the schools' extended functions of treatment and the provision of substitute parental care were therefore being carried out within a framework originally designed for education and training. Results suggested that, as has been found in other children's institutions, this reduced the quality of pastoral interaction between children and staff, and made it difficult for lower level staff to make an impact on children. It also appeared to create dissatisfaction among lower level staff, and possibly contributed to the loss of staff whose training was most appropriate to the school's non-educational functions. The schools which appeared to have made the greatest moves towards balancing the work and house systems, and allowing autonomy to the house units within the school, were seen as most supportive by the boys.

Although many contributing factors could be traced through the history and development of the approved school system, it was felt that results indicated three areas in which the present situation seemed to be rooted in the schools' educational tradition: the senior staffs' desire to retain personal contact with the children; role misconceptions on the part of teachers, and their failure as a group to understand some of the ways in which the role of a parent or a therapist differs from that of a teacher; and the fear that professional co-operation would disintegrate without central control.

It should be stressed that these findings are based on a very small study, and are necessarily tentative. The schools studied were not selected as a representative sample, but voluntarily agreed to help in the research. However other research on approved schools indicates that the characteristics and problems which we found may be widespread (Jones, 1968; Millham *et al.*, 1972). The solution of these three problems is clearly not easy. No one could wish headmasters to become bureaucrats without interest in the well-being of individual children, or teachers to be concerned solely with the academic or technical progress of the children. This would also be a contradiction of the community homes ideal: 'Staff need to take an overall view of the individual child and his treatment needs, rather than a partial view according to their own particular specialisation' (Home Office Advisory Council on Child Care, 1970). The establishment of completely separate and independent house regimes could be seen as potentially threatening to the conception of a home as a community, contributing as such to the children's development of communal responsibility.

Yet the retention of personal interest in children's concerns does not necessarily involve retention of power to programme all everyday decisions. After all, day-school headmasters can exercise such interest without possessing the right to so control the actions of the children's own parents. Personal contact could be maintained as well, perhaps better, through taking a class regularly, or running an activity group, as it can through decisions on report book entries, or weekend privileges. For teachers, the informal contact in the house group during the evenings and weekends enable them to see 'the whole child' without requiring them to operate dual roles in their classrooms or workshops. Our evidence suggested that staff co-operation may well be higher in schools which allow diversity than in those which do not. Many of the problems thus appear to be caused not by insoluble practical difficulties, but rather by an inability to break free of traditional ways of thinking about professional responsibilities and staff relationships.

These are inevitable problems of an attempt to change the function of a system of institutions. The evidence from other research on institutions suggests that attempts to provide one form of care within an organisational framework orginally designed for another are rarely successful, and that redefinition of goals must be accompanied by a 'shake up' in the patterns of power, communication, and role definition, if the expected goals are to be fulfilled (King *et al.*, 1971; Cressey, 1961). Some practical difficulties undoubtedly exist, and the chief of these is probably timing, at what point a desired change should be put into effect. The chance that material facilities, buildings, staffing, intake, and all the other important conditions for success will be simultaneously ideal, is a slim one; invariably something will be missing and this can place the success of the changes at risk, meaning that gambles have to be taken.

> 'Now that John has left, I shall stop having parades. I've wanted to stop them for ages, but it would have been no good, John liked a parade so that the evenings he was on duty there would have been a parade anyway. Now I've got the chance to make the change.'

One headmaster described what happened in his school when, against the wishes of his more traditional staff, he abolished uniform clothing and allowed boys to wear their own things:

> '[Staff] thought it would be chaotic with all these clothes to deal with—so they turned their back—and even encouraged the chaos in a way, just to show what a damn fool I was.'

In this situation the gamble eventually succeeded, and staff accepted it. In another school, where the headmaster had attempted to reduce regimentation by abolishing parades, the staff responded to the independence given to them by lining the boys up to move them to the classrooms. This soon became the dominant pattern of movement in the school, and was imposed by the staff group on new staff who wished to act differently.

> 'I found that I was causing difficulties for other staff. . . . It was things in the routine, lining up for showers. Instead of lining them up I'd let them go up by themselves, and I'd still be downstairs two or three minutes later. The others felt that they would misbehave if we did this, and that the group should move as a whole . . . Perhaps it's better if we all do the same. This is the way I've developed in the year I've been here.'

These problems, on a smaller scale, reflect the whole paradox of the change to community homes: the taking of autocratic action to introduce liberal or democratic processes.

The successful development of the community homes from the approved schools depends on the resolution of these dilemmas. The dilemma over staff autonomy can probably be treated as the crucial one, since it is the one most likely to affect the ability of the schools to attract and retain staff of calibre.

Our results give much cause for optimism. They suggest that some schools appear to have recognised these problems, and are developing organisational structures which are successful in meeting both educational and therapeutic goals. None of the material gives any support to the traditional stereotype of approved schools as punitive or repressive, but on the contrary reflects a high level of concern. It is hoped that the analysis given here suggests ways in which this concern can be used more effectively in the provision of 'a therapeutic approach to social education' (Home Office, 1968).

The research was carried out at a particularly tense stage in the period of transition, the few months immediately before and after the implementation of the 1969 Act. The schools are now over their biggest hurdle of integration with the local child care system. Nevertheless outward structural changes to achieve a better balance between the educational and caring/treatment functions of the school cannot hope to be successful unless they reflect acceptance of the distinct professional skills of the child care staff. In common with other residential workers, child care workers still have a relatively low status. However, the further development of professional training for residential staff should make their acceptance as equals within the community home system considerably easier in the future years.

## Acknowledgments

Our chief debt of gratitude is towards the headmasters, staff and boys in the schools which took part in the research. Members of the Social Services branches of the Department of Health and Social Security gave help and advice at various stages of the project; the original framework for the research was designed by Dr Ian Sinclair who also supervised the project; Jane Troop of the Home Office Statistical Department and John Perry of the Home Office Research Unit carried out the statistical analysis. Helpful comments were received from many research and social services staff both in the

Home Office and the Department of Health and Social Security. However the interpretation in the paper is that of the authors, and does not necessarily reflect the views of the Department of Health and Social Security or of the Home Office.

## References

BARON, G. (1956) *Some Aspects of the 'Headmaster Tradition'*, University of Leeds Institute of Education.

CARLEBACH, J. (1970) *Caring for Children in Trouble*, London: Routledge & Kegan Paul.

CRESSEY, D. R. (1961) *The Prison: Studies in Institutional Organisation and Change*, New York: Holt, Rinehart and Winston.

FIEDLER, F. (1967) *A Theory of Leadership Effectiveness*, New York: McGraw-Hill.

GOFFMAN, E. (1961) 'On the characteristics of Total Institutions', in Goffman, E., *Asylums: Essays on the Social Situation of Mental Patients and Other Inmates*, New York: Doubleday; Chicago: Aldine.

GROSS, N., and HERRIOTT, R. E. (1965) *Staff Leadership in the Public Schools*, New York: Wiley.

HALPIN, A. W. (ed.) (1966) *Theory and Research in Administration*, London: Macmillan.

HARGREAVES, D. H. (1972) *Interpersonal Relations and Education*, London: Routledge & Kegan Paul.

HEAL, K., SINCLAIR, I. A. C., and TROOP, J. (1973) 'The development of a social climate questionnaire for use in approved schools and community homes', *British Journal of Sociology*, 24, 222–35.

HOME OFFICE (1968) *Children in Trouble*, London: HMSO, Cmnd 3601.

HOME OFFICE ADVISORY COUNCIL ON CHILD CARE (1970) *Care and Treatment in a Planned Environment*, London: HMSO.

HOYLE, E. (1969) *The Role of the Teacher*, London: Routledge & Kegan Paul.

JONES, H. (1968) 'Organisation and group factors in approved school training', in Sparks, R. F., and Hood, R. C. (eds), *The Residential Treatment of Disturbed and Deliquent Boys: Proceedings of the Cropwood Round Table Conference*, University of Cambridge, Institute of Criminology.

KING, R. (1968) 'The head teacher and his authority', in Allen, B. (ed.) *Headship in the '70s*, Oxford: Blackwell.

KING, R., RAYNES, N. V., and TIZARD, J. (1971) *Patterns of Residential Care*, London: Routledge & Kegan Paul.

LEVINSON, D. J. (1959) 'Role, personality and social structure', *Journal of Abnormal and Social Psychology*, 58, 170–80.

MARCH, J. G., and SIMON, H. A. (1958) *Organisations*, New York: Wiley.

MILLHAM, S., BULLOCK, R., and CHERRETT, P. (1972) *A Comparative Study of 18 Approved Schools*, Dartington Hall Educational Research Unit, draft report presented to the Department of Health and Social Security.

MORRISON, A., and MCINTYRE, D. (1969) *Teachers and Teaching*, Harmondsworth: Penguin Books.

MUSGROVE, P., and TAYLOR, H. (1969) *Society and the Teacher's Role*, London: Routledge & Kegan Paul.

SHIPMAN, M. (1968) *The Sociology of the School*, London: Longman.

STREET, D., WINTER, R. D., and PERROW, C. (1966) *Organisation for Treatment*, New York: Free Press.

# 5    Varieties of residential nursery experience

Barbara Tizard

## Introduction

Of all residential institutions for children, residential nurseries have probably been the most widely criticised in recent years. For older children group care has always been seen to have some positive aspects; indeed, in England many of those who can afford it send their sons to boarding school from the age of eight. Even for infants both expert and lay opinion tended in the past to prefer institutions to foster homes; institutions were considered more open to the public eye, likely to have higher standards of hygiene and nutrition, and in general more likely to provide adequate care because of their trained and expert staff. Probably this is still the prevailing lay opinion in England. In a recent study of children adopted from institutions after the age of two we found that the natural mothers had expressed a preference for institutional rather than foster care for their infants, and that the adoptive parents, far from being concerned at the potential damage to their child of early institutional care, were full of praise for the expert care and good training he had received.

However, since the onslaughts of Bowlby (1951), Spitz (1949) and Goldfarb (1945), most Western psychologists and pediatricians have held that, despite trained staff and good standards of hygiene, institutional care of very young children is likely to severely and probably permanently damage the development of a wide range of functions. In the cognitive field a marked language retardation and an inability to concentrate have been described; in the field of social relationships young institutional children are said to show an early indiscriminate demand for affection and excessive attention seeking, followed at a later age by a lasting inability to make deep emotional relationships. Although there has been some disagreement about the inevitability and irreversibility of these deficits (the evidence is discussed in Ainsworth, 1962) there is today an almost universal objection amongst Western experts to institutional care of young children.

In discussing the factors responsible for the damage to development many of the earlier writers placed great emphasis on the traumatic effects of separating the child from his mother. Subsequent work has tended to be more concerned with formulating a theory which could explain how the permanent absence of a mother or mother-substitute, as distinct from a separation, could lead to distortions of development. Two main theories have been advanced. Behaviourists have suggested that the retarding factor in institutions is a low level of stimulation, resulting from a low adult-child ratio rather than from the absence of a specific mother figure (Rheingold, 1956, Casler, 1961). The psycho-analytic school maintains that normal growth is dependent upon the early development of an attachment to a specific adult. Bowlby (1971) drew on animal studies to argue that this attachment behaviour serves a biological protective function, and that all primates deprived of the usual mothering experience develop abnormally. The implications of these two theories in terms of public policy for both deprived children and ordinary families are very different. If the second theory is correct almost any mother is better than none: public money should be spent on helping mothers to stay at home rather than on providing day nurseries, and in giving support to weak or disorganised families. The first theory, on the other hand, implies that children would develop more satisfactorily in a stimulating day nursery or residential institution than in an unstimulating family environment.

Theorists of both schools, as well as administrators, have couched their arguments in terms of the effects of 'institutions' as such. Several unstated assumptions are involved, notably that no important differences exist between institutions, and that institutions as such have certain characteristic features which differentiate them sharply from most or all private families. With a few exceptions (e.g. Burlingham and Freud, 1944) the arguments have not been based on a detailed analysis of an institutional environment. Instead, a brief description is usually given of a hospital-type institution with a low staff-child ratio, and the barren environment this provides is contrasted with the rich stimulation and affectionate care to be found in a stable middle-class family with one or two children. Such a comparison is for most present day purposes irrelevant. As far as family environment is concerned, the children likely to enter institutional care tend to come from large disorganised families, often with neglectful or mentally disturbed parents, or from single-parent families living at subsistence level. As far as institutions are concerned, anyone familiar with residential nurseries in England today can hardly fail to be impressed by three facts. First, these nurseries are very different from the grim, sterile institutions described by earlier writers; second, their adult-child ratio is as high as in many families; third, there appear to be quite marked differences between different nurseries. Two important questions therefore arise: to what extent do present-day institutions retard and distort the development of young children, and can differences in the children's development be related to differences between institutional environments? The answer to this second question might enable one to abandon the blunderbuss concept of 'institution' and begin to trace the effects on development of a variety of organisational and social factors.

In an attempt to answer these questions the author and her colleagues have made three studies of children in residential nurseries. In the first, a comparison was made between the development of 2-year-old children who had lived since early infancy in residential nurseries and 2-year-old children living in working-class London families (Tizard and Joseph, 1970). In the second study, three groups of $4\frac{1}{2}$-year-old children, all of whom had been placed in residential nurseries in infancy, were compared; one group had been adopted after the age of 2, the second group had been restored to their natural mothers after the age of 2, and the third group had remained without interruption in residential care. Again, a comparison group of London working-class children living at home was used (Tizard and Rees, 1974).

In both these studies social and emotional as well as cognitive aspects of the child's development were assessed, but in the third study, with which this chapter is principally concerned, only cognitive development was measured (Tizard *et al.*, 1972). In this study an attempt was made to analyse differences between institutions, and the effects of these differences on the behaviour of both staff and children. The conceptual framework used, derived from work by Tizard and his associates in institutions for the mentally retarded (King *et al.*, 1971), was sociological. That is, the nursery environments were analysed in terms of their formal organisational structure, in the expectation that this structure would affect the quality of staff talk and behaviour, and hence the level of development of the children. Earlier writers had suggested that the *amount* of stimulation in the nurseries was inadequate, principally due to the low adult-child ratio. What was novel in the present study was an attempt to relate the level of the children's development to the *quality* of staff behaviour, and to account for differences in staff behaviour not in terms of their personality, training, etc., but in relation to the organisational structure in which they worked. Language was chosen as an index of child development because language retardation is always described as a feature of institutionalism, and because it can be simply and reliably assessed.

## The nursery setting

All the residential nurseries in our study were run by three British voluntary societies which provide care for dependent children.

They were characterised not only by a high standard of physical care but by a concern for the psychological well-being of the children. (These statements are not necessarily true of all British nurseries.)

In many ways the nurseries were quite similar. In response to earlier criticisms, two main changes had been made in all of them during the previous ten to fifteen years. First, an attempt had been made to 'de-institutionalise' child care by dividing the nurseries, most of which now contained only 15–25 children, into small mixed age 'family' groups, each in the charge of one particular nurse. Each group of six children, ranging in age from about 1 year to the upper age limit of the nursery, had its own suite of bedroom, bathroom and living room, with its own nurse and assistant nurse. The average ratio of children to staff, excluding cooks, cleaners and secretaries, was 1·37 with a standard deviation of 0·20. The children had clothes and some toys of their own. Two or more staff were on duty with the group each day; and since they had few cleaning or cooking responsibilities most of their time could be devoted to child care. (Babies under 1 year old were cared for separately.) Second, considerable efforts were made to provide the children with a stimulating environment. Each living room was plentifully supplied with toys and books: outside was a large garden containing further play equipment. Sand, paint and water play were available. The children were always read to at least once a day. Shopping expeditions, excursions, car and bus rides, and occasional weekend visits to the homes of staff members were arranged.

All these changes were made with the aim of making the child's experiences in a residential nursery more like those he would have had in an ordinary family. However, a number of crucial differences remained. None of the nurseries employed men, unless in the role of gardeners. In none of them could the child experience a lasting relationship with an adult, except the matron; junior staff were moved from a group after three to four months, and it was unusual for the nurse in charge to remain for more than two years. Moreover, in all the nurseries close personal relationships between group nurse and child were discouraged.

The matrons gave a variety of reasons for this, e.g. the problems for other staff that such relationships created when the nurse left or was off duty, the problem of jealousy within the group, and the greater difficulty of restoring a child to his mother or placing him for adoption if he did not want to leave his group nurse. Some matrons, recognising the need of both staff and children for closer relationships, had instituted a system of 'nursery mothers', whereby each nurse or student took a particular interest in one child who was *not* in her group—she would take him out when off duty, buy him presents, kiss him goodnight, etc. The strength of the relationship which developed obviously varied widely, but in most senses it could not be regarded as a maternal one.

## Differences between nurseries

Despite many similarities, there were important differences between the nurseries in social organisation. These differences appeared to stem mainly from the depth of conviction of the matron in charge about the benefits of 'Family group' care. Real conviction implied a willingness to allow considerable autonomy to each group. We divided the nurseries into three classes on the basis of the amount of autonomy accorded to the groups. The first class of nurseries, although formally divided into small groups of six, were in fact run by the matron from the centre. Decisions were made on an entirely routine basis or else referred to the matron. Each day was strictly timetabled, the matron would make frequent inspections of each group, and the freedom of the nurse and child was very limited. The children were moved through the day 'en bloc', e.g. the group had to be kept together in the living room, or in the garden, all were taken to the toilet together, the children were not allowed in the bedrooms except when all were taken there at night. The nurse had little more autonomy than the children, e.g. she would have to ask permission to take the children for a walk or to turn on the television set. As in a hospital each grade of staff wore a special uniform, and had separate living quarters, and the nurse's behaviour when off duty was governed by quite strict rules.

In an organisation of this kind the nurse's tasks are so well defined that someone can easily take her place. Such an arrangement is administratively convenient, because staff become interchangeable, and inexperienced staff can be put in charge of a group: but it results in very restricted role-playing by the staff, whose function is reduced to maintaining order and 'minding' the children on behalf of matron. Not surprisingly the nurses often appeared bored; their intellectual and emotional energy was invested elsewhere, and their responses to the children appeared superficial. In this quasi-hospital setting their primary concern often seemed to be the maintenance of order and the imposition of rather high standards of behaviour in certain spheres, e.g. cleanliness, tidiness, and good table manners. Even during play the children were often assigned a passive role, e.g. they might be pushed on a swing, or expected to sit quietly whilst a book was read.

The authors believed that social relationships of this kind would have consequences in terms of verbal interchange; e.g. in a routinised environment one would not expect to hear the children being offered choices, or being given explanations for requests made to them. We expected that a large part of the staff talk in these nurseries would be made up of commands, and of a category of remarks which we called 'supervisory'. These are the kind of remarks which adults make to children when they want to show goodwill but have no real interest in the conversation e.g. conventional verbal accompaniments to certain actions; 'Here you are', 'Off we go'; routine comments; 'Aren't you clever', 'Lucky boy', 'That's nice', 'Did you?'; repetitions of what the child said; and 'social oil' remarks such as 'Thank you' and 'Hullo'.

Both commands and 'supervisory' comments have certain characteristics in common; they tend to involve the use of short simple sentences and restricted and repetitive vocabulary, and they tend not to elicit responses. If such remarks constitute a large proportion of the talk addressed to the children a high level of language development could not be expected in these nurseries.

A marked contrast in organisation was provided by the second class of nurseries, which made a much closer approximation to a family setting. Each nursery group of six children was separately housed in a cottage or self-contained flat, and the staff were responsible for shopping, cooking, making excursions with the children and arranging their own day. The children could move freely about the house and garden and the staff rarely referred a decision to the matron. The nurse in charge did not wear uniform, and her off-duty time was not subject to rules. Her role, in fact, approximated more closely to that of a foster-mother. Since she could plan her own day and was not under constant surveillance she could treat the children more flexibly, and we expected a corresponding difference in her talk to the children. Discussion should become possible on such topics as the day's menu, how to spend the afternoon, or which television programme to watch, and explanations might sometimes be given with requests. The nurse's talk would therefore be more varied and interesting, and we expected the children to both address and answer her more often. In this group of nurseries a higher level of language development was therefore expected.

In the third, intermediate, type of nursery the groups were not independent housekeeping units, but the nurses had more autonomy than did those in the most centralised institutions. In this type of nursery the nurse in charge of the group might be responsible for allocating work amongst the staff in her group, and could make such decisions as whether to take the children for a walk in the afternoon or what birthday presents they should have, without consulting the matron. The main lines of the daily routine were however set out by the matron. It should be noted that even in the most autonomous groups the social structure differed from that of 'hostels' for retarded children (King *et al.*, 1971). There was a marked role and status differentiation between the nurse in charge of the group and her assistant; the junior staff were students or untrained assistants who were assigned to a group for only three to four months, and did not share in decision-making. Social distance was marked: junior staff in all the nurseries wore special uniforms and had separate living quarters. Role differentiation was universal: because the junior staff were transitory the nurse-in-charge tended to give them a larger share of any domestic chores, assuming more of the child care functions herself. No great differences could therefore be expected in the behaviour of the junior staff in different nurseries.

Associated with the differences in autonomy, there were differences between the nurseries in certain other organisational features. In those nurseries where staff autonomy was low, the matrons made less effort to keep the same nurses working in the same groups. Frequently, both students and trained staff did night duty for one or two weeks every two months, and at these times, and when off duty, were replaced by 'floating' staff. In nurseries where the 'family group' concept was taken more seriously greater stability was achieved by employing special night staff, and by appointing two trained nurses to each group, so that when one was off duty the other was on. It seemed likely that low stability would affect staff behaviour in much the same way as low autonomy, since staff who only stayed for a short time with the children would tend to 'mind' them, and the children would tend to talk to them and answer them less often.

Second, in most of the low autonomy nurseries the children were moved on to all-age homes at the age of 4+, so that half or more of each group were under the age of three. In the others, where it was considered important not to separate the child from his nurse and his peers, children could remain until they were seven, and each group had one or two children aged five or older. Because of the burden of physical care, and the more restricted vocabulary and syntax likely to be used with a young group, it seemed likely that the lower the mean age of the children in the group, the lower the level of language development of the children.

Finally, although all the nurseries were generously staffed by most standards, some were better staffed than others; e.g. in the best staffed nurseries there were always at least two staff present with each group of six children, some of whom might be away for part of the day at school, whilst in the worst staffed nurseries only one staff member would be on duty with the group during much of the morning and afternoon. There was some tendency for the high autonomy nurseries to be better staffed ($r = 0.59$, $p < 0.05$). It seemed likely that the better the staff-child ratio, the more often would the staff be able to converse and play with the children, and the better would be the language development of the children.

## The nursery staff

The nurseries we studied were not plagued by staff shortages, the difficulties of non-English-speaking staff, or rapid staff turnover. In all the nurseries the staff were similarly trained, and had a similar education and social background. The nurse in charge of a group was a qualified nursery nurse (NNEB) and her assistant was a student nursery nurse, or a young untrained assistant. Most were the daughters of skilled workers or small shopkeepers or farmers, and all had left school at the age of 15-16 with few formal qualifications. Students usually began training at the age of 17, and were sent to whichever nursery had a vacancy.

The nurseries were rarely short of staff, and indeed all had a long waiting list of applicants. This is because the NNEB training in a voluntary society nursery, which involves obtaining a certificate at the end of two years' practical and college training, has a relatively high status in England. Many of the girls later become 'nannies' in wealthy families. Since each student on entering had to agree to remain for three years, staff turnover in all the nurseries was relatively low. However, few girls remained longer than three years, hence the average age of the staff was very young. It should be noted that because of the universal practice of moving students to another group at the end of three months, and because staff nurses rarely stayed longer than two years, the care of the children passed through many hands.

The matron in charge of the nursery was usually a middle-aged woman, a qualified nursery nurse, often with an additional qualification as hospital nurse (SRN). There was no difference between either the training of the matrons or the educational or social class background of the staff in the three types of nurseries. Students, and in most cases staff nurses also, were allocated to whichever nursery had a vacancy. There was, however, a significant tendency for the nurse in charge of the groups in the least autonomous nurseries to be younger. The ages of the staff nurses in charge of the four least autonomous groups were 19, 19, 20 and 20, whilst in the four most autonomous groups they were 22, 23, 27 and 37. In these nurseries the matrons made a special attempt to recruit more experienced staff to place in charge of a group.

## The children

At the time of our study the majority of the children in the voluntary society nurseries were illegitimate children originally admitted as infants, who had remained without interruption in the nursery ever since. About a quarter were regularly visited by their mothers, who would probably eventually take them home. Most of the other children had been placed in the nursery for adoption, but because of their colour or family history (e.g. of epilepsy or psychopathy) had not been found adoptive homes. Many of these children have however since been adopted. Two thirds of all the children were boys; half were of mixed race or had West Indian parents. There was no information available about the I.Q.s of the parents or the occupation of nearly half of the fathers. Most often the mothers were in semi-skilled or unskilled occupations. There was no evidence that any selective placement of children occurred—infants entering care were sent to whichever nursery had a vacancy.

## Prediction and planning

For the reasons described above we expected to find associations between three aspects of the functioning of the nurseries, the organisational structure, the quality of staff behaviour and the language development of the children. More precisely we expected that the more autonomous the group, the more often the staff would play with the children, rather than passively 'mind' them, the more often they would converse with the children rather than give them orders or make 'supervisory' comments, the more often both staff and children would answer each other's remarks, and the more often children would address remarks to the staff. When the staff were playing with the children, or reading to them, we expected that the more autonomous the group, the more often the child would be assigned an active role in the play or reading situation. Further, we expected that these differences in staff-child interaction would result in superior language development in the children in the more autonomous groups.

Three independent kinds of data were therefore collected. The first, obtained from records and interviews, was concerned with the organisational structure of the nurseries, that is, the autonomy of the groups, the age structure of the groups, staff-child ratio, staff stability, etc. The second, obtained through direct observation using time-sampling techniques, measured the quality of staff talk and behaviour. The third, obtained through formal psychological testing, comprised measures of both verbal and non-verbal cognitive development of the children.

A large number of nurseries were visited in order to establish the autonomy of their nursery groups, as measured by a score based on the number of day-to-day decisions the nurse in charge of the group, and the children, could make themselves. Finally, thirteen nursery groups were chosen, which included the extremes of social organisation found. Five days were spent by an observer in each group, time-sampling the way in which the staff used their time and the remarks which they made to the children. The observer lived in the nursery and tried to make friendly contacts with the staff. Observations were made on alternate mornings and afternoons, either from the time the staff came to dress the children until mid-day, or from mid-day until the children were in bed. The staff working on the group were observed in rotation. During the first ten seconds of every thirty seconds a record of what they did or said was made. Similar records were also made, in rotation, of the children. The techniques and their reliabilities are described in more detail elsewhere (Tizard *et al.*, 1972).

Subsequently a clinical psychologist, who was not part of the research team and not informed about the predictions, tested all the healthy 2–5 year-old children who had been at least six months in the nurseries with the Reynell Development Language Scales (Reynell, 1969) and the non-verbal scale of the Minnesota Pre-School Scale. Of the 85 children tested, 70 per cent had been admitted before the age of 12 months, and only 14 per cent after the age of 2 years. There were about equal numbers of 2-, 3- and 4-year-olds.

## Results

### *Average test scores of institutional children*

Table 5.1 shows that these residential nursery children obtained average scores on both verbal and non-verbal tests. That this finding was not peculiar to the test, tester or children is shown by the findings in a later study of 25 different $4\frac{1}{2}$-year-old children who had been in different residential nurseries of the same voluntary societies since infancy.

The mean Wechsler Pre-school and Primary Scale of Intelligence scores of this group were: Full scale I.Q. 104·9, Verbal I.Q. 105·4, Performance I.Q. 102.6 (Tizard and Rees, 1974). On the Reynell Language tests there was a tendency for nursery children under the age of $2\frac{1}{2}$-years to score slightly lower. The mean Reynell Comprehension score of children aged 2·0–2·5 years was 98·1, S.D. 8·6, whilst that of children aged 2·55–4·95 years was 106·7, S.D. 8·7. This finding was confirmed in another study of 30 residential

TABLE 5.1 *Test scores of 85 residential nursery children*

| | Reynell Comprehension | | | Reynell Expression | | | Minnesota Non-Verbal | | |
| --- | --- | --- | --- | --- | --- | --- | --- | --- | --- |
| | N | Mean | S.D. | N | Mean | S.D. | N | Mean | S.D. |
| All nursery children | 85 | 104·6 | 9·7 | 85 | 98·5 | 9·7 | 54 | 104·9 | 9·6 |
| Girls | 30 | 104·1 | 8·1 | 30 | 98·3 | 7·4 | 17 | 104·5 | 9·7 |
| Boys | 55 | 104·8 | 10·6 | 55 | 98·7 | 10·9 | 37 | 105·1 | 9·8 |
| White children | 39 | 102·6 | 10·0 | 39 | 98·5 | 11·2 | 24 | 101·3 | 11·1 |
| Children of mixed or West Indian parentage | 46 | 106·3 | 9·4 | 46 | 98·6 | 8·5 | 30 | 107·7 | 7·4 |
| | t = 1·70, N.S. | | | t = 0·02, N.S. | | | t = 2·51, p < 0·02 | | |

*Note* For computational purposes the Reynell scales have been given a mean of 100 and an S.D. of 10.

TABLE 5.2 *Structure, staff behaviour and children's test scores in 13 nursery groups*

| Unit | structure* | % of total observations made on staff | | | | | | Mean Test Scores | |
|---|---|---|---|---|---|---|---|---|---|
| | | Talking to children | Playing and reading† | Giving information | Using negative control | Explaining control | Answering child | Reynell Comprehension | Minnesota Non-Verbal |
| 1 | 0·42 | 61·5 | 26·9 | 25·2 | 8·0 | 5·0 | 4·1 | 116·0 | 104·5 |
| 2 | 0·56 | 50·0 | 20·7 | 18·4 | 7·6 | 2·8 | 2·3 | 118·5 | 108·3 |
| 3 | 0·61 | 54·8 | 16·0 | 15·0 | 9·4 | 3·4 | 2·1 | 109·3 | 106·5 |
| 4 | 0·69 | 47·0 | 21·1 | 12·6 | 5·7 | 4·4 | 4·4 | 97·6 | 104·3 |
| 5 | 0·73 | 58·7 | 16·3 | 17·3 | 8·5 | 2·8 | 1·3 | 110·3 | 100·3 |
| 6 | 0·80 | 53·4 | 18·4 | 14·2 | 10·2 | 1·0 | 1·7 | 112·8 | 107·7 |
| 7 | 1·04 | 61·5 | 18·6 | 14·0 | 8·8 | 2·2 | 2·6 | 106·7 | 114·3 |
| 8 | 1·08 | 36·8 | 7·7 | 9·3 | 5·6 | 0·3 | 1·9 | 105·0 | 105·3 |
| 9 | 1·21 | 41·6 | 12·5 | 11·6 | 7·1 | 1·9 | 1·8 | 102·2 | 99·1 |
| 10 | 1·40 | 48·4 | 18·4 | 12·7 | 13·0 | 1·0 | 1·7 | 104·6 | 108·8 |
| 11 | 1·46 | 54·5 | 12·5 | 6·2 | 16·3 | 2·2 | 0·6 | 97·8 | 101·4 |
| 12 | 1·49 | 55·2 | 11·8 | 13·9 | 11·4 | 2·0 | 2·6 | 103·9 | 100·0 |
| 13 | 1·50 | 45·6 | 5·1 | 9·7 | 11·4 | 2·7 | 1·1 | 95·8 | 100·5 |

* Composite score on organisational variables, obtained by principal component analysis (Tizard *et al.*, 1972). A low score denotes high autonomy.
† These observations were made on different occasions from the observations of staff talk.

nursery children aged 24 months, whose mean Cattell Mental age was 22 months (Tizard & Joseph, 1970.) However, nowhere did we find evidence of the gross retardation, verbal or otherwise, described in studies by earlier writers.

### The relationship between the children's test scores and the organisation of the nursery

There were large differences between the verbal, but not the non-verbal scores, of the children in different nurseries (see Table 5.2). The mean language comprehension score of the children in the three most autonomous nursery groups was 115, expressed on a scale having a mean of 100 and a standard deviation of 10, close to that found in children of professional families living at home (social class I and II). The mean language score of the children in the least autonomous nurseries was one-and-a-half standard deviations lower (99·4), and approximates to that found in children living at home in working-class families. It is important to note that on the non-verbal test the mean scores of the children in nurseries with differing autonomy did not differ significantly.

### Quality of staff talk and behaviour

There was no shortage of verbal stimulation; in half of the observation periods the staff observed was speaking to a child. As predicted, there was no significant difference between nurseries in the *amount* the staff talked, but there were very significant differences in the *quality* of talk. Staff in nursery groups which had most autonomy spoke in longer and more complex sentences, made more 'informative' remarks (e.g. telling or asking the child something about present, past, or future activities, naming objects, asking for and giving opinions and explanations), gave more explanations with their commands, gave fewer negative commands, answered the children more often, and were more often answered by the children. Thus the linguistic as well as the social environment differed markedly between the nurseries. In addition, in the groups with higher autonomy the staff spent more time reading to and playing with the children, and doing things with them in which the children were rated as 'active' rather than 'passive'.

### Relationships between children's test scores and staff behaviour

As predicted, there were significant correlations between the mean language comprehension score of the nursery and the frequency of 'informative' staff talk, the frequency with which staff read to and played with the children, the frequency with which the staff answered children's remarks, and the amount of play in which the child was actively rather than passively involved. There were no significant correlations between the mean Minnesota Non-Verbal scores of the nurseries and any of the observational data.

## Discussion

### Institutional retardation

Clear evidence was obtained in two separate studies that children aged from 3–5 years who had been cared for in the residential nurseries of three British voluntary societies since infancy were not retarded on either verbal or non-verbal tests. It should be remembered that most of these were children of lower-working-class parentage: because of their colour or family history they had not been found adoptive homes. It seems likely that intellectually they had, in fact, benefited from their institutional upbringing.

This evidence strongly suggests that the cognitive retardation described in earlier studies was due to lack of stimulation rather than to maternal deprivation as such. Considerable efforts had been made in our nurseries to stimulate intellectual development by organising the children in small mixed age groups, with a high adult-child ratio, and by providing a good deal more in the way of toys, books and reading aloud than can be found in most working-class families. On the other hand substitute mothering in the usual sense was absent. The staff were strongly discouraged from forming close personal relationships with the children and the relationships that did develop were inevitably transitory. At the time of our study only three staff nurses had worked with their group for more than fifteen months. In another study of residential nursery children aged 24 months we found that on the average each child had been looked after by twenty-four different nurses for at least a week (Tizard and Joseph, 1970). Although a quarter of the children were visited by their mothers, these visits were usually very sporadic— only 10 per cent of the children were visited as often as once a week.

Further evidence that the level of the children's language development was not dependent on the development of a close relationship with a specific adult comes from a comparison between the nurseries. There were large and significant correlations between the quality of staff talk and the average language test scores of the children in the different nurseries. However, the nurseries where the children's language development was best were not characterised by closer or more specific adult-child relationships. Some nurseries had, as described above, a system of 'nursery mothers' whereby each member of staff took a particular interest in a child outside her own group. Whatever significance this system had for development was not intellectual; the children in those nurseries (which all had low autonomy) had the lowest mean language scores. All this evidence indicates that an average or above average level of language development is possible despite multiple caretaking and despite an absence of any close relationship with an adult.

The amount of staff talk was sufficient in all the nurseries to promote average development, but the level of development was related to the quality of staff talk. It should be noted that the range of verbal quality was fairly limited; no nurse talked like a graduate mother, and explanations were everywhere unusual. However, in the nurseries where the children's language scores were lowest as much as 75 per cent of staff talk consisted of commands and routine 'supervisory' remarks. These were the nurseries where the staff had least autonomy. Although in general kind and conscientious, these nurses very often appear to be bored. Of course anyone looking after young children is liable to get bored at times, but boredom is particularly likely to occur in a low autonomy unit. There the nurse has no clear function except to maintain order and 'mind' the children. She is not trained as an educator, is discouraged from making close relationships with the children, and cannot interest herself in any of the decisions or diversions which enliven the housewife's life, e.g. cooking or shopping, buying or making the children's clothes, taking them to visit relations or friends. Literally, there is nothing to talk about. And because of her own position in a rigidly hierarchical system, where the maintenance of good order is considered very important, it is also difficult for her to relax her disciplinary grip enough to play with the children.

Because there was a tendency for the nursery groups with higher autonomy to be also better staffed we cannot definitely conclude that it was high autonomy which was responsible for better quality staff and superior language development in the children. However, other evidence gathered during the study supports our hypothesis.

If the staff-child ratio was the crucial variable, rather than autonomy, then one would expect that on occasions when two staff were present with from three to six children, the children would benefit by a much greater output of play, talk of all sorts, and in particular 'informative' talk, than if only one nurse had been present. In fact, analysis of these occasions showed that although the amount of staff talk increased it by no means doubled, and the amount of 'informative' talk and play remained the same.

This was because of the marked staff hierarchy; when two staff were present, it was always understood that one of them was in charge. The attribute of being 'in charge' was not a fixed one, but varied on a minute-to-minute basis. Thus a trained nurse in charge of a group was no longer in charge if joined by a more senior nurse; a student or untrained assistant normally not in charge of a group would be placed in charge when the trained staff were off duty or even left the room. All but the most senior staff could therefore be observed on different occasions in two authority positions. The differences between staff behaviour when 'in charge' and 'not in charge' was similar to, but even more marked than, the difference between the behaviour of the nurses in charge of the most and least autonomous groups. That is, staff on duty but not in charge functioned in a notably restricted way, talking much less and using less 'informative' talk than the nurse in charge.

These effects of staff hierarchy also overrode the effects of training. Regardless of training, whoever was in charge talked more and used more informative talk than the nurse not in charge. The only significant difference between the behaviour of qualified and unqualified staff in charge was a slight tendency for the unqualified staff to play more with the children and allow them to be more active. The original prediction that the behaviour of junior staff would be similar in all nurseries was therefore not confirmed. It was the nurse at that time in charge, whether trained or not, who was affected by the organisation of the nursery. There were no differences between the behaviour of the staff not in charge in the various nurseries, except for their tendency to use more negative commands in the least autonomous nurseries.... All these strands of evidence suggest that, within the limits of the present study, the quality of staff behaviour was determined less by the ratio of staff to children, or by whether the nurse was qualified or not, than by her perception of her position within the authority system.

It is by no means our intention to suggest that staff-child ratio and staff training are factors of no significance, or that the only important variable in an institution is staff autonomy. Children's institutions could and do exist where staff autonomy is high and there is little staff hierarchy, but where nevertheless interactions with the children are minimal or punitive. The evidence of the study suggests, however, that given staff of similar social class, education, training, and goodwill, the social framework in which they are placed has an important effect in determining their behaviour. If given a limited role to perform, they will behave in a limited way. The nurses in the least autonomous nurseries, whose mean sentence length to the children when on duty was four words, could be heard in their own homes talking and playing in a very different way with their young brothers or sisters.

Injunctions to 'Talk more' or to 'Improve your talk' when on duty are thus likely to be of little avail if, as suggested, the nature of the talk depends on the adults' perception of their role in relation to their superiors and to the children.

Again, whilst improvements in staff ratio are likely to be valuable, the size of the contribution of extra staff-members depends on the role to which they are assigned, and the benefit to the children of additional staff may be more limited than would appear at first sight. This is often the case with volunteer help; unless assigned specific tasks or responsibilities the contribution of those who are 'generally helping' a nurse in charge of the group may also be slight and unsatisfying to all.

The evidence reviewed here suggests that intellectual retardation is by no means a necessary feature of institutional upbringing, and that institutions which differ in their social organisation are likely to promote different qualities of staff talk and behaviour, which in turn affect the level of the children's development. This evidence relates only to the children's intellectual development. We made no attempt in this study to discover whether specific abnormalities of social and emotional development are associated with institutional upbringing, and whether and to what extent social and emotional development is affected by different forms of institutional organisation.

## Other aspects of development

We tried to answer the first of these questions in our studies of 2- and 4-year-old children in residential care. The analysis of the 4-year-old study is not yet complete.[1] We found that the major area of difference between nursery and home-reared 2-year-olds lay in their relationships with adults (Tizard and Tizard, 1971). Far from presenting the classical picture of attention-seeking, nursery children at 24 months were less willing to approach or stay alone with strangers, although with familiar adults they were in certain situations more clinging. Their social behaviour might thus be considered in some respects merely immature, except that unlike home-reared children they tended to show affection for a wide range of adults. However, they did not show an indiscriminate demand for affection. Each child had a hierarchy of preferences, as did the home-reared children.

Shyness, clinging, and diffuse attachments can all be related to aspects of the nursery environment. Nursery children tend to see few strangers from outside the institution. Comparatively large numbers of adults care for him—on an average we found that 24 nurses had looked after each of our 2-year-olds for at least a week since he entered the nursery, and during a five-day observation period we found an average of 5·8 nurses (range 4–9) had worked on each group, excluding night staff. No attempt was made in any nursery to reduce the number of adults handling each child by assigning the care of particular children within the group to particular members of staff. Thus a child might be dressed by a different nurse each day, and if four nurses worked on one group during the day a child might be dressed by one, toiletted by a second, taken for a walk by a third, and put to bed by a fourth. It was not uncommon for child care tasks to be allocated by seniority, e.g. the most junior nurse on duty would be assigned to the task of dressing any child who had wet his bed, or changing children who were subsequently wet or soiled. Since close personal relationships were discouraged by the matron, the staff tended to avoid prolonged interactions with any one child, and to distract any child who tried to engineer such an interaction. In such an environment a specific attachment can hardly develop, and it is not surprising that most of the nursery children were reported to be fond of 'anyone who looks after him', rather than a particular nurse.

Nor is it surprising that the nursery 2-year-old clings to his own familiar staff. In the private family the 2-year-old has typically long ago given up crying when his mother leaves the room; instead, he follows her round the house. Should she leave the house, he can confidently predict her return. But in the nursery, 2-year-olds are rarely allowed to follow the staff round the house. Nurses come and go at irregular and unpredictable intervals, often disappearing for days, or weeks, or indeed for ever. In these circumstances the 2-year-old has as little control over the source of his social satisfactions as a non-mobile infant, and it is not surprising that his relationships with adults are correspondingly immature.

However, what is argued here is that abnormalities of development, e.g. excessive shyness, excessive clinging and diffuse attachments at the age of two, are related to particular aspects of the social environment, e.g. limited experience of strangers, multiple caretaking, and constant changes of staff, rather than to 'the institution' as such. Hence changes in the social structure, e.g. reducing to a minimun the number of adults caring for each child, and arranging that when these adults are on duty they care for particular children, should tend to 'normalise' the nursery child's development. Such an approximation to family life could of course only be limited. Unlike mothers, paid staff work a 40-hour week and take holidays; most significantly, they leave the institution for promotion, marriage, or a host of valid personal reasons.

There would thus, in England at least, appear to be no substitute for the stable private family as a resource for long-term adult-child relationships. However, it should be remembered that for many children the actual alternatives lie between some form of residential care and a family which may be not only unstable but grossly neglectful, and sometimes hostile. The problem for the community in these circumstances is to devise an alternative environment in which the child can develop with the least harm, perhaps with benefit. To what extent such an environment can be provided by foster care has not been discussed in this chapter. In any event, every administration has children who cannot be fostered, whether because of a shortage of foster parents, or because of certain characteristics of the child, or because of the problems created by his natural parents. For these children some form of institutional upbringing may be inevitable. We have been able to show that language development in young children need not suffer in institutional care. Experiments aimed at protecting the emotional and social development of the child in residential care need to be encouraged and assessed.

# References

AINSWORTH, M. D. (1962) 'The effects of maternal deprivation', in *Deprivation of Maternal Care. A Reassessment of its Effects*, World Health Organisation, Geneva.

BOWLBY, J. (1951) *Maternal Care and Mental Health*, World Health Organisation, Geneva.

BOWLBY, J. (1971) *Attachment and Loss. Vol. 1: Attachment*. Harmondsworth: Penguin Books.

BURLINGHAM, D. T., and FREUD, A. (1944) *Infants without Families*, New York: International Universities Press.

CASLER, L. (1961) 'Maternal deprivation: A critical review of the literature', *Monographs in Social Research and Child Development*, 26, 1–64.

GOLDFARB, W. (1945) 'Effects of psychological deprivation in infancy and subsequent stimulation', *American Journal of Psychiatry*, 102, 18–33.

KING, R., RAYNES, N., and TIZARD, J. (1971) *Patterns of Residential Care*, London: Routledge & Kegan Paul.

REYNELL, J. (1969) *Reynell Development Language Scales*, Slough, Buckinghamshire: National Foundation for Educational Research.

RHEINGOLD, H. L. (1956) 'The modification of social responsiveness in institutional babies', *Monographs in Social Research and Child Development*, 21.

SPITZ, R. A. (1949). 'The role of ecological factors in emotional development in infancy', *Child Development*, 20, 145–55.

TIZARD, B., COOPERMAN, O., JOSEPH, A., and TIZARD, J. (1972) 'Environmental effects on language development: a study of young children in long-stay residential nurseries', *Child Development*, *43*, 337–58.

TIZARD, B., JOSEPH, A. (1970) 'The cognitive development of young children in residential care', *Journal of Child Psychology and Psychiatry*, *11*, 177–86.

TIZARD, B., and REES, J. (1974) 'The development of children whose first two years of life were spent in institutional care', *Child Development*, *45*, 92–9.

TIZARD, B., and REES, J. (1975) 'The effect of early institutional rearing on the behaviour problems and affectional relationships of four-year-old children', *Journal of Child Psychology and Psychiatry*, *16*, 61–73.

TIZARD, J., and TIZARD, B. (1971) 'The social development of two year old children in residential nurseries', in Schaffer, H. R. (ed.), *The Origins of Human Social Relations*, New York: Academic Press.

# 6   The influence of wardens and matrons on probation hostels: a study of a quasi-family institution

Ian Sinclair

## Introduction

This chapter is based on some research carried out in the 1960s into hostels for adolescent male probationers. The study (Sinclair, 1971) ranged widely, covering, for example, the history and organisation of the hostels, the characteristics and success rates of the inmates, and the problems and attitudes of the staff; but it was dominated throughout by one central fact—the remarkable influence on the hostels of the married couples who ran them. It is with this finding and with its implications that we shall be particularly concerned.

The couples in charge of probation hostels combine the roles of warden and matron with those of husband and wife and this fact helps to explain the nature of their influence and also its theoretical interest. In effect, if not in intention, the pattern provides an example of the increasingly popular 'quasi-family' institution, a somewhat paradoxical entity, since Goffman (1961) at least has argued that the family and the total institution are quite opposed. In keeping with Goffman's view, research on residential institutions has tended to occupy a rather uneasy position in books on organisation theory and to have little connection with studies of parents and children. It is of interest, then, to explore how far places such as probation hostels do operate like families, and in particular how far the influence of the warden and matron is analogous to that of parents.

The following chapter pursues this general topic in three ways:

(1) Innumerable studies have shown the pervasive influence of parents on their children. The impact of staff must clearly be great if it is to be called in any sense parental. We shall, therefore, explore the extent of the warden's and matron's influence.

(2) Children in a true family institution would presumably respond to particular qualities in their housefather just as they would to the same qualities in their own father. In the case of probationers there is a great deal of information on the type of parents who appear to inhibit further delinquency (e.g. Davies, 1969). We shall enquire whether a similar association exists between the delinquent behaviour of hostel residents and the type of warden and matron in charge of them.

(3) In families, parents influence their children, but are also unable to play their own roles adequately without their children's co-operation (Parsons and Bales, 1955, pp. 46–7; Kysar, 1968). This fact gives rise to the possibility of vicious circles so that, for example, a son's recalcitrance can lead to greater antagonism from his father and hence to increased bad feeling between the two of them. We shall examine how far a similar interdependence exists in probation hostels.

The matters just raised have administrative as well as theoretical interest. A child in a large institution has contact with many staff, and while this may be confusing for him and deprive him of the opportunity for close relationships, it also makes him less vulnerable to being let down by any single individual on whom he is largely dependent. In a family, things are quite otherwise. A child suffers deeply when one of his parents dies, leaves, is cruel, quarrels with the other parent, or in some other way fails him. Such children frequently find their way into quasi-family institutions, and if staff in such places really are accepted as standing in place of parents, it is vital that they do not repeat the true parents' mistakes. At the same time, quasi-family institutions are usually highly autonomous, and staff behaviour which might constitute bad parenting is difficult to detect, control or make the grounds for dismissal. Administrators therefore face the difficulty of ensuring that staff power is not misused.

So the task of this chapter is to explore how far the influence of wardens and matrons is analagous to that of parents, and assess the resulting implications for those who attempt to administer similar institutions. Such institutions will not necessarily be penal. At the time of the research, most of the hostel residents were aged less than 17 years on entry. Probation hostels now cater for the age range 17–35. It follows that the conclusions in this chapter do not necessarily apply to existing probation hostels, and indeed in this respect they may be more relevant to hostels and homes operated by local authorities.

## How great is the influence of the warden and matron?

### The warden's position

The research was carried out in the mid-1960s, and dealt with the system of hostels as it was then. In 1966 there were twenty-three of these institutions in England and Wales, most being intended for 19 or 20 probationers, the smallest taking 12 and the largest 24. They were classified by the religion and age of their residents, none of whom, however, was less than 15 or more than 21 on arrival. The residents were sent by the courts, almost universally for the maximum legal period of twelve months, which might later be slightly reduced. As already indicated each hostel was run by the warden with the help of a matron who, with one exception, was also his wife, and of one or two assistant wardens and a non-resident staff including a cook and cleaners.

At the time of the research there were a number of factors which put the warden and matron in a very powerful position. In the first place, the warden was the undisputed professional head of the institution. Unlike the residential staff in social service departments, who are part of a chain of command ending with the director of social services, the warden was responsible not to the principal probation officer but to a voluntary committee, which met once a month and did not exercise professional supervision. True, the hostels were subject to inspection by Home Office officials, but these visited at the most once every six months and exercised little real control, although they were able to check that Home Office regulations were being observed. As will be seen later, this bureaucratic form of control was not sufficient to ensure a uniformly high standard of performance.

A second important factor in ensuring the paramountcy of the warden was the fact that he was not usually faced with long-established, powerfully entrenched staff, whose presence can greatly limit the power of the heads of large residential institutions. In contrast to such places, probation hostels usually had posts for only two assistant wardens and at the time of the research these were often young—the most common age was 22—and very much birds of passage. A survey of 139 assistants showed that half of them left within seven months of arrival. The power of the wardens was correspondingly enhanced.

Third, the wardens had an unusual combination of responsibilities. Subject to their committees' overall control, they carried all the duties associated with an institution's head—representing the hostel to the outside world, determining policy, carrying financial and general responsibility—and at the same time remained in very close touch with the boys. To use a military analogy, they combined the roles of colonel and sergeant and this made them very much the most powerful adult on the residents' horizon, as indeed the father of the traditional family is supposed to be.

## Differences between institutions: empirical evidence

Empirically, the study of the warden's influence was undertaken by demonstrating large differences between the nature and effectiveness of hostel regimes and as far as possible showing that these were unlikely to result from such factors as the hostel committee or location but were related to the warden's attitude and approach. A partial example of this strategy can be taken from a survey of the regimes in operation at sixteen hostels. This found wide differences in the rules, in terms, for example, of the times at which the boys were allowed out in the evenings, the type of dress allowed, restrictions within the hostel, and staff attitudes to allowing the boys to change their work. Punishments were also very varied: reactions to swearing, for example, ranged from the attitude that, 'It is understood that they do not swear in front of the women staff', to deprivation of all privileges for a month. Table 6.1 describes some rules governing the use of equipment and hostel property as they operated in the hostels.

TABLE 6.1  *Variations in customs at 16 hostels*

|  | Yes | No | Yes with qualifications |
|---|---|---|---|
| Boys may turn on TV without permission | 6 | 10 | 0 |
| Boys may turn on radio without permission | 7 | 6 | 3 |
| Boys may go to dormitories without permission | 4 | 11 | 1 |
| Boys may use games equipment without permission | 7 | 8 | 1 |
| Boys may always use more than one room on free evenings | 12 | 1 | 3 |
| Boys may have photographs outside lockers | 12 | 4 | 0 |
| Boys may have pin-ups outside lockers | 7 | 9 | 0 |

In order to summarise the differences suggested by Table 6.1, a 20-item restrictiveness scale was constructed and an equal weight was allotted to the areas of behaviour allowed in the hostel (the items given in Table 6.1), number of hours allowed out for leisure, the rules governing changes of work, and those concerned with another important area of an adolescent's life—dress. This scale correlated highly ($r = 0.65$) with a scale measuring the wardens' attitude towards control, as measured by an attitude questionnaire, and it was shown later that restrictiveness was also related to the boys' behaviour in the hostel and to the level of agreement between warden and matron as to how the hostel should be run.

Differences between the hostels, in atmosphere, staff relationships and other less tangible matters, were, if anything, even more marked

than differences in the rules. Their importance was borne out by
the extraordinary variation in the proportion of boys leaving the
hostels because they absconded or committed a further offence.
This proportion was called the failure rate, a term justified by the
·  ·hat whatever was intended by sending the boys to a hostel, it
,   ·  ·inly not that they should leave as a result of getting into
t:  ·  ·  ·ta on 429 boys who entered seventeen hostels in 1963–4
showed   ·  ·here was a high correlation between failure rate and
two other ₁ sible me·sures of ·egime performance: the proportion
convicted within one   ·  of ·ntering the hostel (r = 0·82) and
the proportion convict···  ·thin, three years of entry (r = 0·69).
Thus although reconviction rate and failure rate are not, as defined
here, identical (a boy can be reconvicted and yet serve his time at
a hostel, or leave as a result of absconding and so fail without being
reconvicted), nevertheless the two rates amount to much the same
thing.

In the course of the research, data were collected on 4,343 boys
who entered hostels between January 1954 and July 1963. The
information was taken from monthly returns which the wardens
made to the Home Office and included details of the residents'
ages, dates of arrival at the hostel and of any abscondings in which
they might be involved, and also of the reasons for which they left,
whether for absconding, the commission of a further offence, or
because their period of residence was completed. This made it possible
to examine the differences in failure rate among 46 regimes and
revealed a startling range from 14·5 per cent to 78·1 per cent.
These variations are set out in Table 6.2.[1]

TABLE 6.2    *Distribution of proportions of boys leaving as a result of absconding or offence in 46 regimes*

| Failure rate % | Number of regimes | Number of boys N | Number of boys % | Average no. of boys per regime |
|---|---|---|---|---|
| 10–14 | 1 | 37 | 0·8 | 37·0 |
| 15–19 | 4 | 200 | 4·6 | 50·0 |
| 20–4 | 4 | 432 | 9·9 | 108·0 |
| 25–9 | 9 | 972 | 22·4 | 108·0 |
| 30–4 | 8 | 738 | 17·0 | 92·3 |
| 35–9 | 5 | 951 | 22·0 | 190·2 |
| 40–4 | 8 | 797 | 18·3 | 99·6 |
| 45–9 | 2 | 59 | 1·4 | 29·5 |
| 50+ | 5 | 157 | 3·6 | 31·4 |
| Total | 46 | 4,343 | 100·0 | 94·4 |

Extensive efforts were made to see whether these variations in failure rate could be accounted for by differences in the type of boy selected. Thus a survey was carried out of 429 boys who entere hostels between June 1963 and July 1964. Background information on them was mainly culled from reports which were made to ~~courts~~ before their admission and which in most cases wou' been available to the wardens at the time they receive for a place. Thirty-six pieces of info~~ion~~ were abst ing the boys' families, background ~~y, criminal~~ other behaviour, and reasons for placeme ~~nre ictors were found~~ to be related to reconviction in the fir ~~ea ys who~~ had left home or had an above average number of pr ious convictions were more likely to be reconvicted, and those who were sent to be removed from very bad homes were less likely—but hostels with high failure rates had not been taking higher or lower proportions of boys with these factors in their backgrounds. In fact there were no apparent differences in selection practice between hostels with high and low failure rates, with the exception that in that particular year the more successful hostels were taking older boys; this finding, however, arose from the accident that some of the hostels for older boys were being particularly successful, a trend which was slightly the reverse of that found over the nine years 1954 to 1963.

TABLE 6.3    *Absconding and offences related to months in which wardens or matrons were on leave or away sick*

| | Months in which hostels open | Abscondings | | Offences | | Abscondings and offences | |
|---|---|---|---|---|---|---|---|
| | | No. | Average per month | No. | Average per month | No. | Average per month |
| Warden/matron absent | 87 | 78 | 0·9 | 55 | 0·63 | 133 | 1·53 |
| Warden/matron present | 258 | 113 | 0·44 | 120 | 0·47 | 233 | 0·90 |
| | | $t = 2·78$; $df = 14$ | | ns | | $t = 2·92$; $df = 14$ | |
| | | $p < 0·01$ | | | | $p < 0·01$ | |

*Note*    t-tests calculated as for correlated means.

One other finding can be mentioned here, partly for its intrinsic interest and partly because, when combined with the findings just given and those of Clarke and Martin (1971) on absconding, it adds further evidence that variation in failure rates cannot be explained by variation in selection. This is the fact that the number of abscondings doubled in months when warden or matron were absent or sick, and the number of criminal charges also increased. This dramatic increase, which is illustrated in Table 6.3 is most unlikely to have arisen from selection factors, and is thus further evidence of the dependence of the hostels on the married couples in charge of them.

It is important to note that failure rates were characteristic of wardens, not of hostels. The differences between successive wardens in the same hostel were as wide as those between wardens in different hostels and there was no association between failure rate and the size, age range or location of hostels. Moreover the warden seemed to determine not only how *many* boys left as a result of absconding or offences, but also *which* ones were most likely to do so. Some wardens had better success with older boys, others with younger ones; some apparently took a lenient view of absconding and took back a high proportion of absconders, few of whom subsequently re-absconded, others took back few absconders and found that even among these most absconded again.

The last two findings deserve, perhaps, a little more discussion. At first sight there is no reason to think that a warden who takes back say 60 per cent of his absconders should find these returned prodigals any more law-abiding than one who takes back 20 per cent. If anything, one would expect that the more lenient policy would lead to a higher proportion of more difficult boys being returned to the hostel and hence to a higher re-absconding rate. In practice, however, the reverse was found to be the case: the higher the proportion of absconders who were given 'a second chance', the lower the proportion of them who got into further trouble. The relevant data are set out in Table 6.4.

The most likely explanation for this phenomenon is that of the self-fulfilling prophecy. Wardens who did not believe that absconders would succeed tended to persuade a court not to return absconders. Absconders who did return justified the warden's opinion by re-absconding.

The explanation of the differences in wardens' relative success with older or younger boys may well be similar. These differences were very highly significant and were therefore most unlikely to be due to chance. Surprisingly, however, although wardens did differ greatly in their tendency to accept older or younger boys, there was no evidence that wardens who selected a high proportion of older boys necessarily did particularly well with them. The explanation put forward in the original report (Sinclair, 1971) still seems the most likely. It was that a warden 'may be equally at home with older and younger boys and thus equally willing to take both groups. But he may react strongly towards or against a particular type of role in the hostel, and some roles, particularly leadership ones, may more often belong to the older boys. Thus older residents may do well or badly according to whether the warden prefers to work with the inmate leadership or keep it in its place.'

TABLE 6.4   *Proportion of residents readmitted after absconding related to proportion of those known to get into further trouble*

| Proportion readmitted | Proportions in further trouble |
|---|---|
| % | % |
| 57 (1) | 49 (14) |
| 56 (2) | 41 (15) |
| 55 (3) | 57 (12) |
| 48 (4) | 65 (8) |
| 45 (5) | 64 (9) |
| 44 (6) | 69 (6) |
| 43 (7) | 53 (13) |
| 41 (8) | 57 (11) |
| 39 (9) | 82 (2) |
| 39 (10) | 28 (16) |
| 35 (11) | 75 (4) |
| 34 (12) | 71 (5) |
| 30 (13) | 78 (3) |
| 27 (14) | 86 (1) |
| 27 (15) | 65 (7) |
| 22 (16) | 60 (10) |
| $\rho = -0.54$, df $= 14$, $p < 0.05$ | |

*Note*   only regimes which took at least 100 probationers are included in this analysis.

These findings underline some of the dangers associated with the quasi-family institution. By devolving so much responsibility on one or two key members of staff they may make it less easy to ensure a uniform standard of performance, and provide the residents with a smaller choice of adults to whom to relate. There may therefore be a greater risk that certain residents feel that the key members of staff have their knife into them and that they themselves have no respite: and indeed the key members of staff may feel the equivalent.

We will return to these problems in the final discussion. For the moment we seem to have shown that, like parents, the warden and matron of a probation hostel had a very considerable influence on their charges. Our next question is whether the qualities demanded of them are those needed by the parents of teenage probationers.

## Is there an analogy between the influence on delinquency of hostels and of families?

*Case studies*

Clearly no family, even the largest and most delinquent, contains eighteen teenage probationers. The question is whether the hostels studied were nevertheless sufficiently similar to a family to encourage demands on the staff similar to those which boys might make of their own parents. Davies (1969) has shown that the probationers who are least likely to be reconvicted most often come from homes where the father is firm but kindly, shows warmth towards the probationer and is agreed with his wife on discipline (see also Davies and Sinclair, 1971). It will be argued below that hostels with low 'failure rates' show very similar characteristics.

In the course of the research, detailed case studies were made of the five regimes that had the lowest failure rates and the eleven which had the highest. It was found that the low-failure-rate regimes all showed a common pattern which could be described as paternalist. The warden was very strict, clearly the dominant person in a hostel where his wife agreed with his policy, and was characterised by a certain warmth towards his charges.

One regime, for example, was described by a member of the committee:

'The warden was a big, hefty, slow-moving fellow . . . and his wife did what he said. He ran a very good hostel. In fact, we went two years without any trouble at all. I'm under the impression that he would walk up to a boy who was giving trouble and say: "If you don't behave yourself I'll give you a belt round the ear'ole." If there was any hint of trouble, he would stamp on it immediately.'

Others confirmed this impression: 'He was the essential authoritarian'. Or again, 'He was as rigid as they come, but with certain good qualities.' The emphasis on consistent discipline is apparent in the warden's reports to his committee and in a contemporary report on the hostel by the principal probation officer:

Despite his stress on discipline, the warden does not seem to have been a cold person. The government inspector noted 'a sense of humour' and a genuine interest in the boys and indeed these are apparent from the warden's reports to his committee, which demonstrate, for example, an understanding of the feeling of worthlessness that troubled some

residents. The matron fitted in with the paternalist pattern.
'She was a very charming person not unduly dominated by her
husband. He was very much the master in his own household
and I think she played along with this. I think the boys saw
her as a mother figure although she was not sloppy.'

The high-failure-rate regimes showed the opposite pattern. In
some the discipline was ineffective and one such was described by a
probation officer who had once worked in it:

'There was a fierce quarrel between the warden and matron
and assistant warden. The boys used to go upstairs to bed and
spit on the staff from over the banisters. Everyone thought me odd
because I ran upstairs after them to stop them. Even then I
couldn't believe that all probation hostels were like this.'

The liaison officer of the hostel had similar views: 'The warden
was a very sick man with a rather sentimental approach to the boys,
and the matron was on the edge of a nervous breakdown. Together
they made a sick pair.' He also thought the assistant warden 'very
disloyal'.

In other high-failure-rate regimes, the troubles seemed to centre
on the matrons:

In two regimes, the warden and matron had problems with their
marriage which in turn probably affected their behaviour. In one,
the matron withdrew almost completely from the hostel and,
according to a temporary assistant, only came into it to shout
at the boys for not cleaning the dishes. In the other, the warden,
possibly in reaction to his matrimonial problems, became
loud-mouthed and insecure, while the matron became provo-
cative towards the boys and obsessional about the house. In
other regimes, the matron usurped her husband's disciplinary
role and was bitterly resented for it.

In other high-failure-rate hostels there was a marked lack of
warmth, and the staff were harsh, sarcastic, or even sadistic. The
warden of the most extreme of these regimes was interviewed by
the present writer, and was remarkably free in describing his methods:

He aimed to induce stress and thought in this way he could
teach the boys to handle stressful situations. His chief method
was the manipulation of uncertainty. Punishments were never

for a fixed duration; spot checks were common; and no boy
knew for certain when or whether he could go for home leave.
The warden might decide that a resident should be kept in but
not tell him until 10 minutes before he was due to go out.
No message could then be given to the resident's girl
friend. 'He may cry, he may scream the place down. They're
soft-gutted, these boys, but they get over it. That way I treat
them like they treat us.' No one could count on avoiding
punishment; one boy might wash a room badly and get no
punishment; another would wash it quite well and get
'something serious'.

## The correlational study

The findings of these initial case studies seemed of such interest
that it was decided to check them against harder evidence. At
fourteen hostels the staff filled in attitude questionnaires and the
warden answered a series of questions about his methods of running
the hostel. This information was then related to the hostel failure
rate.

Technically, the findings can be summarised as follows:

(1)    Wardens who were strict in terms of their rules tended to
have low failure rates ($r = 0·33$, not significant).

(2)    Wardens who were emotionally distant as measured by the
attitude questionnaire tended to have high failure rates: ($r = 0·42$,
not significant).

(3)    Wardens who were strict tended to be emotionally distant
($r = 0·46$, not significant).

(4)    Wardens who could be strict without being particularly
emotionally distant, or emotionally close without being particularly
permissive, had significantly lower failure rates than others (relevant
partial correlations: $r = 0·65$, $p < 0·05$, and $r = 0·67$, $p < 0·01$,
respectively).

Since both warden and matron had filled in an attitude questionnaire independently, it was possible to create a measure of the
difference in attitude between them (in practice this was done by
subtracting the smaller of their scores on a measure of institutional
orientation from the larger). This measure, too, provided some
interesting findings, which can be summarised below:

(1)    Wardens who were strict in terms of their rules tended to
have wives who agreed with them on how the hostel should be run
($r = 0·53$, $p < 0·05$).

(2) Wardens whose wives agreed with them on how the hostels should be run tended to have significantly lower failure rates ($r = 0 \cdot 57$, $p < 0 \cdot 05$).

Thus it seems that 'successful' wardens were likely to be strict, warm, and—in disciplinary matters at least—in agreement with their wives. Their regimes thus approximated to the paternalist pattern suggested by the case studies, and were clearly very similar to the type of family which Davies has shown to be associated with lack of reconviction among delinquent probationers. There is, therefore, evidence that in this respect at least the quasi-family hostel and the family operate alike.[2]

## How interdependent are staff and residents?

### Existence of 'mood swings' in probation hostels

The fact that the successful warden was warm and firm does not prove that these qualities were the cause of his success. Firmness and supportiveness are less properly seen as attributes of a particular man than as descriptive of a relationship between one man and others. No doubt some people find it easier to be firm, but firmness carries with it the presumption of effectiveness. Thus a person whom others persistently disobey would not be seen as firm, but rather as weak, rigid, nagging, or in some other way ineffective. These facts underlie the point made in the introduction that the various members of a family depend on each other for the successful performance of their roles, with the result that families are liable to vicious circles which can bring strife to potentially happy units. Probation hostels are subject to similar processes.

Most institutions are prone to what might be called mood swings. These oscillations have been noticed in therapeutic communities (Rappoport, 1961) and American correctional schools (Jesness, 1965) and they occur even though staffing, structure and clientele remain largely unchanged. As will be seen, the swings were particularly marked in probation hostels. To understand them it was thought necessary to take account of what can be called the control system of the hostel, which consisted of those people likely to react if the hostel started to run into difficulties. Data on this were gathered from similar records to those used in the case studies, combined with 92 semi-structured interviews with staff and others connected with hostels and a certain amount of direct observation.

A bad patch often began when a new warden took up a post and faltered in establishing his position. He could find such temporary fumblings hard to repair. Almost inevitably he was compared unfavourably with his predecessor, being seen, for example, as harsh rather than permissive, or soft rather than firm. If he was seen as harsh, the residents might abscond, set up a barrier between themselves and the staff, or in extreme cases defy the staff to their faces. If he was seen as soft, delinquency could become more open, bullying, kangaroo courts and even organised stealing become rife, and the staff be defied not occasionally but continually, and by low- as well as high-status boys. Faced with such defiance the warden had a difficult task. If he increased punishment, he increased resentment, if he continued with a reprimand he was seen as nagging, if he did nothing he might be despised. More seriously, he was likely to feel increasingly threatened and to react, depending on his personality, with ill-judged aggression or equally ill-judged withdrawal, either of which of course made matters worse, resulting in either the cold or the chaotic situations that have been described.

As already stated, problems within the hostel were likely to affect not only the warden but also the rest of the staff. All, there-fore, were equally in danger of losing sight of the wood for the trees, and indeed the warden could find it particularly difficult to handle a situation in which the residents upset his wife. In such circum-stances, the reactions of those outside the hostel were vitally import-ant. But, for a variety of reasons, others were ill-placed to help. As has been seen, the committee did not usually provide professional supervision, and an attempt on their part to do so in troubled times could easily be handled clumsily or seen as snooping. The probation service, the professional group most closely connected with the hostel, usually differed in training and philosophy from the wardens, and there was an awkward conflict of responsibilities. The warden was responsible for the running of the hostel, but the probation officers had responsibilities for individual boys within it. As a result, the warden could wish the court to punish an absconder so that others might be deterred; the probation officer, being concerned for the individual absconder, could disagree, and such conflicts were clearly more likely to arise when there were many abscondings or offences. So, also, were difficulties with the police, who could be called on to collect absconders from different towns, and with employers, who found that hostel boys were increasingly unreliable. The situation, therefore, contained a number of vicious circles made worse by a general tendency to attribute all that went on in the hostel to the warden's personality. The following is an example of such events:

The warden was a former Chief Petty Officer, who reacted
to his appointment in charge of a hostel by imposing a rigid

discipline backed up by an aggressive hectoring approach which seemed to others to stem from personal tension as much as from disciplinarian beliefs. The residents reacted to this with superficial conformity, a considerable amount of absconding and delinquency, and finally a mass refusal to go to work combined with a joint protest to a sympathetic liaison probation officer. This incident was resolved and the warden turned for support to a local psychiatrist whose blunt manner appealed to him, and whose understanding enabled the warden to modify his techniques and make use of his own good qualities. The final years of this regime were marked by very firm discipline tempered with warmth, and an almost complete absence of delinquency.

The second regime illustrates a hostel recovering from a breakdown in discipline:

The warden took over a hostel that had been run on very strict lines, and attempted to introduce a more relaxed atmosphere. The consequence of this was an outbreak of fights, kangaroo courts, bullying, and defiance of the staff. One resident threatened the warden with a knife, and, surviving a summons for this incident, proceeded more or less to take over the hostel, treating the other boys as his servants. The probation officer and the committee reacted to the situation by blaming the warden, and the warden experienced an understandable loss of morale. A change was produced by a decision to close the hostel down for repairs. Following this, the warden took in younger boys, whom he found easier to control, imposed a stricter regime, and mended his relationship with the probation service. Table 6.5 shows the dramatic difference in the incidence of absconding and offences before and after the hostel shut down.

TABLE 6.5   *Improvement in performance in one regime*

| | Absconded or offended | | Did not abscond or offend | | Total | |
|---|---|---|---|---|---|---|
| | N | % | N | % | N | % |
| Admitted up to shut-down | 25 | 57 | 19 | 43 | 44 | 100 |
| Admitted after shut-down | 24 | 28 | 62 | 72 | 86 | 100 |

The bad patches just discussed did not necessarily, of course, coincide with the warden's arrival. The chain of events might be set off by a warden's illness, the matron's new baby and her consequent anger at being forced to be a matron as well as a mother, disloyal assistants, or a combination of particularly difficult boys. Nor is the evidence for the oscillations simply anecdotal, convincing though the accounts of such changes can be. As illustrated above, the proportion of residents getting into trouble can be strikingly different at different points in a warden's regime. An analysis of thirty-two regimes[3] showed conclusively that hostels did go through bad patches, in the sense that failure rate was sometimes much greater in one half of a warden's regime than in another, and these differences were most unlikely to arise through chance ($\chi^2 = 59 \cdot 67$; $df = 32$; $p < 0 \cdot 001$). This analysis, however, did not prove that the warden's individual characteristics had no effect. Wardens differed in their liability to 'bad patches'. A rather elaborate analysis demonstrated that whereas there was no doubt that, even given the same warden, hostels did go through epidemics of absconding or offending, under some wardens these were more frequent or more serious than under others.

## Administrative implications

### The administrative problems

Our analysis of probation hostels, then, highlighted three aspects: their dependence on the warden and matron, the almost parental qualities demanded of these members of staff, and the interdependence of staff and residents. All this amounts to a claim that probation hostels did operate in many ways like families, and, as suggested in the introduction, this raises problems for administrators.

In the first place, like families, the quasi-family institution is very variable. This variability faces the administrator with the problem of ensuring a uniformly high standard of performance. His dilemma is made more difficult by the fact that one convenient method of control, the use of rules and routines, is either largely ineffective or alternatively implies a type of institution which is the opposite to what he wants. The difficulty is that the success of the quasi-family institution depends on relationships, and whereas bureaucratic control tends to produce an impersonal atmosphere, its absence does not ensure a happy one. Other forms of control are difficult to apply. Thus, although government inspectors sometimes noticed that relationships in a probation hostel were poor, they were rarely able to provide much help in this area, and their effective action was often limited to ensuring that fire and Home Office regulations were obeyed.

The tensions, crises and moods of the small quasi-family hostels are a second source of difficulty which inevitably places a strain on the staff and which can again be contrasted with the situation in larger, more bureaucratic, institutions. Such organisations usually provide their lower-level employees with defences against the anxiety endemic in human relationships, expecting their staff to react to clients less as people than as the owners of problems or of inferior social roles. Thus, rotation of staff makes them less likely to form spontaneous relationships with clients from whom they must soon be separated; the principle of division of labour avoids the conflict inherent in combining expressive and instrumental roles; and the hierarchical system lessens the risks of manipulation by ensuring that those in direct contact with clients have little discretion in granting their requests. Indeed, involvement between staff and client may be penalised informally by the staff culture, formally by the hierarchy, or personally through the pain which staff face when they themselves are transferred or their clients leave, die, suffer distress, or let them down.

Whether or not the situation just described applies in all large institutions, it is certainly harder to maintain it in a small quasi-family one. In the hostels studied, for example, the warden provided both discipline and support, carried responsibility for the health and well-being of his charges, for day-to-day financial transactions and for representing the hostel to the court, the probation service, and the outside world in general. He had to face the moral conflicts resulting from his powerful position, the role conflicts inherent in the disciplinary and supportive aspects of his job, and the human conflicts resulting from his continuous, many-faceted involvements with the residents. His home was not a refuge but his place of work. Problems in the hostel affected not only the warden but his wife, and unlike others he could not often refresh himself by talking to people not immediately connected with his work.

The matron, too, had her difficulties. She was the only woman in a household of men. She had an ambiguous relationship with the assistants, who might or might not defer to her as the warden's wife. She had to combine the role of matron with that of wife and sometimes mother, and balance the claim of her own family against that of the residents, many of whom had very ambivalent attitudes towards women. Both she and the warden were likely to work very long hours (at the time of the research, for example, some wardens had been working from 5.30 a.m. to 11.0 p.m. for weeks, almost without relief).

The following quotation from a matron may illustrate the reactions which sometimes (certainly not always) characterised hostel staff:

'These boys all want so much of you. With twenty boys coming in you can't give it. It's terribly difficult in a year to get to know them all. They are all so different. It's hard work to have time for them and we mustn't spend five minutes longer with Jack than with John . . . [When we came] it was terrible. My husband had told me I had lived a sheltered life, but I didn't realise such things went on. I said to my husband: "We've got to get out of here. I don't care if we have to move the furniture out into the street." The language I heard! And the boys are so big, they tower over you . . . . My husband and I hardly have any time together. I've got three young girls and I hardly ever see them. I get very tired, especially when I have to do the cooking. I find I get a terrible pain and was worried that it was a heart or cancer or something. I went to the doctor and he said it's nothing else—just fatigue. You just go on—you just have to, especially with the staff. It's very difficult to get an assistant with any sense. The only person I've ever met in this area is the minister's wife and she's a very busy person. I've got a friend at a children's home up the road, but we only talk to each other on the telephone most of the time. The only ones locally who come to our door come to complain.'

The quotation just given illustrates neatly the strange cross between family and institution which constituted hostels of this kind. The feeling that, 'These boys all want so much of you' and that one has neither time nor emotional resource to meet their needs must be familiar to most parents. So, too, must the difficulty of spending more time with one child than another. Yet parents are usually less troubled with delinquent behaviour, with conflicts between their marriage, their family, and their job, and with severe social isolation. These latter problems are institutional in origin. It is in its combination of family and institutional stress and in its lack of the usual institutional defences that the peculiar problems of the quasi-family institution lie.[4]

## The requirements for an administrative solution

A frequent response to the problems just raised is to call for more training for residential staff. The reliance on training for the control of performance is a central feature of many professions—particularly those such as psychiatry where there are great difficulties in checking the professional's results, so that the public must rely on his ethical code and professional competence. No doubt more training is needed for residential staff, not least to raise their status. But the training must be appropriate and is certainly not sufficient on its own without other measures. Trained staff cannot be expected to function in intolerable situations, or to be attracted to them. Moreover, their human responses cannot be trained out of them, and insofar as they remain human they will continue to be involved with their charges, with both good and bad results. Thus it is unfortunate that residential work, like teaching, has not on the whole developed a supervisory system capable of handling the inevitable involvement of front-line staff with their clients.

Measures of performance constitute a further method of control which has some promise, and probably some use. The probation hostel study provided one such measure and this could be supplemented by others, for example the social climate questionnaire described elsewhere in this book. It is significant, however, that these measures have not been used to evaluate the performance either of the hostel system as a whole or of individual wardens, and in both cases the reasons are probably the same. Measures of performance are most useful where means exist to help poor performers to improve. However, those concerned with probation hostels have little idea how a high failure rate can be reduced; thus to advise a warden of his high failure rate may simply increase anxiety that is already excessive and invite a defensive reaction that he has more than usually difficult boys or a particularly advanced regime.

In the long run, the control of quasi-family institutions can only be tackled by selecting the right staff, ensuring that the qualities demanded of them are not superhuman, and providing them with sufficient supervision and support. Within this general framework a variety of different policies are possible. Thus administrators can attempt to attract more, and hence possibly more capable, staff (for example, by increasing pay, introducing secondment schemes from other fields of social work, or in the case of probation hostels by not insisting that warden and matron be married).[5] They can make it easier to remove those who cannot cope with the strains of residential work (again through secondment schemes or probationary periods). They can try to reduce the strains (for example, by employing more staff to reduce the number of hours worked, or altering the role requirements by making it easier to remove very difficult residents, or otherwise relaxing disciplinary demands of the job). Finally, they can set up a flexible system which supports rather than harasses staff when particularly severe strains arise. Among other things, this implies a consultative, supportive form of supervision, more like that prescribed by social work theory and including, where possible, the discussion of tensions among the staff.

The last point is particularly important. In the present writer's opinion, the mistakes of residential workers are less the result of faults of character or training than of human reactions to almost intolerable stress. It follows that such workers must be supported, not simply told what to do or trained and left to get on with it. They should, of course, be friendly, firm and understanding, have insight into their own prejudices, realise their own part in provoking absconding, see—where appropriate—distress behind aggression, and withstand stress and lack of sleep. But in a world where they, or anyone else, found things that easy, few residential institutions would be needed.

# References

CLARKE, R. V. G., and CORNISH, D. B. (1972) *The Controlled Trial in Institutional Research*, London: HMSO.

CLARKE, R. V. G., and MARTIN, D. N. (1971) *Absconding from Approved Schools*, London: HMSO.

DAVIES, M. (1969) *Probationers in their Social Environment*, London: HMSO.

DAVIES, M., and SINCLAIR, I. A. C. (1971) 'Families, hostels and delinquents, an attempt to assess cause and effect', *British Journal of Criminology, 11*, 213–29.

GOFFMAN, E. (1961) *Asylums: Essays on the Social Situation of Mental Patients and Other Inmates*, New York: Doubleday; Chicago: Aldine.

JESNESS, C. (1965) *The Fricot Ranch Study*, California Department of Youth Authority, *Research Report 47*.

KYSAR, J. E. (1968) 'Reactions of professionals to disturbed children and their parents', *Archives of General Psychiatry, 19*, 562–70.

PARSONS, T., and BALES, R. F. (1955) *Family Socialization and Interaction Process*, Chicago: Free Press.

RAPPOPORT, R. N. (1961) *Community as Doctor. New Perspectives on a Therapeutic Community*, London: Tavistock.

SINCLAIR, I. A. C. (1971) *Hostels for Probationers*, London: HMSO.

SINCLAIR, I. A. C., and SNOW, D. (1971) 'After-Care Hostels receiving a Home Office grant', in *Explorations in After-Care*, London: HMSO.

# 7 Measurement of treatment potential: its rationale, method and some results in Canada

Tadeusz Grygier

## Introduction: the purpose and the setting

A new measuring instrument, subsequently named the Measure of Treatment Potential (MTP), was developed between 1961–4 in the course of a comprehensive study on social adjustment, personality and behaviour in Ontario training schools. The primary function of the MTP is to compare various treatment units and to isolate some elements of the methods, populations and situations that help or hinder them. Treatment units were 'houses', 'cottages', 'linguistic groups' or, sometimes, small schools that permitted and enhanced social interaction between the children and the staff. In all, 967 subjects were drawn from 6 boys' training schools (corresponding to approved schools in England), 1 training centre for young men (corresponding to a borstal) and 4 training schools for girls. White Oaks, a school for young boys, was established later and studied separately, since it involved some modification of the MTP procedures. This is reported on pp. 154–6; in Appendix D; and elsewhere (Grygier et al., 1968).

Institution size ranged from 15 girls in one school to 200 boys in another; size of the units varied from 14 to 37. Between units, the average age of the children ranged from $14 \cdot 03$ to $16 \cdot 13$ years in the training schools and from $18 \cdot 53$ to $19 \cdot 50$ years in the training centre. All of the children in the new school for young boys were under the age of twelve.

The staff/pupil ratio for the male institutions varied from $0 \cdot 24$ to $0 \cdot 74$. In the new school for young boys it exceeded unity: in this case there were more staff than pupils. Three training schools were restricted to children of Roman Catholic faith and were administered by religious orders. One of these was 'bilingual': most of the staff spoke both English and French and the pupils were divided into two linguistic groups, one predominantly French and the other English. All other schools were unilingual: English, like most of the schools in the Province of Ontario.

## Rationale of the MTP

In recent decades 'treatment' has become the goal of training school programmes. No matter what structures and treatment methods have been developed, the relationships between wards and staff are seen as a determining factor in effecting behavioural change. If the institution is composed of two separate normative systems, that of the staff (representing a model of law-abiding behaviour) and that of a delinquent subculture in opposition to the staff, the peer group of children may have the power to impede or negate any positive goals which the institution may have set.

This is often the case in correctional institutions for adults. Clemmer (1940) states that prison culture is organised around the values of its most persistent and least amenable members. Moreno and Jennings (1947) report that in prisons and reformatories the most popular inmates have an outstanding record of antisocial activity; those who wish to be reformed remain unchosen in sociometric tests. Schrag (1954) reports that the most popular leaders of prison inmates, as defined by replies to his sociometric questionnaire, proved to have spent more years in prison, to have had longer sentences remaining to be served, to have been more often charged with crimes of violence, and to have been more frequently recidivists. Studies by Goffman (1961), McCorkle and Korn (1954), Polsky (1962), Morris and Morris (1963) and Sykes (1958) confirm the sociometric data reported on adult male prisoners. Jennings (1943) observes that the girls with high sociometric status tend to disobey the training school staff and to assert their own independence.

All this is understandable. When a prisoner or a young delinquent is labelled by society in unfavourable terms and is thrown into an unfamiliar environment, he in turn rejects those who represent the rejecting society. He limits his communication to members of his own 'society of captives' (McCorkle and Korn, 1954; Sykes, 1958) and restricts as far as possible his communication with his captors (McCleery, 1961). Under these circumstances there can be no true treatment: positive influence requires communication and acceptance.

Harmony, communication and mutual acceptance appear to be prerequisites of successful treatment; they seldom exist in large prisons, but in training schools the situation appears to vary. In more progressive schools the social system of the delinquent boys is not necessarily opposed to authorities and may even support them (Street *et al.*, 1966). There is seldom much point in measuring a constant; but once variation can be detected by observation, it becomes evident that a more objective measure could be useful, especially since what is termed progressive by some observers may be perceived as undisciplined by others.

Clearly, assessment of the therapeutic potential and total social climate of an institution requires an objective, empirical device. This instrument has to be capable of measuring the extent of staff/ ward cleavage or, conversely, the degree of correspondence of attitudes and goals. The MTP developed by the author satisfies these criteria; it is based on the premise that if a delinquent in an institution meets with the approval of his peers whenever he offends against the official culture, and with disapproval whenever he tries to co-operate, he is likely to reject therapy in favour of acceptance by the delinquent subculture. If, on the other hand, the attitudes of staff and delinquents coincide, the efforts of the staff will be reinforced by the concensus of those undergoing treatment.

As Cusson (1968) notes, the underlying concept of the MTP is interpersonal experience based on agreement and mutual respect. Under these conditions the delinquent learns to establish a relationship of trust and co-operation. He understands that relations other than those based on exploitation and power exist. He realises that an order is not issued on a whim and that obedience is not necessarily humiliating. He learns to co-ordinate his actions with others in order to pursue a common goal. In this context, 'the other', whether staff member or peer, ceases to be either a menace or a victim. He becomes one who shares the same values and obeys the same laws. Acceptance of and respect for others become possible.

## Structure of the MTP

The MTP is composed of two separate measures, one representing the status of the children among their peers (the sociometric questionnaire), and the second the behaviour rating of the child by the training school staff (Appendices A and B). 'Treatment potential' may be operationally defined as:

A correlation between the attitudes of wards towards the behaviour of their peers (as measured by the sociometric questionnaire) with the attitudes of the staff towards the wards' behaviour (as expressed in behaviour ratings) is an index of the treatment potential of a unit.

In developing the MTP it was assumed that standards of behaviour to which the staff gave only lip service would not suffice; these would have to be overtly expressed in their daily contacts with the children. The behaviour ratings were regarded as a measure of the attitudes of staff towards the children; a child was ranked in his group according to the value system of the rater. Models of behaviour deemed desirable or undesirable were embodied in the personalities of the children as seen by the staff rather than in abstract qualities which the staff might declare to be the goals of their treatment.

We were not interested in superficial conformity on the part of the children, whether in verbal statement or action, but sought underlying attitudes which may reflect their predominant values. Verbal statements, especially those under some form of compulsion, have doubtful validity. The delinquent verbally accepts standards of conduct he rejects in action. Conforming behaviour in a situation which demands conformity and implies enforcement is an unreliable indicator of future behaviour. Only underlying attitudes, measured in such a way that the subject does not realise how much he is revealing, can give us a clue to the degree of potential for behavioural change. The sociometric questionnaire was constructed to be an indirect measure of the children's attitudes towards each other and is based on the premise that personalities embody life styles with implicit value orientations. A sociometric choice is also a statement, but it is a statement of intended action and not merely of professed values and norms. A positive attitude towards a peer is taken as indirect but active approval of his values and behaviour.

There is nothing original or daring in these assumptions. Northway (1944) maintains that sociometric status is an indicator of conformity to group habits and incorporation of group values. True conformity implies acceptance of the group norms that prescribe group conduct (Grygier, 1966; Homans, 1950, 1961; Sellin, 1938), as well as the roles its members are expected to play (Parsons, 1951; Parsons and Shils, 1951). In a subcultural setting of society's rejects the captives are, in fact, expected to overplay their roles: armoured by their defence mechanisms (Lavallee and Mailloux, 1965) and driven by the forces of 'social progression' (Grygier, 1965b, 1966) they will tend to amplify their deviance from the norms of the society at large (Wilkins, 1969). For this reason the clash of values, norms and expectations in a correctional setting has a particularly pernicious effect: it releases dynamic forces leading to progressive deviance, forces much more powerful than the static, formal constraints of the official system.

The two constituent variables of the MTP, the behaviour ratings and the sociometric questionnaire, are both intended to reveal attitudes towards the behaviour of individual children within each unit; the former represents that of the correctional authorities; the latter that of the children under their charge. Where there is a high positive correlation between the two variables, a correspondingly high degree of agreement on values is postulated. As Bridgman (1927, 1945) says, any concept is synonymous with the corresponding set of operations, and two operations may be said to be equivalent if they lead to the same numerical results. A low or negative correlation indicates a negative subculture operating in opposition to the staff.

The question the MTP was intended to answer was whether children adopt a set of attitudes towards their own behaviour which corresponds to the attitudes of the staff to the children's behaviour. It was assumed that the correlation coefficient between these two sets of attitudes could provide a measure of both the potential and short-term effects of treatment. If resocialisation is an interactive process, in which the wards and those in charge are trying to find—or to avoid—a common language, every part of the process may be both the cause (the potential) and the effect of treatment. There is, in fact, little use in postulating causality in the strict sense, provided the process is understood and measured. Everything that correlates with the process may be its cause, its effect, or simply an associated variable—the MTP is assumed to assess the process of interaction at a given moment, no less and no more.

## Components of the MTP

### The sociometric questionnaire

A method of establishing various aspects of sociometric status, previously designed by the author and I.J. Croft (1956), was further refined for use with training school subjects. The sociometric method requires testees to have constituted a reasonably distinct group over a long enough period to have developed feelings and attitudes towards each other. For this reason the children were studied in the groups in which they usually participated and where they knew each other intimately.

Thirty-six such training school units were measured in this research (not including the new school for young boys which was studied later). Testing included as many as possible of those children who could follow the instructions and who were sufficiently stabilised within their reference group to present a reliable pattern of social relations. Those not eligible included: children of subnormal intelligence (I.Q. below 80); those with a reading level below grade six; those displaying marked inability to concentrate; those awaiting placement; those in residence for less than one month; those having returned from placement or absconding within two weeks prior to testing; those under twelve; or unavailable on the day of testing. Whenever possible, the researcher conducted testing in classrooms.

Names of all the eligible children in the unit were listed on the blackboard. The children sat at individual desks. If a pupil disregarded instructions or otherwise spoiled the answer sheet, his answers were discounted; but he remained as a possible choice in the questionnaire (Appendix A).

The first step in scoring was to list the names from the blackboard. First choices were given a weight of 3, second choices 2, and third choices 1. This provided preference (positive) and rejection (negative) scores. The acceptance scores (WA) were calculated by subtracting the rejection scores (WR) from the preference scores (WP); the result could be either positive or negative. The emotional response scores (WE) were arrived at by adding preference and rejection scores, disregarding plus or minus signs. This method provides the sociometric measures set out in Table 7.1. The method of calculation shows that the WA and WE scores are dependent upon WP and WR. The latter two scores are conceptually independent but tend, as might be expected, to correlate negatively. The letter W, preceding the letter indicating the type of score, distinguishes the weighted raw scores from standard scores, which were named P, R, A and E respectively. The standard scores were obtained by using a fixed normal distribution with a mean of 3. Within each unit, a score of 5 was assigned to a child who was most liked (P), least rejected (R), most positively accepted (A), or towards whom there was the greatest emotional response (E). There was only one score 5 and one score 1 (the opposite of 5) in most groups tested, although larger groups had two extreme scores at each end. The distribution of other scores followed the *Procrustean Table to Stretch Data on* (Appendix C).

TABLE 7.1

| Score | | Attribute measured |
|-------|--|--------------------|
| WP | (preference) | Being frequently chosen as liked (friend) |
| WR | (rejection) | Being frequently chosen as disliked (rejected) |
| WA | (acceptance) | Being frequently chosen as liked rather than disliked |
| WE | (emotional involvement) | Being chosen as liked *or* disliked |

*Behaviour ratings*

In each of the 36 units where the sociometric questionnaire was administered the staff member presumed to be closest to the pupils was asked for behaviour ratings of the children under his charge. The rater was usually a house master or mistress in the case of residential units, or the most immediate supervisor where the unit consisted of a grade or cultural/linguistic grouping.

The staff rater was given the same list of names that had appeared on the blackboard for the children completing the sociometric questionnaire. The researcher did not define the standards of conduct; he explained that the raters were to base their choices on their own criteria. The same distribution of ratings that had been fixed for the sociometric scores was issued.

The object of the forced normal distribution for sociometric scores and behaviour ratings was, in part, to increase standardisation and comparability of results. Otherwise, children popular in a large group would invariably score higher than the most popular children in a smaller group; rejected children would be most rejected in the largest groups, and so on. The rigid standardisation imposed on the raters allowed subjective 'response sets' to be reduced.

The method used for assessing the MTP components in the school which was studied separately is explained in Appendix D. In this special case, techniques were adapted to younger children in a setting where more than one staff member was in close contact with them.

## Calculating the MTP

When the results of the sociometric test and the behaviour ratings were compiled, each child, in each unit, had 5 scores: one behaviour and four sociometric scores. The first represented the attitude of the staff towards the child; the latter four represented the combined attitudes of the other children towards the child. In order to arrive at the MTP for a unit it was necessary to determine the extent of agreement between the two sets of attitudes. This was calculated by correlating the behaviour rating scores with one of the standard sociometric scores; in our case the acceptance scores (A) were chosen as the most appropriate. By means of a new formula for product-moment correlation, called Plato's r (Grygier, 1965a), correlations were calculated with a minimum of error and in considerably reduced time.

One additional step was necessary because correlation co-efficients are not normally distributed: in order to compare unit

MTPs with related factors and to employ standard tests of significance the correlation coefficients had to be converted to z scores, which have a normal distribution.

The final index number derived from the calculations represents the degree to which the pupils adopt a set of attitudes towards their own behaviour corresponding to the attitudes of the staff.

## Reliability and validity

### The sociometric questionnaire

Any measure of repeat reliability of sociometric findings may be questioned as a matter of principle. Indeed, the founder of sociometry, J. L. Moreno (1934) and, more recently, Evans (1966) and Northway (1967), assert that the ordinary concepts of reliability and validity applied to psychological tests have no meaning in the field of sociometry, which is said to measure unstable current behaviour.

When the questionnaire was developed for the original study in a British secondary modern school, Croft and Grygier (1956) did establish the reliability of their sociometric scores. But since reliability depends on the population tested and upon its particular circumstances, it must be re-examined whenever the population or the circumstances differ from those for which reliability data are available.

Four training school units were retested after an interval of three months to determine the stability of the sociometric scores. The sociometric scores represent the children who are recipients of sociometric choices and not the children taking the test, they therefore applied to those not available for retesting, provided the latter were still known to the testees and their names were on a list. On retest the same names were listed whether or not each child was available.

Our sociometric scores on retest thus came from a smaller number of children and represent a smaller number of actual choices; but they concern the same number of children as recipients of sociometric choices and have, therefore, the same fixed distribution of standard scores.

The results of the test-retest reliability investigation for the sociometric questionnaire are set in Table 7.2. It can be seen that all sociometric scores are moderately stable, except (as with the second group) where the purpose and structure of the group has changed.

TABLE 7.2 *Test-retest correlations of sociometric scores in four training school units*

| Group | P | R | A | E |
|---|---|---|---|---|
| 1 A typical house in a training school for boys | 0·70* | 0·50 | 0·70* | 0·70* |
| 2 A house converted into a centre for disciplinary problems in a training school for girls | 0·25 | 0·05 | 0·30 | 0·40* |
| 3 A house for young girls in a training school for girls | 0·70* | 0·75* | 0·75* | 0·40* |
| 4 A house in a training school for young boys | 0·72* | 0·50* | 0·67* | 0·56* |

* $P < 0·05$.

Other evidence of the reliability of the sociometric questionnaire might be inferred from an examination of the consistency of choices made by each testee in response to the different items within the single test run. The children seemed to choose their favourites irrespective of the function suggested in the question (see questionnaire, Appendix A). This suggests that each of the functional questions was simply an alternative form of the basic question: 'Which boys/girls do you like best?', and the repetition of choices may in itself be considered a measure of test reliability.

## Behaviour ratings

In determining the attitudes of the staff towards their pupils, behaviour was rated by the staff member most closely associated with the unit in question. No individual supervisor was asked to rank the behaviour of the same children again, and so repeat reliability of behaviour ratings is unknown.

Inter-rater reliability is another matter. The ranking of behaviour may vary considerably, depending upon which staff member is questioned. When the MTP was pre-tested at a private centre for disturbed children, several staff members were asked to rank the behaviour of the children. The staff were not in agreement about the ratings of individual children. A similar divergence was found by Maurice Cusson (1968) in a Quebec training centre when he collected behaviour rating data from three staff members within each unit. In deciding which set of rankings was most representative among those presented by the unit's chief supervisor and by his two assistants, Cusson argued in favour of the rating given by the chief supervisor, partly because he had the greatest power within the unit and was the most closely identified with authority. If Cusson's contention is correct, then our use of the 'House Master' or his equivalent is probably justified.

## The MTP in England and Quebec

The MTP provides a correlation coefficient (converted to its z score equivalent) between the sociometric acceptance scores of pupils within each unit and the behaviour ratings of the responsible staff person. In order to establish its repeat reliability (stability) both component measures have to be reapplied. This was done only once: a unit of girls was retested on both constituent measures, but between testing times the unit had undergone restructuring for the purpose of intensive treatment. The resulting drop in the MTP was attributed to the differing structure, and the retest could not be considered useful as a measure of reliability.

In the pioneer investigation of a form of this instrument in a modern secondary school, Croft and Grygier (1956) presented some prima facie evidence for its validity. They found that in 'normal' classes sociometric scores correlated positively with behaviour ratings, while in classes exhibiting academic and behavioural problems such correlations were reduced to zero.

The most extensive exploration of concurrent validity of the MTP has been reported in the Province of Quebec by Cusson (1968). He used three criteria: (a) assessments by the director and assistant director of the institution under study, (b) participant observation, and (c) a penetrating study of attitudes of the boys receiving the highest Preference scores on the sociometric questionnaire.

The first criterion was the evaluation by the director and assistant director of a large 'Centre de ré-éducation' (a cross between an approved school and a borstal in England). Cusson asked them the following question: 'According to you, which are the cottages that function best?' This was a general question which left directors free to use their own evaluation criteria. Cusson learned later that, for the directors, the cottage that functions well is the one where the boys are disciplined, participate in group activities and co-operate with the educators. These characteristics correspond to what the MTP is supposed to measure.

When the cottages (16 in all) were ranked and compared with the rank order of the MTP measures, the following correlations were obtained: director correlated 0·56 with assistant director and 0·75 with MTP; assistant director correlated 0·43 with MTP.

The correlation between director and assistant director was inflated, because the two had met frequently and discussed the functioning of the units Cusson asked them to assess. The correlations of the MTP were suppressed, because Cusson used Preference instead of Acceptance scores; this reduced the range of MTP scores and consequently the size of the correlation coefficients. If agreement on effective functioning rather than a single measure of it were to be the criterion of validity, it could be argued that either the opinion of the director or the MTP was most valid. Even if we assumed the director's assessment to have the highest validity, a correlation of 0·75 with the MTP of a reduced range would indicate a very high validity of our measure.

Cusson also used another variant of the same criterion. He asked the two directors to rank jointly the cottages according to the quality of supervision by cottage staff.

The results are reproduced in Table 7.3.

TABLE 7.3

| Rank of supervision | MTP score | Rank of supervision | MTP score |
|---|---|---|---|
| 1 | 0·62 | 9 | 0·28 |
| 2 | 0·55 | 10 | 0·16 |
| 3 | 0·55 | 11 | 0·11 |
| 4 | 0·48 | 12 | 0·05 |
| 5 | 0·40 | 13 | 0·00 |
| 6 | 0·40 | 14 | −0·22 |
| 7 | 0·34 | 15 | −0·32 |
| 8 | 0·28 | 16 | −0·39 |

In this case, the ranks correspond almost perfectly. Cusson also found that the teachers (*éducateurs*) who, according to the directors and objective data, underwent the most severe selection before appointment to the staff headed the cottages with relatively higher MTP. On the other side of the staff—pupil interaction, the MTP in cottages where the directors had placed relatively less aggressive boys ranged from 0·0 to 0·62 with the mean of 0·38; in the cottages to which more aggressive boys had been sent the MTP ranged from −0·39 to 0·16, with the mean of −0·10.

The second criterion used by Cusson was participant observation. He chose two cottages, one with the MTP of 0·55 and the other —0·39, and worked for several months in each of them. He noted that in the cottage with the high positive measure of treatment potential the boys communicated more willingly and frequently with the 'educators', and accepted directives more readily. In the cottage with the negative measure of treatment potential the boys were more influenced by their own leaders and manifested hostility towards the educators. In this cottage the educators remained on the fringe of the group's life and the group formed a solid block, immunised against any influence of the staff. The educators were passive and self-effacing, and intervened only in cases of serious disorder. They seldom organised group activities, demanded only the minimum from the boys and made concessions for the sake of peace. The boys performed their tasks badly and complained; they often used 'guerilla tactics' of harassment, minor provocations or rowdy or demonstrative group activities in which the educator, faced with universal hostility, could only punish the whole group or let the matter drop. The strategy of the group was to exhaust the teacher's patience, undermine his self-confidence, break his will and reduce his taste for any intervention. The objectives were reached when, faced with a hostile group that never missed a chance to ridicule and humiliate him, the educator became immobilised. Left to themselves, the boys gathered around a little gang, dominated by the most delinquent members of the group. The picture was entirely reversed in the cottage with the high positive measure of treatment potential.

The third criterion was the assessment of the leaders, i.e. of the boys with the highest Preference scores. The top sociometric choices are, of course, neither typical representatives of their group nor even necessarily leaders. Natural leaders exert authority and influence, and are capable of leading the group according to their own design (Homans, 1961). Expressive leaders, on the other hand, are more influenced than influential. Both types symbolise group tendencies; they do not represent them in the same way in which a random sample represents a population. Top sociometric scorers, as the expressive leaders, are symbolic in this way. In the institution studied by Cusson the two top sociometric choices in each cottage tended to be also group leaders. Cusson interviewed each of them separately and then compared the favourites of the cottages with MTP above the median $(0 \cdot 25)$ with those from cottages of presumably lower treatment potential. He asked a number of significant questions, cited in Table 7.4. The figure on the right indicates the average number of positive responses from the favourites in the high and low MTP groups of cottages.

The trend is obvious, and becomes even more apparent in replies to the semantic differential type of questions. Here the leaders were asked to place themselves on a scale to indicate where they were

TABLE 7.4

| Interview question | High MTP | Low MTP |
|---|---|---|
| Do you think that some educators have helped you to become a man? | 2·00 | 0·71 |
| Are the educators just? | 1·43 | 0·85 |
| Do you accept being placed here? | 1·50 | 0·71 |
| Do you think your behaviour has improved since you came here? | 1·85 | 0·85 |

before coming to the training centre and, separately, at the time of the study, both with respect to the contrasting characteristics: lazy/industrious; quarrelsome/placid; not-serious/serious; disobedient/obedient; mischievous/not-mischievous. The tendency of the responses was to indicate a positive evolution (with the exception of 'seriousness' in the low MTP group), but the general average of differences in ratings was 8·6 in the high MTP group and only 2·86 in the low MTP group. It is apparent that the leaders of the cottages with a high MTP have a more positive attitude towards their superiors and tend to believe that their behaviour in the institution has improved.

It has to be recognised, of course, that favourites in a group are not merely representatives of the social forces operating within the group. Some sociometric studies (Bonney, 1943; Northway, 1944, 1946, 1947; Northway and Widgor, 1947; Perrin, 1963; Wu, 1964) have concentrated on personality characteristics as determinants of popularity. However, personality may be conceived as a coherent system of attitudes and behaviour patterns and, in this sense, the leader's personality is representative of dominant values and behavioural trends in the group.

## Indications of validity in Ontario

An unreported study in units of an adult institution administered by the Ministry of Correctional Services of Ontario resulted in similar findings. Units with a high MTP were described by researchers as co-operative, friendly and cordial, while units of low MTP exhibited opposite characteristics. These findings were substantiated by the fact that units with high MTP tended to choose their own supervisors as favourites, while members of other units were not so conclusive in their choices of 'favourite'. In this study an additional questionnaire established the sociometric status of the staff members for each unit of the inmates.

A more objective measure of concurrent validity was confirmed in our study. When the MTP was computed for each training school, the administrator of Ontario training schools, who was well acquainted with the schools, was asked to rate them according to his estimate of their therapeutic impact. His rank-order for the boys' schools corresponded precisely to that of the MTP. He was unable to distinguish between the treatment potential scores of girls' schools, most of which were very low, not significantly different from zero; the exception was one school for young girls, which had a high MTP and was assessed by him accordingly.

These findings of concurrent validity for the MTP provisionally confirmed our theoretical assumption that a correlation between sociometric and behaviour measures is an indication of the treatment potential of the group undergoing training. However, it was understood that acceptance of staff values by the children is not simply the result of the quality of the training school staff, let alone its superintendent. Treatability depends upon many factors. It was also realised that even if the measure is reliable and valid in relation to short-term effectiveness, it is desirable to assess the measure as a predictor of long-term effects.

## Predictive validity

Two pilot studies examining the post-release behaviour of children from Ontario training schools were conducted. The first was not specifically designed to measure the predictive power of the MTP, but allows for comparison of follow-up data on two schools of differing MTPs. The second tested the hypothesis that boys released from units of high MTP have lower rates of recidivism than boys released from units of low MTP.

### Social adjustment

'A Study of White Oaks Village', by Tom de Swaaf (1968), was an examination of the psychological and behavioural changes in boys released from two different training schools. One group was composed of all the boys who had graduated from White Oaks since 1966. The school had a relatively high MTP (0·62). All the boys in the experimental group in de Swaaf's follow-up study were residents of White Oaks when the MTP testing was conducted (see Appendix D).

Control subjects were drawn from one of the traditional training schools. These subjects were matched with the experimental subjects in terms of age, length of time since release, and time spent at the school. It was, however, difficult to control for the latter variable as the boys from White Oaks remained in the school longer than subjects from the traditional school.

The instrument used to measure personality change was the Bristol Social Adjustment Guide (Stott, 1960) administered to the respective teachers of each boy at three stages in his schooling: before training school, during training school, and at the time of the follow-up. The period covered in the community was less than one year after release from the respective schools.

The sample from the traditional school achieved, on average, a relatively greater degree of improvement in the first period, between the Guide 1 and Guide 2 measures. Both groups exhibited less maladjustment during training than before committal, but the White Oaks boys improved less. The trend in the second period, between the Guide 2 and Guide 3 measures, is different. After release, boys from the traditional school generally regressed to a considerable extent, whereas the White Oaks graduates continued to progress in a positive direction towards lesser maladjustment.

All White Oaks subjects were members of the school at a time when its MTP of 0·62 was recorded, in 1967. On the other hand, members of the control group were not resident at the traditional school when the MTP testing was conducted at that school in 1964. Nor were all the subjects in the control group necessarily members of one unit, since they were selected to match the experimental subjects. However, it is not unlikely that most were drawn from a common group since, in this particular traditional school, the treatment unit was defined by school grade for the purpose of establishing the MTP. Also, one of the key factors in matching was age; all the White Oaks boys were 12 years of age or younger, and so were the controls.

The over-all MTP for the traditional school was 0·36 and it was lower for units of younger boys. There is no evidence that the training environment at the traditional school underwent any particular changes prior to the selection of the control subjects.

If de Swaaf is correct in attributing the difference in mean adjustment of the two groups to qualitative factors involved in the divergent social climates, it might be concluded that boys from the school of higher MTP show better adjustment after training than those from the school of lower MTP.

This is unlikely to be affected by the bias on the part of the training school raters. On the contrary, when different sets of raters were used, during the stay of the boys at the school (Guide 2), the raters of White Oaks Village appeared to be more severe (the maladjustment scores of their pupils declined less than those of the boys in the traditional school). On the other hand the White Oaks graduates *may* have received better scores after their return to the community because White Oaks was generally regarded as a success and its 'treatment' more effective. The researcher should be aware of these pitfalls but can never entirely avoid them.

One more caveat remains. A serious problem of experimental control was encountered in comparing the two schools: White Oaks attempted to establish a more intensive system of after-care than other schools. It may be that this after-care system, rather than the institution itself, was responsible for improvement after release; but it is at least probable that the new school had a better treatment potential, and that this potential was measured by the MTP and was realised in the follow-up period.

## Recidivism

Recidivism data were collected in 1970 with the co-operation of the Royal Canadian Mounted Police, who provided information on adult offences; and from training school files, which provided data on correctional intervention after graduation. An attempt was made to include all the original subjects from boys' training schools: of the 379 boys of the original study, only five were missing from the follow-up. The remainder had spent at least two years in the community before the follow-up, and all were over 18 years of age.

Recidivism was operationally defined in five different ways, all related to the type of disposition and length of time between release from the tested unit and the first intervention. This method was used in preference to the frequency of further intervention, since recidivism was to be related to the dynamics of the subjects' experience only in the unit which was tested for the MTP. Examining behaviour after later correctional treatment would confuse the issue because the influence of subsequent correctional environments was not known.

An inverse relationship between the MTP and recidivism was expected: the higher the MTP of a unit, the lower the number of recidivists. However, no significant association was found between the MTP and recidivism, regardless of how the latter was defined. The measures showed a lack of consistent discrimination, possibly due to intervening variables (some of which were investigated) or, perhaps, to the difficulties inherent in any study of recidivism involving juveniles.

Two explanations for the negative findings were tested. The first was a suspected intervening variable: the average age of subjects in their training school units. In its simplest form, this had to be rejected since the average age of subjects in the six schools under study was almost the same. It was, therefore, not associated either with recidivism or with the MTP.

The other explanation involved a possible change in treatment policies during the 24 months between the first and last administration of the MTP. Boys included in the early testing programme exhibited a different pattern of recidivism than those tested towards the end of the programme. They tended to be subject to intervention earlier, within two years, to a significantly greater extent than boys tested later. The different pattern of recidivism could be interpreted as an effect of improved treatment, especially in terms of increased after-care services which may have retarded the return to deviant behaviour.

The third explanation for the negative findings is purely methodological. Therapeutic efforts were concentrated on the children who needed them most: the young starters, absconders, and those who committed more serious offences. This was exemplified in the training schools dealing with the youngest children and in the small maximum security school which housed relatively older boys considered to be the most difficult to treat; many of these were transferred from other training schools because of their serious behavioural problems. The relatively high MTP results for these schools reflect more intensive therapeutic efforts, without which these schools might have had even higher recidivism rates. Since no association was found between recidivism and the MTP, it may be that, in fact, treatment was successful since the results for these schools could have been expected to be worse.

Obviously, the effects of classification and differential intensity of care may interfere with attempts to find a direct association between the MTP as a measure of therapeutic impact, and recidivism as a criterion of later success or failure. When correctional policy is effective in equalising recidivism potential, prediction must take this factor into account.

Ancillary findings indicated that, independently, each of the component measures of the MTP has predictive power. Boys who were well accepted in their units were less apt to become recidivists, as were boys who received the best behaviour ratings. The relevant correlation coefficients were statistically significant.

These results contradict some widely held opinions. It is often assumed that all institutions housing delinquent children preserve and intensify a delinquent sub-culture; if this were true the most delinquent, most recidivism-prone boys would have been the most popular—as is the case with many adult institutions (Clemmer,

1940; Schrag, 1954; Sykes, 1958). It is often assumed that good behaviour is merely expedient behaviour, typical of the chronic recidivist; if this were true of training schools, the best behaved children would have had a relatively high recidivism rate and not the lowest, as was the case.

### Correlates of the MTP

Three items of readily accessible hard data thought to be associated with effectiveness of treatment—age of pupils, size of institution, and staff/pupil ratio—were examined as possible correlates of the MTP.

It is generally accepted that the age of the offender correlates with his prognosis: the earlier he started his delinquent career, the more likely he is to recidivate. On the other hand, it has been claimed that the younger the child or adult offender, the better are the short-term treatment effects. Our measure offered a ready means of assessing the validity of this assumption.

When the mean ages of boys in all training schools and of the young adults in the training centre were correlated with the MTP, the correlation coefficient was $-0 \cdot 72$; with the size of the institution and the staff/pupil ratio kept constant, the partial correlation was even higher: $-0 \cdot 90$. In other words, age appeared to be an extremely important determinant of treatment potential as defined by our measures, at least for this combined population of boys and young men. Cusson (1968) also reports higher MTP for cottages housing younger boys. Girls' schools were not examined since they were fewer in number and the average age of pupils was almost constant.

Similarly, the relationship between staff/pupil ratio and the MTP could not be examined in girls' schools because there were only four schools and little variability in staffing: only one, a private Roman Catholic school, differed by having a much lower staff/pupil ratio. With the boys' schools there were marked differences, varying from $0 \cdot 24$ to $0 \cdot 74$. When the staff/pupil ratios for all the boys' schools and the training centre for young offenders were correlated with the MTP, the correlation coefficient was $0 \cdot 45$; with age and size of institution kept constant the partial correlation coefficient increased to $0 \cdot 64$. Thus, staff/pupil ratio appeared to be closely associated with treatment potential.

Size of the institution was the next factor examined. It was hypothesised that size would correlate negatively with the MTP. For the male institutions the correlation coefficient of $-0 \cdot 40$ confirmed this assumption. With the boys' age and staff/pupil ratio constant the correlation was, however, reduced to $-0 \cdot 19$. In these same institutions, staff/pupil ratio correlated −0·74 with the size of the institution, which was the probable reason for the original high correlation of size with MTP and for its subsequent reduction. The results were no doubt affected by one school, the previously mentioned maximum security training school for boys with serious behavioural problems. This was a relatively small institution with a high MTP, which also had a very high staff/pupil ratio.

The situation in girls' schools was different. MTP results in one institution indicated that it was outstandingly effective. This was a small school for a maximum of 20 girls, but its staff/pupil ratio did not differ significantly from the average. In contrast to the smallest boys' school, the smallest girls' school contained wards who, according to the classification committee, had a good chance of adjusting to an open setting. If one took into account 'progression effects', the girls selected as good risks would be expected to respond to treatment even without a high staff/pupil ratio, and the encouraging MTP results may well reflect a likelihood of success which was present from the start, or at least from the moment of their classification.

## MTP differences between schools and units; White Oaks Village

Contrary to the expectation that the MTP would be negative in training schools, a conclusion drawn from Croft and Grygier's (1956) studies in the modern secondary school, our results for Ontario were positive in all of the boys' schools and one of the girls' schools. This might be interpreted as an indication that most Ontario training schools tend to have a therapeutic social system in which the standards of behaviour upheld by the staff are reinforced or accepted by the pupils themselves. In the case of the training schools for girls, with one exception, there was neither agreement nor disagreement between staff and pupils about desirable conduct. Most of the correlations were positive, but only one in twelve significantly so.

Results in one of the girls' units were particularly illuminating. The house was in a period of unrest at the time of the study and was subsequently turned into a special treatment centre for disciplinary problems. All but two girls of the research group remained in the house and problem children from other houses were added. The sociometric questionnaire was then re-administered to the girls originally in the house and correlated with behaviour ratings by staff. The MTP dropped from low positive to zero.

These results are not unique. They indicate the dangers of

classification and grouping of delinquent children in undesirable terms. With other data, on both offender groups and 'normal' children, they suggest that any classification or allocation reinforces the characteristic that was the basis of selection. A juvenile delinquent, already labelled in derogatory terms, feels even more alienated when singled out as a special problem or 'hard-core case'. Inevitably, he becomes progressively more anti-social. This phenomenon of 'social progression' based on a variety of data (mainly from England, but also from this research), has been described in greater detail in several publications (Grygier, 1965b, 1965c, 1966). Under a different term, 'deviance amplification' has also been described by Wilkins (1969).

The theory of social progression strengthens the expectation that no lasting effects can be expected when wards and staff radically disagree on what is desirable. No such disagreement was found in our data, although the MTP results in girls' training schools indicated a poorer prognosis than the results in boys' schools. If our measures are valid it follows that, although fewer boys than girls are sent to training school, the girls are less ready to accept the staff as models and consequently are more difficult to treat. It does not follow that they will become persistent offenders: other factors may preclude this.

Some MTP results for boys' schools were unexpected. For example, boys in one school were subject to maximum security precautions because of their serious behaviour problems. Except for its small population, this school resembled an adult institution, and the MTP was expected to reveal the existence of a 'delinquent subculture' of hostile pupils working out a value system in opposition to the norms established by the staff. One could also expect 'deviance amplification' effects. This was not the case; the MTP of 0·62 for this school was relatively high.

This finding is significant; it suggests that a high degree of custodial control may have beneficial results when applied to youngsters who have demonstrated an inability to operate in an open setting or to those whose lack of personal controls has made them a danger to society. Within the constraints of the small maximum security institution with a high staff/pupil ratio their behavioural goals were not discordant with those of the staff. The extent to which this positive treatment orientation would carry over after graduation could not be determined.

White Oaks Village was opened shortly after our study was completed, and organised in accordance with the research data taking into account our MTP studies. This school was designed for boys under the age of twelve, the early starters, who usually constitute a high risk category. Basic to the structure of White Oaks were two factors which our measure has shown to be associated with treatment effects: small population and high staff/pupil ratio. The school was composed of cottages housing no more than ten boys, each with a staff of five house parents. In addition, the school employed a number of administrative, professional and supervisory staff, who related to the entire complex of five cottages. The total number of staff exceeded the number of boys.

This unique situation, in which a new school for children who start their delinquent careers at an early age was established to incorporate factors thought to be associated with effectiveness of treatment, needed careful evaluation. When this was done, MTP results for all cottages were in a positive direction, and for the school as a whole the index of $0 \cdot 62$ reached a high level of significance (Grygier *et al.*, 1968).

Just as the study of a small school for young children confirmed MTP validity, its application in several large institutions for serious adult offenders showed its limitations: co-operation was so poor that sociometric status could not be determined (Grygier, 1975). If it had been determined and MTP calculated, the results might have been invalid.

In most training schools in Ontario and in the training centre in Quebec we assumed that agreement on standards of behaviour implied acceptance of adult standards by the children. This kind of agreement indicates high treatment potential. Operationally, however, the MTP defines only *agreement* on standards: it does not define the *nature* of these standards. In Cusson's study, in a cottage with negative MTP, the educators evidently rejected the standards of the delinquent gang and merely submitted passively to their rule, but in Polsky's (1962) study cottage parents seem to have accepted the standards of the bullies.

It is apparent that the assessment of treatment potential by MTP cannot always be valid. In institutions where the staff are not only weak and passive but possibly corrupt a high MTP may mean that the underworld, led by the most experienced, most violent or most sophisticated criminals, has succeeded in dominating the value system of the whole unit.

Barring these circumstances, a high MTP indicates a climate of co-operation regarded by senior administrators as conducive to effective functioning. Those under their care are disciplined, participate in common activities and co-operate with the staff. The most popular boys have positive attitudes towards their supervisors and towards the whole institutional experience; they also believe that they have made progress on the road to resocialisation. After their stay in a training school with a high MTP, delinquent children adjust to a normal school better than before treatment.

The high MTP units are small, and the staff/pupil ratio is high. The staff are well selected, imaginative and self-reliant; the children are young, relatively less aggressive, and respond readily to staff leadership. Other characteristics of units of high treatment potential await further research.

## The impact of the studies of treatment potential on social policy in Canada

(a) Although the Measure of Treatment Potential refers always to total units and not to individual children, both its components—the sociometric status and the behaviour rating—refer to individuals. As was confirmed in a later study (Blanchard, 1971), low sociometric and behaviour scores are predictors of later adult criminality. In the original study it was found that the children labelled 'incorrigible', 'unmanageable' or in similarly derogatory terms rather than 'adjudicated' by courts for criminal acts resented their detention in training schools more than the others did, and tended to reject their whole environment. Their behaviour and sociometric scores were correspondingly low. This finding has radically changed juvenile delinquency legislation. The Training Schools Act of 1965, drafted by the author and now in force in Ontario, abandons the North American concept of the 'state of delinquency' in favour of a distinction between criminal offences and what might be called in England 'care and protection' cases. Bill C-192, introduced by the Federal government but not yet enacted, follows the same principle. The Ontario Training Schools Act is the first law in Canada, and possibly in the world, based on empirical research.

(b) Within two weeks of having been informed of the MTP data showing that large institutions have a lower treatment potential, Hon. Allan Grossman, then Minister of Reform Institutions of Ontario, announced a change of building plans: no training schools for more than 125 children and no reformatories for more than 200 inmates would be built in the future. This policy has been in existence now for nearly ten years.

(c) In accordance with the same findings, Dr Grossman's[1] successor, Hon. Sylvanus Apps, introduced a network of 'group homes', for children who can adjust to an informal setting in a small group but cannot be handled at home or by foster parents.

(d) A small training school for young children (White Oaks Village) was organised in accordance with the findings of treatment potential studies. Its MTP is high.

(e) The largest boys' training centre in the Province of Quebec, studied by Cusson (1968), has been re-structured in accordance with his MTP data.

(f) Large correctional institutions for adults under the jurisdiction of the Ontario government are being replaced by smaller units.

(g) The data showing that young maladjusted children have the worst prognosis without treatment but the best chance of improving following treatment (they have the highest MTP) has led to an increased emphasis on treatment facilities for the 'younger set'.

(h) Private training schools in Ontario, suffering from inadequate funds and, consequently, a low staff/pupil ratio and low MTP, have received increased assistance.

(i) Selection and training of staff have improved: this is a general trend, occurring coincidentally with the MTP findings.

Other recommendations await implementation:

(i) Routine sociometric and behaviour evaluation of children rejected by their peers and staff.

(ii) Further research, to determine the effect of the new policy on the children, their parents, the administration of justice and the social services.

(iii) Recognition at the federal level of the fact that for some individuals a small and well-staffed maximum security institution may offer not only community protection but the internal security necessary for effective treatment. Recent appointments indicate the possibility of policy changes in this area.

(iii) Comparative studies of MTP on a cross-cultural basis, especially those comparing Canadian training schools and *écoles de protection* with their English equivalents.

## Acknowledgments

The author was assisted by Mrs Jane Gibson, graduate and Research Assistant of the Centre of Criminology, University of Ottawa, and Mrs Margaret Guarino, Information Officer of the Ministry of Correctional Services, Province of Ontario, Canada. The studies in Ontario were supported by the above Ministry; those in Quebec were carried out by Dr Maurice Cusson of the University of Montreal.

## Appendix A

*The sociometric questionnaire*

The following questions are about your likes and dislikes. Always choose 3 names from the boys in this group—all names are on the blackboard and you cannot choose any other. Read the whole list of questions through before making your choice. WHAT YOU WRITE DOWN IS SECRET AND WILL NOT BE SHOWN TO ANY OTHER BOY OR STAFF MEMBER.

### LIKES

Write first the name of the boy you like most, then the name of the boy you like second best, then the third best.

A.   Which boys do you like most?

1................................    2................................    3................................

B.   With which do you like to play most?

1................................    2................................    3................................

C.   With which would you like to go on a trip most?

1................................    2................................    3................................

D.   With which would you like to be photographed most?

1................................    2................................    3................................

### DISLIKES

Write first the name of the boy you like least of all, then the names of the two boys you like next least.

E.   Which boys do you like least?

1................................    2................................    3................................

F.   With which would you like to play least?

1................................    2................................    3................................

G.   With which would you like to go on a trip least?

1................................    2................................    3................................

H.   With which would you like to be photographed least?

1................................    2................................    3................................

## Appendix B

*The behaviour rating form*

Instructions are as follows: Read the list below and choose the boy (or girl) whose behaviour you most like. Put 5 against this name on the left hand margin. Then choose one whose behaviour you like least and put 1 against this name. Then choose —— children whom you regard as next best behaved and mark 4 against each of their names. Choose —— children whose behaviour you dislike and mark 2 against each of their names. You should be left with the names of —— children whose behaviour you regard as average: mark 3 against each name. If you do not remember a boy well you should assume that he is about average and mark him 3.

## Appendix C

*Procrustean table to stretch data on*

| N | f(X = 1) | f(X = 2) | f(X = 3) | f(X = 4) | f(X = 5) | $\Sigma(X - 3)^2$ |
|---|---|---|---|---|---|---|
| 12 | 1 | 3 | 4 | 3 | 1 | 14 |
| 13 | 1 | 3 | 5 | 3 | 1 | 14 |
| 14 | 1 | 3 | 6 | 3 | 1 | 14 |
| 15 | 1 | 4 | 5 | 4 | 1 | 16 |
| 16 | 1 | 4 | 6 | 4 | 1 | 16 |
| 17 | 1 | 4 | 7 | 4 | 1 | 16 |
| 18 | 1 | 4 | 8 | 4 | 1 | 16 |
| 19 | 1 | 5 | 7 | 5 | 1 | 18 |
| 20 | 1 | 5 | 8 | 5 | 1 | 18 |
| 21 | 1 | 5 | 9 | 5 | 1 | 18 |
| 22 | 1 | 5 | 10 | 5 | 1 | 18 |
| 23 | 2 | 5 | 9 | 5 | 2 | 26 |
| 24 | 2 | 6 | 8 | 6 | 2 | 28 |
| 25 | 2 | 6 | 9 | 6 | 2 | 28 |
| 26 | 2 | 6 | 10 | 6 | 2 | 28 |
| 27 | 2 | 6 | 11 | 6 | 2 | 28 |
| 28 | 2 | 7 | 10 | 7 | 2 | 30 |
| 29 | 2 | 7 | 11 | 7 | 2 | 30 |
| 30 | 2 | 7 | 12 | 7 | 2 | 30 |
| 31 | 2 | 7 | 13 | 7 | 2 | 30 |
| 32 | 2 | 8 | 12 | 8 | 2 | 32 |
| 33 | 2 | 8 | 13 | 8 | 2 | 32 |
| 34 | 2 | 8 | 14 | 8 | 2 | 32 |
| 35 | 2 | 8 | 15 | 8 | 2 | 32 |

*Procrustean table to stretch data on—continued*

| N | f(X = 1) | f(X = 2) | f(X = 3) | f(X = 4) | f(X = 5) | $\Sigma(X - 3)^2$ |
|---|---|---|---|---|---|---|
| 36 | 2 | 9 | 14 | 9 | 2 | 34 |
| 37 | 2 | 9 | 15 | 9 | 2 | 34 |
| 38 | 2 | 9 | 16 | 9 | 2 | 34 |
| 39 | 3 | 9 | 15 | 9 | 3 | 42 |
| 40 | 3 | 9 | 16 | 9 | 3 | 42 |
| 41 | 3 | 10 | 15 | 10 | 3 | 44 |
| 42 | 3 | 10 | 16 | 10 | 3 | 44 |
| 43 | 3 | 10 | 17 | 10 | 3 | 44 |
| 44 | 3 | 11 | 16 | 11 | 3 | 46 |
| 45 | 3 | 11 | 17 | 11 | 3 | 46 |
| 46 | 3 | 11 | 18 | 11 | 3 | 46 |
| 47 | 3 | 11 | 19 | 11 | 3 | 46 |
| 48 | 3 | 12 | 18 | 12 | 3 | 48 |
| 49 | 3 | 12 | 19 | 12 | 3 | 48 |
| 50 | 3 | 12 | 20 | 12 | 3 | 48 |
| 51 | 3 | 12 | 21 | 12 | 3 | 48 |
| 52 | 3 | 13 | 20 | 13 | 3 | 50 |
| 53 | 3 | 12 | 21 | 13 | 3 | 50 |
| 54 | 4 | 13 | 20 | 13 | 4 | 58 |
| 55 | 4 | 13 | 21 | 13 | 4 | 58 |

$$\text{Plato's r (correlation coefficient)} = \frac{\Sigma(X - 3)(Y - 3)}{\Sigma(X - 3)^2}$$

## Appendix D

*MTP testing in units of young children*

The method described in this appendix was followed at White Oaks Village, where none of the children was over age twelve. The component measures for the MTP are conceptually the same as those described in the section on the structure of the MTP (pp. 143–7), but the testing techniques had to be adapted to the age of the boys. Five adults were equally close to the residents in each of the small cottage-style units.

The first adaptation involved assessment of sociometric status. In most cases the boys were too young to complete the sociometric questionnaire. Use was made of an alternative method, called the Two Houses Technique, which was devised by Dr V. Szyrynski

(1963) to reveal the dynamics of interpersonal relations within a family. It was modified to serve as an equivalent to a sociometric test. The 'family' under scrutiny at White Oaks was the group of boys and staff living in each cottage in the training school setting rather than the nuclear family which was the object of Szyrynski's investigations.

Each child was given a stamp in the form of a human figure and asked to enumerate the children who belonged to his cottage; he placed a stamp at the top of a large sheet of paper each time a person was named. The interviewer wrote the appropriate name under each figure. Omissions were noted, suggested to the child, and then added to the diagram.

Next, the interviewer drew two houses in the middle of the paper and told the child that members of his cottage now had two houses to live in. The child was asked to place each of his cottage members, including himself, in one of these two houses. Each figure was again stamped under its own house. The child's attention was subsequently drawn to the house in which he placed himself, and he was asked whom he would invite from the other house to visit his house. The question was repeated until all those originally placed in the other house had been invited in turn.

The opposite situation was then introduced. Each child was asked to go back to the initial division of his cottage members. He was asked to imagine a hypothetical situation which would necessitate the removal of members from his house; the reasons suggested included circumstances such as: the house is too small, a bed has broken down, another bed has broken down, or this is just for a short visit. If a child absolutely refused to send anyone away he was asked to say whom he would least like to send away and so on, until an order of sending away was established. The question was repeated until everyone from his house had been sent to the other house except himself.

Scoring was based on three factors: initial placement in the house of the child taking the test; the order of the invitation to visit the child's house; and the order of departure from his house. At each successive step, each person staying at the same house as the child tested received one point. The total score for each child was then calculated and placed in rank order. In this manner, the sociometric status for each boy in each house was determined and the results were subjected to the same normalising procedure used in those schools where the questionnaire was administered.

The second adaptation of the MTP method at White Oaks concerned the staff behaviour ratings. In this case, the staff members in close contact with the children were numerous, and all house personnel participated individually in assessing behaviour ratings. This provided two separate methods for calculating the MTP. The first made use of cumulative behaviour ratings by ranking the children on the basis of total scores, adding together the individual scores assigned by each supervisor. The combined values for this component were then ranked and correlated with the sociometric status of the children to provide an MTP based on the cumulative evaluations of the staff.

The second method produced an MTP index relative to each individual set of staff behaviour ratings. This method of calculation resulted in a number of different values for the MTP which corresponded to the number of staff raters. The separate correlations were then averaged to provide a single value representing the MTP as a mean sociometric/staff rating correlation. As expected, in most cottages this mean correlation was lower than that derived from the cumulative behaviour ratings.

# References

BLANCHARD, JANE LOUISE (1971) 'Long-term validity of the Measure of Treatment Potential: a follow-up study of boys released from training schools in Ontario', unpublished Master's Thesis in Criminology, University of Ottawa.

BONNEY, M. E. (1943) 'The constancy of sociometric scores and their relationship to teacher judgments of social success and to personality self ratings', *Sociometry*, 6, 409–23.

BRIDGMAN, P. W. (1927) *The Logic of Modern Physics*, New York: Macmillan.

BRIDGMAN, P. W. (1945) 'Some general principles of operational analysis', *Psychol. Rev.*, 52, 246–49.

CLEMMER, D. (1940) *The Prison Community*, Boston: Christopher House.

CROFT, I. J., and GRYGIER, T. (1956) 'Social relationships of truants and juvenile delinquents', *Human Relations*, 9, 439–66.

CUSSON, M. (1968) 'Relations sociales dans les pavillons d'un centre de rééducation', unpublished Master's Thesis in Criminology, University of Montreal.

EVANS, KATHLEEN (1966) *Sociometry and Education*, London: Routledge & Kegan Paul.

GOFFMAN, ERVIN (1961) *Asylums: Essays on the Social Situation of Mental Patients and Other Inmates*, New York: Doubleday; Chicago: Aldine.

GRYGIER, TADEUSZ (1965a) 'Plato's r: A new formula based on old principles', *Proceedings of the Social Statistics Section, 1965*, Washington, DC: American Statistical Association, 2–7.

GRYGIER, TADEUSZ (1965b) 'The concept of social progression', in *Criminology in Transition*, Tadeusz Grygier, Howard Jones and John Spencer (eds), London: Tavistock, 153–93.

GRYGIER, TADEUSZ (1965c) 'The concept of the "state of delinquency" and its legal and social consequences', *Wayne Law Review*, 2, 627–59.

GRYGIER, TADEUSZ (1966) 'The effect of social action', *British Journal of Criminology*, 6, 269–93.

GRYGIER, TADEUSZ (1975) 'Correlates of trust in correctional workshops: a research report', *Cananian Journal of Criminology and Corrections*, 17, 99–107.

GRYGIER, TADEUSZ, GUARINO, MARGARET, NEASE, BARBARA, and SAKOWICZ, LOUISE (1968) 'Social interaction in small units: new methods of treatment and its evaluation', *Canadian Journal of Corrections*, 10, 252–60.

HOMANS, GEORGE C. (1950) *The Human Group*, New York: Harcourt-Brace.

HOMANS, GEORGE C. (1961) *Social Behaviour: its elementary forms*, New York: Harcourt, Brace and World.

JENNINGS, HELEN (1943) *Leadership and Isolation*, New York: Longman.

LAVALLEE, C., and MAILLOUX, N. (1965) 'Mécanismes de défense caractéristiques des groupes de jeunes délinquants en cours de rééducation', *Contribution à l'étude des sciences de l'homme*, 6, 52–66.

MCCLEERY, R. H. (1961) 'The governmental process and informal social control', in *The Prison*, by D. Cressey (ed.), New York: Holt, Rinehart and Winston.

MCCORKLE, L. W., and KORN, R. (1954) 'Resocialization within walls', *The Annals of the American Academy of Political and Social Sciences*, 293, 88–98.

MATZA, D. (1964) *Delinquency and Drift*, New York: Wiley.

MORENO, J. L. (1934) *Who Shall Survive?* Washington: Nervous and Mental Disease Monograph Series, no. 38.

MORENO, J. L., and JENNINGS, HELEN (1947) *Sociometric Control Studies of Grouping and Regrouping*, New York: Sociometry Monographs, no. 7, Beacon House.

MORRIS, T., and MORRIS, PAULINE (1963) *Pentonville*. London: Routledge & Kegan Paul.

NORTHWAY, M. L. (1944) 'Outsiders: a study of the personality patterns of children least acceptable to their age mates', *Sociometry*, 7, 10–25.

NORTHWAY, M. L. (1946) 'Personality and sociometric status: a review of the Toronto studies', *Sociometry*, 9, 233–41.

NORTHWAY, M. L. (1967) *A Primer of Sociometry*, University of Toronto Press.

NORTHWAY, M. L., and WIGDOR, B. T. (1947) 'Rorschach patterns related to the sociometric status of school children', *Sociometry*, 10, 186–99.

NORTHWAY, M. L., et al. (1947) *Personality and Sociometric Status*, New York: Sociometry Monographs no. 11, Beacon House.

PARSONS, TALCOTT (1951) *The Social System*, Chicago: Free Press.

PARSONS, TALCOTT and SHILS, EDWARD (eds) (1951) *Toward a General Theory of Action*, Cambridge, Mass.: Harvard University Press.

PERRIN, DALE (1963) 'Personality interaction in correctional treatment', unpublished M.S.W. thesis, University of Toronto.

POLANSKY, N., LIPPITT, R., and REDL, F. (1950) 'An investigation of behavioral contagion in groups', *Human Relations, 3,* 319–48.

POLSKY, H. W. (1962) *Cottage Six,* New York: Russell Sage Foundation.

SCHRAG, C. (1954) 'Leadership among prison inmates', *American Sociological Review, 19,* 37–42.

SELLIN, T. (1938) *Culture Conflict and Crime,* New York: Social Science Research Council.

STOTT, D. H. (1960) 'The prediction of delinquency from non-delinquent behaviour', *British Journal of Delinquency, 10,* 195–210.

STOTT, D. H. (1963) *The Adjustment of Children: Manual to the British Social Adjustment Guides,* Hodder & Stoughton.

STREET, D., VINTER, R. D., and PERROW, C. (1966) *Organization for Treatment,* New York: Free Press.

SWAAF, T. DE. (1968) 'A Study of White Oaks Village', Report to the Department of Reform Institutions, Toronto.

SYKES, GRESHAM (1958) *Society of Captives,* Princeton University Press.

SYKES, GRESHAM, and MATZA, D. (1957) 'Techniques of neutralization: a theory of delinquency', *American Sociological Review, 22,* 664–70.

SZYRYNSKI, VICTOR (1963) 'Investigations of family dynamics with the "Two Houses Technique" ', *Psychodynamics, 4,* 68–72.

WILKINS, L. T. (1969) *Evaluation of Penal Measures,* New York: Random House.

WU, EVAN HOI (1964) 'Personality and social roles of supervisors in their schools', unpublished M.S.W. thesis, University of Toronto.

# 8 The measurement of staff-child interaction in three units for autistic children

Lawrence Bartak and Michael Rutter

## Introduction

Infantile autism is a severe disorder of development which was first described systematically by Kanner (1943). He outlined the main clinical features as an inability to develop normal relationships with people, a delay in speech acquisition together with non-communicative use of speech after it develops, repetitive behaviour with distress at any change, good rote memory and normal physical appearance. The condition differed from most other serious disorders of childhood in that the abnormalities were present from early infancy, with (usually) no prior period of normal development. Kanner suggested that infantile autism was due to some inborn defect.

Since Kanner's original account, a large body of clinical and experimental research has confirmed the validity of the syndrome (Rutter, 1974). The basic biological cause of the disorder remains unknown but there is now extensive evidence that autism is associated with a specific cognitive defect involving the use and understanding of language. It seems likely that this defect leads to the development of the social and other abnormalities, although this hypothesis has not yet been adequately tested and the precise mechanisms remain uncertain.

With the increasing evidence that autism may be due to specific cognitive defects (Rutter and Bartak, 1971), there has been increasing attention to the measures required to aid more normal social and linguistic development in the pre-school child and those needed to avoid the development of secondary handicaps (Rutter and Sussenwein, 1971). Especially with young children, emphasis has been placed on working with parents in the home using behavioural modification techniques in a developmental and social context (Schopler and Reichler, 1971; Howlin et al., 1973; Rutter, 1973).

With older children, the presence of cognitive defects has inevitably led to a focus on the possible value of educational techniques. Follow-up studies indicated that special schooling was associated with appreciable social, as well as scholastic, benefits (Lockyer and Rutter, 1969; Rutter et al., 1967). In the last decade there has been a rapid growth in the number of special schools and classes for autistic children, but in spite of the availability of techniques for evaluation (Tizard, 1966) there have been few attempts to assess the efficiency of different forms of treatment (educational or other) for autistic children (Goldfarb, 1969). This chapter describes the methods used in a study designed to compare the effects of three different approaches to the education of autistic children.

At the time the investigation began there had been a variety of studies of treatment for autistic children (see Bartak and Rutter, 1973), but most of these suffered from a number of limitations common to many educational studies (Guskin and Spicker, 1968). There were only three investigations which had attempted to provide a direct comparison between different treatment regimes. Ney (Ney, 1967; Ney *et al.*, 1971) compared operant conditioning and play therapy and found that the former led to greater improvement over a six-month period. There was no follow-up so the findings are of limited relevance with respect to educational progress. Goldfarb *et al.* (1966) compared matched groups of psychotic children in day and residential treatment. The sample was not restricted to autistic children and there were no measures of the treatment regimes in the two settings. Wenar *et al.* (1967) compared unmatched groups of autistic children in three treatment settings. There was some evaluation of the treatment regimes but comparisons were unsatisfactory in view of the initial differences between the children in the three units. Accordingly, there was a need for a comparative investigation which would relate differences in special educational approaches to the progress of autistic children, after having taken into account any initial differences between the children. Our study was designed to do that.

## Study design

The special units which had been set up for autistic children in the United Kingdom varied considerably in their theoretical orientation, emphasis on formal teaching, degree of structure, segregation or mixing with other children, and in the type of relationship the staff provided for the children.

Some units were based on the view that autism was an emotional disorder associated with failure in the early development of parent-child relationships, while others regarded autism as a developmental or 'organic' disorder involving handicaps in language and perception. The main difference in teaching concerned the division between those who considered that the prime aim should be the fostering of a strong emotional bond between adult and child (formal teaching beginning only when that had been established) and those who saw the main need as deliberate teaching of specific skills.

There were also differences in structuring in that some workers emphasised the need for a permissive flexible environment allowing the autistic child to develop in his own way whereas others believed that a firm external structure should be imposed just because the handicaps of the autistic child prevented him from developing internal controls in the usual way. In some units autistic children were mixed with other children to provide better communication and social interaction as well as normal peer models. In others, it was thought that mixing only served to dilute the special care needed and that most pre-adolescent autistic children were unable to make use of peer interaction. Some therapists felt that a one-to-one relationship was crucial at all times (necessitating a one-to-one staff-child ratio) while others argued the need from the outset to plan progression from a one-to-one interaction to individualised teaching in a small group setting (so allowing a lower staff-child ratio).

The aim of the study was to evaluate the different effects of varying approaches to special educational treatment, and, in particular, to assess the amount of educational progress made by autistic children, to relate this to the nature and extent of the child's handicap and to the type of treatment regime, and to determine how far educational progress was associated with social and behavioural progress.

In order to answer these questions a search was made for sizeable well-established units which differed in their style of approach along the dimensions outlined above. Three units were selected for study (see Bartak and Rutter, 1971 and 1973, for a fuller description).

*Unit A* was chosen as an example of one using regressive techniques with minimal attention to the teaching of specific skills. A child psychotherapist was in charge of a number of lay workers each of whom, under direction, attempted to develop a close interpersonal relationship with the child allotted to them on a one-to-one basis.

*Unit B* was an autonomous educational unit with several classrooms in which a permissive classroom environment was used to combine special educational methods with regressive techniques. No standard structure was imposed. Rather, an attempt was made to match the regime to the needs of the individual. Such regimes might vary from a fairly structured task situation to a free play setting. Autistic children were mixed with children with other difficulties on the rationale that non-communicating children need the company of verbally communicating children who, while disturbed, nevertheless form relationships and follow normal childhood interests. In this unit, it was considered that, to a large extent, the child should set his own pace.

*Unit C* was a school solely for autistic children and exemplified the approach in which perceptual, motor and cognitive handicaps were seen as primary and around which education was to proceed. It was thought that the child's environment must be structured, organised and logical rather than permissive. The main emphasis was placed on teaching the child specific skills using techniques which aimed to circumvent the perceptual and cognitive defects.

The study involved three stages. First, the children were studied during 1967 using a combination of interview, observation and psychometric methods. This served both to identify the children meeting the diagnostic criteria for autism (Rutter, 1971)[1] and to provide a baseline against which to measure progress. Second, there was a systematic study of the characteristics of each unit using time-sampled observations in the classroom. These observations were made on two occasions, once in the middle of the study and once towards the end, to determine whether there had been any important changes in teacher-child interaction during the course of the investigation. Third, the children were followed up twice, once in 1969 after some 20 months, and once in 1970–1, giving a $3\frac{1}{2}$–4 year follow-up to assess their educational, social and behavioural progress. A combination of psychometric techniques, classroom and interview observations and systematic reports from the parents was used. In order to assess the various aspects of the child's development which might be differentially influenced by the contrasting regimes in the three units, a wide range of measures was used to determine the children's progress. The majority of the children remained in their original unit throughout the whole of the study. About a third transferred during the follow-up period to units outside the study and they were examined at their new units at follow-up. Further details are reported elsewhere (Rutter and Bartak, 1973).

Fifty children were finally included in the study: 6 boys and 2 girls at unit A, 10 boys and 8 girls at unit B, and 18 boys and 6 girls at unit C. The mean age of the children at outset was roughly the same in all three units (7–9 years) and there were no statistically significant differences between units in this respect. Nevertheless, units A and B had a greater proportion of young children and unit C was the only one with adolescents. The mean non-verbal I.Q. was 48 at unit A, 52 at unit B and 66 at unit C, the difference between B and C being statistically significant at the 5 per cent level. In both units B and C most children had I.Q.s in the education- ally subnormal range but the majority of the severely retarded children were at unit B and the few children with I.Q. above 90 were all at unit C. In all three units about half the children were without useful speech at the beginning of the study. The period of time the children had been attending the units prior to the start of the study was closely similar in all units (a mean of 21 months in A, 19 months in B and 18 months in C). In summary, the children were roughly comparable across the three units but there were some differences at the extremes of the ranges of age and intelligence which had to be taken into account in assessing the children's progress.

The methods used to assess the children are described elsewhere (Bartak and Rutter, 1973), as are the findings on differences between units in children's progress (Rutter and Bartak, 1973). In this chapter, there will be a focus on the issues involved in the measurement of staff-child interaction in units for children with severe developmental handicaps, rather than on the progress of the children. However, in assessing the utility of our measures of interaction it is important to know that there were major differences between the units in the progress of the children. With respect to scholastic skills, children in unit C made the most progress and those in unit A the least. There was more on-task behaviour in unit C and more parallel or co-operative play in free-play situations. However, although children in all three units showed social and behavioural progress as measured outside school on the basis of parental reports, there were no significant differences between the units in this respect. With all aspects of progress, but especially with the three 'Rs', the child's initial level of intelligence was crucial. Progress was much greater for children with an I.Q. over 50.

## Previous measures of teacher styles and techniques

A wide variety of techniques for assessing teachers and teacher-pupil interaction have been described. Argyle (1967) has argued for the need to study social and professional skills in the same way that any other type of skill (motor, cognitive or perceptual) might be studied. Runkel (1958) has adopted a similar standpoint in his framework for classroom interaction. The teacher's personal history is seen as influencing his choice of educational goals, which determine his frames of reference against which teacher-child interaction must be viewed. The interaction involves the teacher's behaviour, the child's responses and the feedback to the teacher which regulates and guides his subsequent acts.

Assessment of teaching goals has been greatly aided by the production of taxonomies of educational objectives (Bloom *et al.*,

1956 and 1964). With respect to teaching in ordinary schools, much attention has been focused on teacher roles and expectations (e.g. Gross *et al.*, 1958; Biddle *et al.*, 1966; Oliver and Butcher, 1968) on teacher attitudes (Cook *et al.*, 1951; Oliver and Butcher, 1962; Butcher, 1965; McIntyre and Morrison, 1967) and personal characteristics (see Morrison and McIntyre, 1969). Several studies have utilised supervisor ratings of teaching skills but these have not achieved a satisfactory consensus on what makes a 'good' teacher (Robertson, 1957).

These approaches have provided information of interest and value, but with regard to the specialised problem of the education of autistic children, it seemed likely to be more fruitful to concentrate first on the details of teacher-child interaction. The questions of how the interaction is influenced by the teacher's personal background, theoretical orientation and training were best left for later investigations.

Early studies of classroom interactions since the work of pioneers such as Parten (1932) and Thomas *et al.* (1933) made it clear that it was impossible to record every detail of what happened in a class. Ethologists have attempted to produce continuous descriptions of on-going behaviour in order to highlight the processes of interaction and to determine, without prior restriction, both what types of behaviour are important and how they cluster together (Hutt and Hutt, 1970). This is a valuable technique in the stage when measures are being developed but it suffers from limitations concerning both quantification and comparability. The same applies to methods utilising ratings made after the teaching session, such as that devised by Ryans (1960).

As a means of dealing with these problems, methods were devised for the immediate recording of certain predetermined activities or categories of behaviour as they occur in specified units of time (Medley and Mitzel, 1958; Medley, Impelletteri and Smith, 1966; Duthie, 1970; Flanders, 1965, 1968, 1970). In the Medley scheme activities are checked every time they occur during a five minute observation period. Teacher statements are classified under headings such as *rebuking*, *directing*, *informing*, and the style of the teacher's response to child statements is noted according to such categories as *supporting*, *approving*, *neutrally rejecting*, and *critically rejecting*. This provides a detailed and discriminating measure of teacher-pupil interaction but it does not adequately reflect *sequences* of interaction.

The Flanders scheme, by recording every three seconds, is better designed for that purpose. It uses ten categories for classifying different types of talk by both teachers and children. These include *praises or encourages, asks questions, criticises or justifies authority, talk by students in response to teachers,* and *student talk-initiation.* Like most other schemes, emphasis is placed on the recording of what the teacher says. Less attention has been paid to the detailed recording of non-verbal behaviour, perhaps because this plays a smaller part in teacher-child interaction in ordinary schooling. The Flanders system has the limitation that it does not specify which child is included in the interaction, but it can be modified to produce this information (Wragg, 1970).

The scheme, and others like it, is straightforward and has been very widely applied for both research and the training of teachers (Amidon and Hough, 1967; Brandt, 1972). The technique of using specified categories of behaviour in conjunction with time-sampling provided a useful framework within which to study interaction in autistic units, but the emphasis on verbal interaction, and especially on student-initiated verbal interaction, made the categories rather unsuitable for direct application.

The same considerations applied even more forcefully to the use of audio-taped recordings of classroom interactions, such as that which was employed by Barnes (1969). The language of autistic children is both seriously retarded and deviant, and there is little verbal interchange in the classroom (Bartak *et al.*, 1975). Moreover, the analysis of tape-recordings is very time consuming and significant events are easier to detect at the time when the observer can make use of visual cues than afterwards when he is solely dependent upon sound recording which may be very difficult to understand because of the high degree of ambient noise in a group setting.

More subtle, but less easily measured, aspects of teaching skills have been assessed by Kounin (1970) who used ratings to assess such variables as '*overlapping*' (the ability to cope with two issues at one time), '*smoothness*' (ability to move smoothly from one activity to another), '*group alerting*' (the degree to which the teacher maintains the children's interest and involvement) and '*accountability*' (the degree to which the teacher holds the children accountable and responsible for their task performance). These add an important dimension to the more molecular approach of Flanders but are designed for a group teaching session rather than for the more individualised setting in autistic units.

The measures discussed so far concern only teacher-child interaction in the classroom but other aspects of school life can also have a very important influence on the children's development. Hargreaves (1967) has used participant observation with great effect to study social relations in one school. The method provided valuable insights into the ways in which the attitudes of staff and of pupils, together with the social structure of the school, led to serious divisions within it. Poor relationships among staff are a frequent source of complaint by teachers (Rudd and Wiseman, 1962) but this is such a delicate issue that Hargreaves felt obliged to omit reference to relations between teachers in his report.

With residential schools, the quality of child care is also crucial. In their study of children's homes and hospitals, King, Raynes and Tizard (1971—see also Chapter 3 in this volume) not only developed valuable measures of child management practices, but also showed their importance. As only one of the units in our study took an appreciable number of children for weekly boarding, this could not constitute an important part of our comparisons between the three units.

It was concluded that studies of teacher-child interaction in ordinary classrooms provided a sound basis from which to devise measures for use in autistic units, but because of the very different nature of the teaching task, they could not be applied without considerable modification. Accordingly it was necessary to develop new measures specifically designed for the purpose.

## Choice of measures

In devising measures of teacher-child interaction for the study, it was necessary first to determine the characteristic approaches in the three units as seen by their staff. Accordingly close attention was paid to the descriptions of the approach followed in these and other units for autistic children (Alpert and Pfeiffer, 1964; Clark, 1968; Cordwell, 1968; Dundas, 1968; Elgar and Wing, 1969; Furneaux, 1966 and 1969; O'Gorman, 1970; Stroh, 1968; Williams, 1968). There were discussions with the staff at each unit and extensive informal observations were made in the three units during the pilot stage of the study.

In unit A considerable emphasis seemed to be placed on the *style* of interaction with the child. Staff were instructed that the quality of their relationship with the child constituted a crucial aspect of the treatment programme. There was an explicit focus on physical contact and on the effective components of staff-child interaction. This, together with the emphasis placed by other workers upon non-verbal elements in social interaction (Bugental *et al.*, 1970; Mehrabian and Wiener, 1967; Mehrabian, 1972), meant that our measures needed to include systematic assessments of the emotional tone involved in both verbal and non-verbal communications. Earlier work had shown that this can be measured reliably, and that the measures have considerable predictive validity for the affect shown in situations other than those in which it is measured (Brown and Rutter, 1966; Rutter and Brown, 1966). Six point unipolar unidimensional scales had been used in these studies but pilot work showed that such fine ratings could not be made reliably when based on very short segments of behaviour, as required by techniques for assessing sequences of teacher-child interaction. Accordingly, a three-point bipolar scale, much simpler but based on the same principles, was developed.

In contrast to unit A, the staff in unit C seemed to place most emphasis on the *content* and *purpose* of interactions. They stressed the clear setting of goals and the need to structure the situation to achieve these goals. It was necessary, therefore, to provide measures which assessed these aspects of the interaction. Examples of such categories were available in the Medley, Flanders and several other schemes. These were adapted to be more suitable to the nature of the teaching and the context of staff-child interaction in autistic units. Measures of different types of staff behaviour concerned frequently occurring activities and for this purpose time sampling is most appropriate. After experimenting with both shorter and longer time periods, fifteen-second time intervals were eventually selected as most suitable for our purposes.

The staff at unit C also emphasised the need to lead children into more constructive task-oriented activities and to discourage deviant and inadequate behaviours which interfere with school work, meaningful play (i.e. not solitary stereotyped repetitive activities), or group interaction. As a consequence it was necessary to provide measures of how staff *responded* to different child behaviours. In ordinary classes, the total amount of praise and disapproval is generally less important than how these are distributed, that is which behaviours are encouraged and which discouraged (Becker *et al.*, 1967). It seemed likely that this would also be the case in autistic units so measures were devised to assess the contingent qualities of staff responses to children's behaviour. This required the assessment of staff reactions to what were sometimes infrequent behaviours, so that event sampling was more appropriate (Brandt, 1972). In this case events were defined in terms of the children's behaviour.

Unit B particularly stressed the value of the interactions between autistic children and other children. Although these could only occur in that unit (as units A and C did not take more than the occasional non-autistic child), it appeared important to assess the frequency and nature of such interactions in order to provide some gauge as to their likely importance.

Observations in the pilot stage indicated that the detailed teaching methods used did not vary greatly between the units so that less attention was paid to their assessment. The amount of time spent in classroom teaching, however, did vary considerably, so that an analysis was made of time-tabling in order to provide measures of the duration of time spent in different activities. In all three units very little use was made of formal discipline or punishment so that no specific measures were devised to assess this aspect of schooling (although, of course, the scales on staff responses are relevant to this issue).

## Description of measures

### Types of staff behaviour

A scale based upon time samples was constructed to assess both what the staff said and did with the children and also *how* they did so. Series of 15-second time samples, alternating with 15-second recording periods were built up. Each series consisted of sixteen such alterations without breaks. Sequences of such series were built up so as to sample systematically, in representative fashion, all unit activities and all staff members.

TABLE 8.1    *Staff behaviour (time-sampling)*

| Categories | Examples |
|---|---|
| No interaction | Teacher correcting school work at his desk |
| Plays with | Co-operative play with child |
| Works with | Helps child to set out equipment, prepare materials |
| *Acts of instruction* | |
| Questions | Asks child question about task |
| Directs | Gives child order |
| Instructs | Shows how to do something |
| *Acts of approval* | |
| Verbal approval | Tells child he is good |
| Physical reward | Fondles, hugs child |
| Privilege | Tells child he can have some reward, e.g. going out to play |
| *Acts of disapproval* | |
| Restrains | Physically restrains child's movements |
| Physically punishes | Hits child |
| Verbal disapproval | Tells child he is naughty |
| Other | Tells child he will lose some benefit, e.g. stay in and work |

Teacher activities were recorded according to a list of operationally defined activities (listed in Table 8.1). They were grouped as acts of instruction (e.g. asking questions, showing how to do something), playing with the child, acts of approval (saying something approving, cuddling the child) and acts of disapproval (e.g. making disapproving statements or gestures). In this scale, several different staff behaviours could be recorded in a given 15-second observation period. Thus a staff member might smile, say 'Good boy' and pat the child simultaneously. All three events would then be recorded. With all verbal acts, tone of voice was recorded as *warm*, *neutral* or *critical*.

## Staff responses to child behaviour

A second measure, based on event sampling, was devised to assess how staff responded to different types of behaviour shown by the autistic children. This required a linking of child behaviours (which defined the event) and the teacher behaviours which immediately followed. For this purpose the class was observed and each time a child in interaction with a member of staff behaved in one of a specified list of ways (see Table 8.1) the staff response was recorded, provided it occurred within 30 seconds of the child's behaviour. At this stage a choice had to be made between the teacher as primary focus or the child as primary focus. Because the main aim was to compare units, it was decided to base the measure on staff rather than children. Child behaviour/staff response sequences were recorded so that there were at least fifty sequences for each member of staff. These sequences were built up to cover a representative selection of unit activities over different times of day and days of the week. It was noticeable, however, that within units there were differences in how staff responded to different children. Initially, it had been hoped to assess the effect of these differences by taking comparable measures with the child as the focus and then comparing children's progress within units, but resources did not permit this.

The children's behaviour was coded under four main headings, each of which was sub-divided into socially acceptable and deviant behaviour. Thus, *general* activity was differentiated according to whether the child was carrying out the activity intended for him, or whether he was turning away from such activities. Similarly, *affect* was subdivided into appropriate smiling, friendly behaviour on the one hand and tantrums and the like on the other. *Language* was subdivided into communicative utterances on the one hand and, on the other, non-communicative vocalisations, echolalia, neologisms or other inappropriate utterances. Finally, a special category was included for *toileting behaviour*. Acceptable behaviour included the child's indicating the wish to go to the lavatory, as for example, by saying 'toilet', or getting up from his seat and attracting the adult's attention while clutching his own trousers. Unacceptable behaviour in this area mostly consisted of the child wetting or soiling himself in the classroom. In piloting this scale, few responses in the final category were observed. However, we noticed that staff tended to react strongly to this class of behaviour when it did occur and it was considered desirable to make provision to record it separately.

The staff response was characterised according to a number of categories of *approval* or *disapproval*, both verbal and non-verbal, together with additional categories of *attention* and *learning*. Verbal approval and disapproval were defined by the verbal content of the staff response (e.g. saying 'that's a good boy'). Tone of voice was recorded in each case using the three-point scale described above.

Non-verbal approval or disapproval was subdivided into physical gestures involving contact such as fondling and cuddling or restraining or striking the child, and bodily expressions such as facial expression and gesture, e.g. smiling, frowning. *Attention* was only recorded when the staff member made no other response to the child but did turn to him, walk over to him or look at him and meet his gaze with no particular gesture, facial expression or use of voice.

In order to ensure that the measures provided as valid a reflection as possible of the staff and children in each unit, we spent prolonged periods in each unit observing behaviour before the measures used in the analysis were started. The directors of the units had been told at the outset that observations would be made on a variety of classroom activities, both of children and of staff, but never knew what was being recorded on any particular occasion.

### Evaluation of measures

Any assessment of the value of measures of staff-child interaction must include evaluations of inter-observer reliability, temporal stability and validity.

In the case of continuous scales, much work has been done on the development of tests of agreement, notably through the use of intra-class correlations (Cronbach *et al.*, 1972). However, for measures including qualitative distinctions such tests are less satisfactory.

Measures of association, such as provided by the chi square and the contingency coefficient, may be used and, for two category scales, they are equivalent to measures of agreement. When scales include more than two categories, measures of association are less satisfactory.

The assessment of agreement between observers is further complicated by the distinction between overall measures of agreement and measures of agreement for each scale category. When overall agreement is only moderate it will usually be necessary to obtain both. The statistic $k$ has proved to be a useful and convenient measure of overall agreement (Everitt, 1968) and, when required, it can be partitioned to assess agreement for individual categories (Light, 1971). A comparison of the frequency with which each observer rates each category can further differentiate low reliability due to rating threshold differences and low reliability due to random variation. As with the partition of $k$, this will be necessary when $k$ is low in order to locate the source of the unreliability.

In the present study, an overall $k$ was calculated to test inter-observer agreement overall for the main components of each of the scales used. For the time-sampling scale assessing staff behaviour, $k$ was computed over the categories shown in Table 8.2 (but excluding tone of voice), and was $0 \cdot 87$. (All measurement of agreement between observers was based upon series of observations carried out by two independent observers[2] trained in the use of each scale.) Inter-observer agreement for tone of voice used by staff assessed by time-samples was determined separately and $k$ equalled $0 \cdot 77$.

With the event-sampling of staff-child interactions, agreement was first determined for the child behaviour categories, and $k$ was found to be $0 \cdot 91$. However, since inspection of the data showed that the majority of disagreements between observers were over whether behaviour was adaptive or deviant, and since other categories were collapsed down to these two for much of the main analysis in the study, $k$ was re-calculated. This time agreement was assessed only for adaptive and deviant categories and $k$ equalled $0 \cdot 88$.

Within each child behaviour category of adaptive and deviant behaviour (as judged by one of the observers), agreement was then measured for staff response categories excluding tone of voice and for tone of voice separately (as for the time-sampling of staff behaviour). For staff responses to adaptive child behaviour $k$ was $0 \cdot 79$ and for tone of voice in verbal responses to adaptive behaviour it was $0 \cdot 81$. In the case of deviant child behaviour, $k$ was $0 \cdot 90$ for classification of staff responses and $0 \cdot 80$ for tone of voice. These results indicate that both scales showed satisfactory inter-rater reliability.

For the scales to be used as a reflection of the enduring characteristics of staff-child interaction, it is necessary to show that the ratings have temporal stability as well as reliability. As the main interest was in the features which characterised units, rather than in the interactions of individual staff members, stability of measures was assessed by unit (as distinct from by staff member) over a two-year period. It will be appreciated that over a period as long as two years there was considerable staff turnover as well as develop-ments in unit policy. Accordingly absolute stability was not to be expected. Even so, the differences between the units in staff-child interaction on the first occasion were very similar to those found on the second occasion (Bartak and Rutter, 1971, 1973), indicating satisfactory long-term stability.

Finally, the evaluation of measures must include consideration of their validity. For obvious reasons, this could not be assessed directly. However, it was important to check that the measures reflected characteristics of the units as seen by other observers and by us during the pilot stage. This could not be evaluated quanti-tatively but enquiries indicated a close correspondence between the features as seen and the features as measured. Probably the major reflection of validity is predictive validity. To assess this directly would require an experimental design, but it was important and relevant that the measured differences between the units bore a logical relationship to the follow-up findings on the progress of the children (Rutter and Bartak, 1973).

## Results

### Types of staff-child interaction

TABLE 8.2    *Staff behaviour (time-sampling, 1969)*

| Acts* | Units A | B | C |
|---|---|---|---|
| Acts of instruction | 51 | 127 | 120 |
| Plays with child | 26 | 5 | 0 |
| Acts of approval | 59 | 37 | 14 |
| Acts of disapproval | 11 | 10 | 10 |
| Total units of observation | 160 | 103 | 150 |

   * Figures in body of table refer to acts per 100 15-second observation periods.
   The figures do not add up to 100 per cent as more than one act could occur in each observation period.

The first point that emerged from the time-sampling of staff be-haviour was the high rate of staff activity in all three units. For most of the time, the staff were actively doing something with the children. In less than one in six 15-second samples was there no interaction recorded. This illustrates the demanding nature of the job performed by the staff and also reflects the problems of autistic children in working or playing without immediate and direct supervision. The children's response to staff requests to carry out an activity was studied. In units B and C the children usually complied but they only persisted in the activity for an average of less than three minutes. The children in unit A complied less often with instructions and when they did comply they did so on average for less than two minutes. The possible reasons for this difference between unit A and the other two units are considered elsewhere (Rutter and Bartak, 1973). However, the findings from all three units indicate the necessity of close supervision of autistic children. This will only be possible where there is an adequate number of staff.

TABLE 8.3  *Type of staff instruction (1969)*

| Type of instruction | Units A | B | C |
|---|---|---|---|
| Questions child | 12 | 25 | 14 |
| Directs child | 29 | 62 | 65 |
| Shows child | 10 | 40 | 41 |

Figures in body of table refer to acts per 100 15-second observation periods.

At units B and C, most of the interaction consisted of some kind of act of instruction, directing the child being the most frequent, followed by showing the child something, and third by some kind of questioning (Table 8.3). Unit A was quite different in this respect. Acts of instruction were significantly less frequent and playing with the child was relatively more frequent than in the other units. However, this difference is a function of the fact that unit A was not primarily an educational unit. When the behaviour of the teacher at unit A was examined, the results were very similar to those for the staff of the other two units, there being a high level of acts of instruction and very little play.

The amount of disapproval shown (Table 8.2) was similar in the three units but there were marked differences in the frequency of approval. Acts of approval were much more frequent at unit A than at either of the other two units. At unit A, acts of approval far outweighed acts of disapproval, in unit B acts of approval also outnumbered acts of disapproval in 1969 but at unit C approval and disapproval were about equally frequent. By 1971, the pattern at unit B was similar to that for unit C.

TABLE 8.4    *Type of staff approval (1969)*

| Type of approval | Units A | B | C |
|---|---|---|---|
| Tells child he is good | 13 | 14 | 12 |
| Fondles or hugs child | 38 | 20 | 1 |
| Other | 9 | 3 | 1 |

Figures in body of table refer to acts per 100 15-second observation periods. The differences between units with respect to physical expressions of approval are statistically significant at the 1 per cent level.

In all units telling the child he was good was the commonest method of showing approval (Table 8.4). However, in units A and B, physical demonstration of approval such as hugging the child were also frequent. In B these accounted for 55 per cent of expressions of approval and in unit A for 64 per cent. In sharp contrast, at unit C they accounted for only 7 per cent of acts of approval. This marked difference was also found when interaction was measured for the second time near the end of the study in 1971, but there was one notable difference. Early in the study, physical demonstrations of approval were more frequent and, overall, they occurred more frequently than verbal approval. This was not so at the end, when physical acts of approval made up 24 per cent of all acts of approval, in contrast to the earlier figure of 54 per cent over all units. The explanation probably lies in the age of the children. Hugging may be a more appropriate form of approval in younger children and the children were nearly four years younger at the outset than at the end of the study. Nevertheless, at all stages in the study, the relative differences between the units remained the same. Physical approval was common at unit A, frequent at unit B and rare at unit C.

TABLE 8.5    *Tone of voice (1969)*

| Tone | Units A | B | C |
|---|---|---|---|
| Neutral | 73 | 87 | 79 |
| Critical | 0 | 3 | 21 |
| Warm | 27 | 10 | 0 |

Figures in body of table refer to percentage of verbal interactions.

Similar differences were found with respect to tone of voice (where the findings are based on a total of 635 verbal interactions). At unit A, warm tone was frequently evident (Table 8.5), it was less common at unit B, and was very rare at unit C. Conversely, critical tone of voice was common at unit C, less common at unit B and very rare at unit A.

In summary, these results indicate that the staff at unit A spent much of their time in warm approving play with the children, whereas instruction was the main activity at the other units. Units B and C differed largely in the way the children were instructed, warmth and physical approval being more characteristic of unit B.

## Staff responses to different child behaviours

Event sampling of staff responses to children's behaviour showed that in all three units acceptable behaviour was generally followed by staff approval. But the units differed in their responses to deviant behaviour. At units B and C, deviance was generally followed by disapproval but this was not the case at unit A. In that unit, deviance was as likely to be followed by approval as by disapproval. Thus it seemed that children there might find it difficult to discriminate right and wrong since behaviour of all kinds was liable to be followed by praise. These results for the 1971 sampling of staff behaviour are shown in Figure 8.1.

An examination of the tone of voice used by staff corroborates these findings. Figure 8.2 shows the tone of voice used by staff in response to acceptable and to deviant behaviour in each unit.

Two points are evident with respect to unit A. First, critical tone was never expressed in response to either acceptable or deviant behaviour. Second, the staff response was similar for both acceptable and deviant behaviour, many verbal responses being expressed warmly whatever the child's behaviour.

The pattern at unit C was quite different. The staff clearly differentiated between acceptable and deviant behaviour. Deviant behaviour quite commonly resulted in critical tone and only rarely in warmth. For acceptable behaviour, neutral tone of voice predominated and warmth and critical tone both occurred with about the same low frequency.

In unit B, tone of voice was most clearly used as a differential response to children's behaviour. Acceptable behaviour was followed by warmth in nearly a third of cases and critical tone was never used. When the child's behaviour was deviant, critical tone was employed 26 per cent of the time and warmth only 7 per cent.

There is a further aspect of staff behaviour that needs to be taken

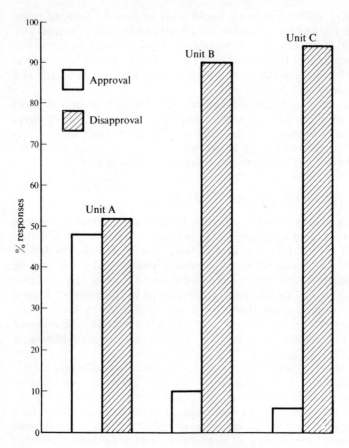

FIGURE 8.1   *Teachers' response to deviant behaviour*

into account in this connection, and that is the extent to which the words used and the tone of voice give the same message. Verbal responses by staff in each unit were grouped as matching (disapproval with critical tone and approval with warm tone), non-matching (all responses with neutral tone) or discordant (disapproval with warm tone or approval with critical tone). Again, the three units showed clear differences. At unit A, 38 per cent of responses were matching but 9 per cent were discordant and involved disapproval uttered in warm tone of voice. At unit C, tone and context were generally in agreement (6 per cent discordant) but the majority of responses (76 per cent) were given with neutral tone and as

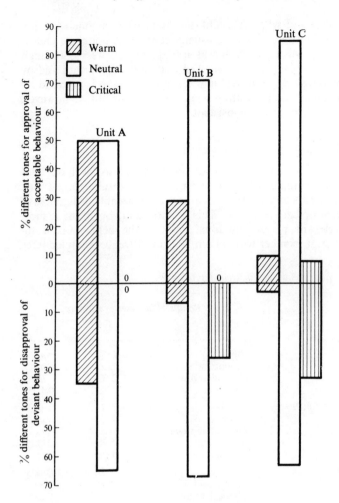

8.2   *Teachers' tone of voice in three units*

Figure 8.2 shows verbal approval in particular was usually given in a flat tone of voice. In unit B only 2 per cent of responses were discordant and 28 per cent were matching. This finding obtained at the end of the study contrasted with those obtained for unit B in 1969 when there was a tendency for critical remarks to be said warmly (21 per cent discordant, 36 per cent matching).

These findings may be summarised by describing unit A as one in which indiscriminate warmly expressed approval tended to be given regardless of what the child did, and unit C as one in which approval and disapproval were usually contingent upon the child's behaviour, but where warmth was infrequently expressed through tone of voice. At unit B, staff showed quite a lot of warmth and by the end of the study, approval and disapproval were being used by staff in a highly discriminating way. Early in the study, however, unit B staff had been less consistent.

## Staff behaviour—individual differences

The findings on staff-child interaction discussed so far have been based upon averages achieved by pooling the results for all staff in each unit. This approach has demonstrated sizeable differences in staff behaviour between units. This is important, but what is more directly relevant to an individual child is the behaviour of the particular staff member with whom he is most frequently in contact.

TABLE 8.6    *Staff behaviour—individual differences*

| Unit | df | Variable | Results of analyses of variance | |
|------|-----|----------|------|------|
| | | | F | p |
| A | 5,17 | approval | 1·83 | ns |
| | | disapproval | 1·59 | ns |
| | | physical approval | 2·12 | ns |
| | | warm tone | 3·92 | 0·025 |
| B | 6,19 | approval | 3·77 | 0·025 |
| | | disapproval | 1 | ns |
| | | physical approval | 1·57 | ns |
| | | warm tone | 5·89 | 0·005 |
| | | critical tone | 1·65 | ns |
| C | 7,24 | approval | 5·26 | 0·005 |
| | | disapproval | 1·66 | ns |
| | | physical approval | 55·42 | 0·001 |
| | | warm tone | 23·24 | 0·001 |
| | | critical tone | 3·46 | 0·02 |

It was not practicable to carry that kind of analysis very far because staff left and joined all three units during the course of the study, and because children changed classes. However, although it was not possible to relate individual differences between children to those between staff, some analysis of differences between staff within each unit was carried out. For each individual, data from time-sampling of staff behaviour at final follow-up were arranged to give the percentage of 15-second time periods in which any acts of *approval* or acts of *disapproval* occurred. In addition, the percentage of time periods in which *physical demonstrations of approval* (e.g. hugging) occurred was established for each individual, as were the percentages of all verbal interactions with *warm* and *critical tone* of voice. Thus, scores on 5 measures were available for each individual in all units. In addition, several replicate scores were available on each measure since each replicate was based upon a series of observations and the total time samples were built up from several such series obtained over a number of occasions. Within each unit and for each measure it was thus possible to do an analysis of variance between individual staff (using the variance within staff across replicates as an estimate of error). Results of these analyses are shown in Table 8.6. In the case of unit A, no analysis was possible for *critical tone of voice* since no member of staff was observed to use it.

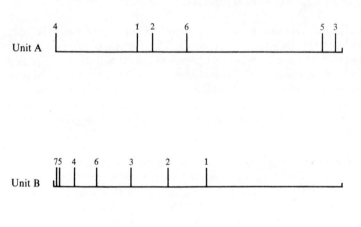

FIGURE 8.3    *Staff differences in use of warm tone of voice (1971)*

These results show that although there are significant differences between individuals in each of the units on at least one variable, most of the differences occurred at units B and C. In order to find out where the differences lay in each unit and to identify which members were contributing most to the variance between staff for each variable, the Newman-Keuls studentised range test (Kirk, 1968) was carried out on each set of data which had yielded a sign ificant F ratio.

(a) *Acts of approval (all)*     Unit A staff did not show any differences. For u nit B the studentised range test showed that the only differences between staff lay between the least approving teacher and each of the two m ost approving teachers (p $< 0\cdot05$) so that the significant F ratio was based on the whole range of scores. No single individual emerged as different from all other staff. At unit C the pattern was quite different. Here the test indicated that the most approving teacher was different from every other membe r of staff (p $< 0\cdot01$) including the next most approving teacher. No differences between any other teachers were significant.

(b) *Physical demonstrations of approval*     Unit C staff were the only ones to show individual differences. The Newman-Keuls test indicated that one teacher was more physically demonstrative of approval than any others (p $< 0\cdot01$) including the next most demonstrative member of staff and that no other differences between teachers were significant. The teacher concerned was the same person who stood out in the analysis for acts of approval, and in fact was the head of the unit.

(c) *Warm tone of voice*     At unit A the person with the lowest percentage of warm responses differed from each of the two members of staff with the highest percentages (p $< 0\cdot05$) and no other differences were significant, so that the significant F ratio was based on the whole range of scores and no single person stood out.

At unit B a similar result obtained. The test showed that three staff members with the lowest percentages of warmth each differed significantly from the two staff members who showed the highest percentages. Again, no single person stood out in contrast to all others.

Unit C again was different. In this case the head differed as before from every other member of staff (p $< 0\cdot01$) including the teacher with the second highest percentage of warm responses and no other differences were significant.

(d) *Critical tone of voice*     At unit A no verbal responses which were recorded included critical tone. At unit B there were no significant differences between staff members. For unit C the test indicated that, once again, a particular member of staff differed significantly from each other teacher. One teacher showed the highest incidence of critical tone of voice and differed from the next five most critical teachers at the 5 per cent level of probability and from the two least critical teachers at the 1 per cent level. No other differences between staff were significant.

These results of analysing individual differences between staff in the three units show that unit C contrasted with the other two. Although there were a number of differences between individual members of staff at units A and B, no single staff member emerged as very different to others in each unit. Moreover, at unit C two teachers did emerge as being different. The head of the unit differed from all other staff in using all kinds of approval including warm tone of voice and physical demonstration of approval more frequently. One of the other senior teachers similarly differed from all other staff of unit C including the head by virtue of the high rate of occurrence of critical tone in his verbal responses. It is noteworthy that this teacher's rate of acts of disapproval of all kinds was again the highest of all teachers at unit C. Although the analysis of variance for disapproval yielded a non-significant F ratio, this result is in keeping with the striking result for critical tone. It is unlikely that these differences between the head and this senior teacher were due to differences in the children they taught as both tended to take difficult children.

These findings suggest that children were likely to encounter rather varied teacher behaviour at unit C. The head took new children when they first joined the school, so that the initial teacher-child interaction experience by school entrants was fairly uniform in style. However, after that, when transferred to other staff, children were likely to receive less warmth and less positive physical contact, and might receive considerably more criticism.

It should be emphasised that the measures apply strictly to warmth and criticism as *demonstrated* so that no conclusions are possible about any teacher's *feelings* of warmth. What was assessed was the professional style of teacher-child interaction rather than any aspect of teacher personality, concerning which we have no data.

It should be remembered that it was not possible to compare the heads of units A and B with other staff as, unlike the head of unit C, they did not take an active role in regular work with children.

These findings have important implications, not only for children's experience in unit C but also with regard to staff communication. In so far as the head wished the staff to treat the children in a similar fashion, there seems to have been some failure to communicate some aspects of what they should do. There was a lack of uniformity in the staff use of warmth and physical contact with the child, in spite of a reasonable consistency in the way staff praised approved behaviour and criticised deviant behaviour. It is noteworthy that, as the teacher who stood out as different from both the head and other staff was senior, the senior staff provided rather conflicting models for new teachers.

### Child-child interaction

As a special point was made in unit B concerning the mixing of autistic children with children showing other problems, the inter-action of autistic and non-autistic children at this unit was speci-fically studied. Three hundred and sixty 15-second observations were made during free play periods and in only five of these observa-tions was any interaction observed between autistic and non-autistic children. All five involved some kind of positive interaction and no hostile or negative interchanges were seen during the systematic observations. The non-autistic children at unit B usually played together in one area while the autistic children were usually engaged in solitary activities elsewhere. These results are in keeping with the finding (Rutter and Bartak, 1973) that there is little interaction between autistic children. It seems that there is also little interaction with other non-autistic children.

### Changes over time in teacher behaviour

As already noted, staff-child interaction when measured at the end of the study was generally similar to that measured in the middle of the study. However, there were a few changes which require mention. At unit A more of the children's time was spent with the teacher at the end of the study than was the case earlier, and the other staff had become somewhat more directive. For example, there were 89 acts of instruction per 100 units time compared with 51 per 100 units time earlier in the study. Even so, this is still appreciably below the rates for units B and C at any time in the study. At unit B, there was some tendency at the beginning for critical remarks to be said warmly but this was not so at the end. The third change concerns the frequency of physical expressions of approval. Although the relative difference between the units was the same throughout the study, there was a drop in the absolute level of physical approval at the end of the study. As noted above, the explanation probably lies in the age of the children.

We were also concerned with interactions between residential staff and children at units B and C, and assessed these with the scales we have described above. These results are detailed elsewhere (Bartak and Rutter, 1973).

## Overview

Previous studies have shown that it is possible to provide objective measures of teacher-child interaction in ordinary schools. The present investigation has shown that quantification of staff-child interaction is also possible in specialised units for autistic children. It has extended the type of measures available in its development of tools for assessing the contingencies of staff responses to child behaviours and in its demonstration of the utility of examining individual differences between staff in their style of interaction with the children.

While objectivity is of considerable importance (Tizard, 1966) it is equally important that it should not be purchased at the price of loss of sensitivity. However, our results show that it is possible to use quantitative scales to assess variations in emotional tone as well as nuances in changes over time and in individual differences in styles of interaction. Thus, the measures are sensitive not only to differences between units but also to staff differences within units and to changes in staff behaviour over time. Techniques such as these could be employed therefore to assess responses to teacher-training in special education.

The three units differed strikingly in their theoretical orientation and these differences were associated with characteristic patterns of staff-child interaction. Staff in unit A set out to develop close interpersonal ties with the autistic children and they were observed to show the most uncritical indiscriminating warm approval of their children's behaviour. Conversely, unit C staff sought to teach specific skills and they were found to be less emotionally demonstrative but to systematically vary their responses according to whether or not the children were behaving in a way consistent with the educational goals which had been set.

The follow-up findings showed that, as judged by tests of reading and of arithmetic/mathematics, the children in unit C had made the most scholastic progress and those in unit A the least. In all three units the children's understanding of what they had learned lagged behind their mechanical skills but the three units did not differ in this respect. In free-play situations the children at unit C showed more parallel or co-operative play. In all units the children showed considerable social and behavioural progress but their behaviour at home (as assessed from parental reports) did not vary by unit. The results suggest that an autistic unit with a high staff-child ratio and large amounts of specific teaching in a well-controlled classroom situation is likely to bring the greatest educational benefits. However, if these benefits are to extend to the child's behaviour at home special attention is likely to be needed with respect to school-home co-operation and collaboration.

Throughout, 'structure' seems necessary in the sense that there should be a task orientation so that the staff decide what the child should be doing. This may mean that a child is encouraged to engage in play with other children rather than stand on his own carrying out solitary stereotypies or it may mean that he is encouraged to read or take part in constructional tasks. Whereas the normal child may well be able to profit by the opportunity to discover things for himself, the autistic child's handicaps impede him in this and he needs to be *taught* how to make use of opportunities. The content of the tasks, of course, needs to be set in terms of individual needs and neither rigidity nor rote learning are implied. Nor is there any implication of 'discipline' or 'coercion'. Encouragement, praise and interest are usually the best ways of getting a child to do something. What is important is that the teacher makes some decision on what is most helpful for the child and then takes the appropriate action to bring about the desired effect (Rutter and Bartak, 1973).

As well as differences between units in the children's progress, there were striking differences between children. Scholastic progress was much greater for children with an I.Q. over 50. However, even for children with I.Q. under 50, the type of unit still mattered in that the autistic children with severe mental retardation made most behavioural progress in the more structured setting of unit C. The findings on the progress of the children in the three units are discussed in more detail elsewhere (Rutter and Bartak, 1973).

The analysis of the professional skills of the teacher (specialised or otherwise) is an urgent, if not to say overdue, task (Goldhammer, 1969; Bijou, 1969; Sarason, 1971) and methods such as those outlined in this chapter would appear to provide a useful element in such an analysis. Investigations of teaching skills should be of practical as well as theoretical value. Other studies have suggested that teachers involved in special education differ in their approach to handicapped children and that these differences may influence the children's educational progress (Jones, 1966; Guskin and Spicker, 1968). Our own study provided follow-up evidence which showed that autistic children's scholastic attainments differed markedly according to the type of educational unit at which the children were placed (Rutter and Bartak, 1973).

There are additional aspects of teacher behaviour which might usefully be examined in any further studies in this area. The follow-up study clearly indicated (as have previous studies—Lockyer and Rutter, 1969) that autistic children have difficulty in understanding what they learn. There is a tendency for material to be learned by rote and the basic concepts may not be appreciated or compre-hended by the child. It would be useful to focus specifically on those aspects of teaching which aid understanding and also to assess the extent to which the teacher receives feedback on how much the child has understood of what he was taught.

Autistic children present many and varied problems of behaviour. Our measures assessed the extent to which teachers were consistent and discriminating in showing approval or disapproval in response to different behaviours according to the extent to which the be-haviours were adaptive or maladaptive. However, not all behaviours have the same origin and it would be instructive to determine how skilled teachers were in identifying problem behaviour and in making a functional analysis to find out the source and contingencies of the deviant behaviour.

Impaired understanding of language is one of the most character-istic features of infantile autism, at least in the early school years. Presumably, children will learn better if they can understand what the teacher says. With autistic children, the teacher's use of gesture, demonstration and short simple sentences might all be important in this context.

With any kind of teaching, one of the most important tasks is gaining and holding children's interest and attention. Even casual observation in schools makes it very clear that teachers vary greatly in this skill. It would be important, therefore, in future studies not only to assess this skill but also to delineate the factors in teaching which led to success in holding children's interest.

In the meantime, a start has been made in assessing some of the crucial aspects of teacher-child interaction as they influence the scholastic and social progress of autistic children attending special units. Teaching is an art, but it is an analysable art (Bijou, 1969).

## *Acknowledgments*

The study was supported in part by grants from the Department of Education and Science and the Gulbenkian Foundation. We are most grateful to the three units for autistic children for their full co-operation at all stages of the investigation and for their for-bearance in allowing extensive classroom observations. Permission was kindly granted by the *Journal of Child Psychology and Psychiatry* and by Churchill-Livingstone to reproduce material included respectively in Bartak, L. and Rutter, M. (1973), 'Special educational treatment of autistic children: a comparative study. I. Design of study and characteristics of units', and in Bartak, L. and Rutter, M. (1971), 'Educational treatment of autistic children', in Rutter, M. (ed.), *Infantile Autism: Concepts, Characteristics and Treatment*. The materials used in this chapter form part of a thesis being submitted by one of us (L.B.) for the degree of Ph.D in the University of London.

# References

ALPERT, A., and PFEIFFER, E. (1964) 'The treatment of an autistic child', *J. Amer. Acad. Child Psychiat.*, *3*, 594–616.

AMIDON, E. J., and HOUGH, J. (1967) *Interaction Analysis: Theory Research and Application*, Reading, Mass.: Addison-Wesley.

ARGYLE, M. (1967) *The Psychology of Interpersonal Behaviour*, Harmondsworth: Penguin.

BARNES, D. (1969) *Language, the Learner and the School*, Harmondsworth: Penguin.

BARTAK, L., and RUTTER, M. (1971) 'Educational treatment of autistic children', in Rutter, M. (ed.), *Infantile Autism: Concepts, Characteristics and Treatment*, London: Churchill.

BARTAK, L., and RUTTER, M. (1973) 'Special educational treatment of autistic children: a comparative study. I. Design of study and characteristics of units', *J. Child. Psychol. Psychiat.*, *14*, 161–79.

BECKER, W. C., MADSEN, C. H., ARNOLD, C. R., and THOMAS, D. R. (1967) 'The contingent use of teacher attention and praise in reducing classroom behaviour problems', *J. Spec. Educ.*, *1*, 287–307.

BARTAK, L., RUTTER, M., and COX, M. (1975) 'A comparative study of infantile autism and specific developmental receptive language disorder: I. The children', *Brit. J. Psychiat.*, *126*, 127–45.

BIDDLE, B. J., ROSENCRANZ, H. A., TOMICH, E., and TWYMAN, J. P. (1966) 'Shared inaccuracies in the role of the teacher', in Biddle, B. J. and Thomas, E. J. (eds), *Role Theory: Concepts and Research*, London: Wiley.

BIJOU, S. W. (1969) 'Promoting optimum learning in children' in Wolff, P. and MacKeith, R. (eds), *Planning for Better Learning*, Clinics in Developmental Medicine No. 33, London: Heinemann/SIMP.

BLOOM, B. S., ENGELHART, M. D., FURST, E. J., HILL, W. H., and KRATHWOHL, D. R. (1956) *Taxonomy of Educational Objectives: the Classification of Educational Objectives. I. Cognitive Domain*, London: Longman.

BLOOM, B. S., ENGELHART, M.D., FURST, E. J., HILL, W. H., and KRATHWOHL, D. R. (1964) *Taxonomy of Educational Objectives: the Classification of*

*Educational Objectives. II. Affective Domain*, London: Longman.

BRANDT, R. M. (1972) *Studying Behaviour in Natural Settings*, New York: Holt, Rinehart and Winston.

BROWN, G. W., and RUTTER, M. (1966) 'The measurement of family activities and relationships: a methodological study'. *Human Relations, 19*, 241–63.

BUGENTAL, D. E., KASWAN, J. W., and LOVE, L. R. (1970) 'Perception of contradictory meanings conveyed by verbal and non-verbal channels', *J. Pers. Soc. Psychol., 16*, 647–55.

BUTCHER, H. J. (1965) 'The attitudes of student teachers to education', *Brit. J. Soc. Clin. Psychol., 4*, 17–24.

CLARK, G. D. (1968) 'Educational treatment of psychotic children', in Mittler, P. J. (ed.), *Aspects of Autism*, London: Br. Psychol. Soc.

COOK, W. W., LEEDS, C. H., and CALLIS, R. (1951) *Minnesota Teacher Attitude Inventory*, New York: Psychological Corporation.

CORDWELL, A. (1968) 'Educational techniques likely to benefit autistic children', in *Autism, Cure Tomorrow, Care Today*, Warradale, S. Australia: Autistic Children's Assn.

CRONBACH, L. J., GLESER, G. C., NANDA, H., and RAJARATNAM, N. (1972) *The Dependability of Behavioural Measurements*, New York: Wiley.

DUNDAS, M. H. (1968) 'The one to one relationship in the treatment of autistic children', *Acta Paedopsychiat., 35*, 242–45.

DUTHIE, J. H. (1970) *Primary School Survey: a Study of the Teacher's Day*, Edinburgh: HMSO.

ELGAR, S., and WING, L. (1969) *Teaching Autistic Children*, Guidelines for Teachers No. 5, College of Special Education and Nat. Soc. Autistic Children, London.

EVERITT, B. S. (1968) 'Moments of the statistics kappa and weighted kappa', *Brit. J. Math. Statist. Psychol., 21*, 97–103.

FLANDERS, N. A. (1965) *Teacher Influence, Pupil Attitudes and Achievement*, Washington DC: Cooperative Research Monograph no. 12.

FLANDERS, N. A. (1968) Interaction analysis and in-service training', *J. Exper. Educ., 37*, 126–33.

FLANDERS, N. A. (1970) *Analyzing Teacher Behaviour*, Reading, Mass.: Addison-Wesley.

FURNEAUX, B. (1966) 'The autistic child', *Brit. J. Disord. Commun., 1*, 85–90.

FURNEAUX, B. (1969) *The Special Child*, Harmondsworth: Penguin.

GOLDFARB, W. (1969) 'Therapeutic management of schizophrenic children', in Howells, J. G. (ed.), *Modern Perspectives in International Child Psychiatry*, Edinburgh: Oliver & Boyd.

GOLDFARB, W., GOLDFARB, N., and POLLACK, R. C. (1966) 'Treatment of childhood schizophrenia', *Archs Gen. Psychiat., 14*, 119–28.

GOLDHAMMER, R. (1969) *Clinical Supervision. Special Methods for the Supervision of Teachers*, New York: Holt, Rinehart and Winston.

GROSS, N., MASON, W. S., and MCEACHERN, A. W. (1958) *Explorations in Role Analysis: Studies of the School Superintendency Role*, London: Wiley.

GUSKIN, S. L. and SPICKER, H. H. (1968) 'Educational research in mental retardation', in Ellis, N. R. (ed.), *International Review of Research in Mental Retardation*, *3*, 217–78, New York: Academic Press.

HARGREAVES, D. H. (1967) *Social Relations in a Secondary School*, London: Routledge & Kegan Paul.

HOWLIN, P., MARCHANT, R., RUTTER, M., BERGER, M., HERSOV, L., and YULE, W. (1973) 'A home-based approach to the treatment of autistic children', *J. Aut. Childhd Schiz.*, *3*, 308–36.

HUTT, S. J., and HUTT, D. (1970) *Direct Observation and Measurement of Behavior*, Springfield, Ill.: Chas. C. Thomas.

JONES, R. L. (1966) 'Research on the special education teacher and special education teaching', *Except. Child.*, *33*, 251–7.

KANNER, L. (1943) 'Autistic disturbances of affective contact', *Nervous Child*, *2*, 217–50.

KING, R. D., RAYNES, N. V., and TIZARD, J. (1971) *Patterns of Residential Care*, London: Routledge & Kegan Paul.

KIRK, R. E. (1968) *Experimental Design: Procedures for the Behavioural Sciences*, Belmont, California: Brooks-Cole.

KOUNIN, J. S. (1970) *Discipline and Group Management in Classrooms*, New York: Holt, Rinehart and Winston.

LIGHT, R. J. (1971) 'Measures of response agreement for qualitative data: some generalizations and alternatives, *Psychol. Bull.*, *76*, 365–77.

LOCKYER, L., and RUTTER, M. (1969) 'A five to fifteen year follow-up study of infantile psychosis. III. Psychological aspects', *Brit. J. Psychiat.*, *115*, 865–82.

MCINTYRE, D., and MORRISON, A. (1967) 'The educational opinions of teachers in training', *Brit. J. Soc. Clin. Psychol.*, *6*, 32–7.

MEDLEY, D. M., IMPELLETTERI, J. T., and SMITH, L. H. (1966) *Coding Teacher Behaviour in the Classroom: A Manual for Users of OScAR 4V*, New York: Division of Teacher Education in the City University of New York.

MEDLEY, D. M., and MITZEL, H. E. (1958) 'A technique for measuring classroom behaviour', *J. Educ. Psychol.*, *49*, 86–92.

MEHRABIAN, A. (1972) 'Non-verbal communication', in Cole, J. K. (ed.), *Nebraska Symposium on Motivation*, Lincoln, Nebraska: University of Nebraska Press.

MEHRABIAN, A., and WIENER, M. (1967) 'Decoding of inconsistent communications', *J. Pers, Soc. Psychol.*, *6*, 109–14.

MORRISON, A., and MCINTYRE, D. (1969) *Teachers and Teaching*, Harmondsworth: Penguin.

NEY, P. (1967) 'Operant conditioning of schizophrenic children', *Canad. Psychiat. Assoc. J.*, *12*, 9–15.

NEY, P. G., PALVESKY, A. E., and MARKELY, J. (1971) 'Relative effectiveness of operant conditioning and play therapy in childhood schizophrenia', *J. Aut. Childhd Schiz.*, *1*, 337–49.

O'GORMAN, G. (1970) *The Nature of Childhood Autism* (2nd edition), London: Butterworth.

OLIVER, R. A. C., and BUTCHER, H. J. (1962) 'Teachers' attitudes to education

—the structure of educational attitudes', *Brit. J. Soc. Clin. Psychol.*, *1*, 56–69.

OLIVER, R. A. C., and BUTCHER, H. J. (1968) 'Teachers' attitudes to education, *Brit. J. Educ. Psychol.*, *38*, 38–44.

PARTEN, M. B. (1932) 'Social participation among pre-school children', *J. Abnorm. Soc. Psychol.*, *27*, 243–69.

ROBERTSON, J. D. C. (1957) 'An analysis of the views of supervisors on the attributes of successful student teachers', *Brit. J. Educ. Psychol.*, *27*, 115–26.

RUDD, W. G. A., and WISEMAN, S. (1962) 'Sources of dissatisfaction among a group of teachers', *Brit. J. Educ. Psychol.*, *32*, 275–91.

RUNKEL, P. J. (1958) 'A brief model for pupil-teacher interaction', in Gage, N. C. (ed.), *Handbook of Research on Teaching*, 126–7, London: Rand McNally.

RUTTER, M. (1971) 'The description and classification of infantile autism', in Churchill, D. W., Alpern, G. D., and DeMyer, M. K. (eds), *Infantile Autism. Proceedings of the Indiana University Colloquium*, Springfield, Ill.: Chas. C. Thomas.

RUTTER, M. (1973) 'The assessment and treatment of pre-school autistic children', *Early Child Development Care*, *3*, 13–29.

RUTTER, M. (1974) 'The development of infantile autism', *Psychol. Med.*, *4* 147–63.

RUTTER, M., and BARTAK, L. (1971) 'Causes of infantile autism: some considerations from recent research', *J. Aut. Childhd Schiz.*, *1*, 20–32.

RUTTER, M., and BARTAK, L. (1973) 'Special educational treatment of autistic children: a comparative study. II. Follow-up findings and implications for services', *J. Child Psychol. Psychiat.*, *14*, 241–70.

RUTTER, M., and BROWN, G. W. (1966) 'The reliability and validity of measures of family life and relationships in families containing a psychiatric patient', *Soc. Psychiat.*, *1*, 38–53.

RUTTER, M., GREENFELD, D., and LOCKYER, L. (1967) 'A five to fifteen year follow-up of infantile psychosis. II. Social and behavioural outcome', *Brit. J. Psychiat.*, *113*, 1183–99.

RUTTER, M., and SUSSENWEIN, F. (1971) 'A developmental and behavioural approach to the treatment of pre-school autistic children', *J. Aut. Childhd. Schiz.*, *1*, 376–97.

RYANS, D. G. (1960) *Characteristics of Teachers, Their Description, Comparison and Appraisal*, Washington DC: American Council on Education.

SARASON, S. B. (1971) *The Culture of the School and the Problem of Change*, Boston: Allyn & Bacon.

SCHOPLER, E., and REICHLER, R. (1971) 'Developmental therapy by parents with their own autistic child', in Rutter, M. (ed.), *Infantile Autism: Concepts, Characteristics and Treatment*, London: Churchill.

STROH, G. (1968) 'The function of in-service training with management of disturbed children', *J. Child Psychol. Psychiat,.* *9*, 189–201.

THOMAS, D. S., LOOMIS, A. M., and ARRINGTON, R. E. (1933) *Observational Studies of Social Behaviour. Vol. I. Social Behaviour Patterns*, Connecticut: Yale University Institute of Human Relations.

TIZARD, J. (1966) 'The experimental approach to the treatment and up-bringing of handicapped children', *Develop. Med. Child Neurol.*, *8*, 310–21.

WENAR, C., RUTTENBERG, B., DRATMAN, M., and WOLF, E. (1967) 'Changing autistic behaviour. The effectiveness of three milieus', *Archs Gen. Psychiat.*, *17*, 26–34.

WILLIAMS, S. (1968) 'The educational programme at North Ryde', in *Autism, Cure Tomorrow, Care Today*, Warradale, South Australia: Autistic Children's Assn.

WRAGG, E. C. (1970) 'Interaction analysis as a feedback system for student teachers', *Education for Teaching*, *81*, 38–47.

# 9 A conceptual scheme for the comparative analysis of residential institutions

Spencer Millham, Roger Bullock and Paul Cherrett

## Historical background

Sociology, which claims for itself the widest of perspectives, still remains fragmented into various sub-disciplines such as the sociology of education, politics or industry and there is little cross-fertilisation between them. One of the areas accorded considerable attention in the past fifteen years is the sociology of complex organisations, a term which includes a wide variety of institutions such as factories, schools, hospitals and even concentration camps. While many writers have identified and related certain features of these organisations, the early theories about organisations formed part of more general sociological perspectives. Max Weber's pioneering essay on bureaucracy, for example, was part of a wider theory of social change and explored the increasing rationalisation of developing societies. C. Wright Mills (1957) in his analysis of elites was similarly concerned with the wider social structure, and the empirical findings of Bernstein (1971) on the effectiveness of teaching are related to considerations of knowledge as a social construct.

Many writers who have studied complex organisations, however, have ignored these wider implications for a concern with the social structure of the institutions. Merton (1957), for example, has turned from grand theory to the establishment of empirical truth. Other writers have followed suit. Goffman (1961), for example, has explored features of total institutions and in 1961 the American sociologist Amitai Etzioni strove to bring order into empirical chaos and, using the concepts of Parsons, attempted to relate elements of the social structure of organisations. He hypothesised the ways in which sociological dimensions such as goals, methods of social control and the commitment of inmates were interrelated. Inevitably, subsequent empirical work has cast doubt on a number of the relationships he hypothesised. Studies of organisations following the work of Burns and Stalker (1961) do not demonstrate the coherence and stability that Etzioni's framework would imply.

Other critics have suggested that the issue of conflict is absent in both Etzioni's work and that of other members of the so-called structural/functionalist school of sociologists. In their writings the parts of the structure fit together perfectly and conflict is minimal.

It is suggested that behaviour is role-determined and that the individual is an automaton programmed to respond mechanically to the demands of the organisational structure, be he a teacher, a student or a worker. This does not accord with what is clearly observable in complex organisations and much recent sociology now stresses the ways in which individuals and groups within the organisation perceive, evaluate and react to their social situation. Particularly influential here have been the works of Mead (1934) and Berger and Luckmann (1967) who suggest that an individual's behaviour is not simply determined by outside forces or evoked by internal impulses, as some psychologists would maintain, but results from his interaction with others. Their perspectives suggest that a member of any organisation defines and evaluates his situation and that this is an important factor in determining behaviour. He does not simply respond to social pressures in the manner of some robot. Such a summary obviously oversimplifies the complexities of these contrasting sociological approaches and the reader can look else-where, such as to the work of Silverman (1970), for a more elaborate elucidation of these differing sociological perspectives, but there has been a move away from a systems approach to a phenomenological standpoint.

The approach to the sociology of residential institutions we offer in this chapter will develop some of the ideas presented by these writers and develop a conceptual framework by which residential institutions can be both studied and compared. It sets the stage for social interaction and suggests the wider functions that different institutions have for society and the way in which these functions are reflected in the structure of organisations. Concepts such as goals, roles, controls and informal social systems will be discussed in the course of this exposition. As an approach, the framework may appear to employ many features of structural/functionalist sociology but a closer examination should reveal that our perspective tries, in both concept and method, to consider the dynamic implications of the individual's definition of his social situation. Thus conflict and change are not excluded from our concepts (Lambert *et al.*, 1970). It would be wrong to present such a framework without making the reader aware of the deficiencies that appear in any theoretical construct when tested by research. Hence the theoretical approach is accompanied by some indications of where we feel it is inadequate. Our approach will be subsequently illustrated by looking at the ways in which new members are assimilated into complex organisations, a process called by some writers 'socialisation'.

It is natural that any theoretical approach will be constantly revised in the light of empirical study and that the ideas presented in these chapters reflect the specialist interest of this Research Unit which has been examining various kinds of residential institutions since 1964. The Unit has made a study of seventy boarding schools for ordinary children, and from 1968 has been undertaking a project which examines eighteen residential institutions for deprived and delinquent boys. But during the process of research we have been able to study some other organisations. For example, some educational institutions are run by religious groups or by the armed services, and long stays in these various communities have enabled us to gain insights into the workings of religious orders and the armed services. Similarly, our work on the approved schools has directed our interests to mental hospitals and prisons as well as to non-residential institutions such as industrial units, hostels and day schools. This approach, therefore, has a wider base than the residential schools which have been our chief concern and which provide most of our illustrations.

Initially it is important to lay out certain elements of the social structure, to delineate key areas of the organisation. With this classification in mind it is then possible to hypothesise certain relationships between these structural elements and to explore them empirically. For example, is it true that the greater the size of the organisation, the more difficult becomes communication or the more alienated become the lesser participants?

## Goals

Like Etzioni, we begin by assuming that institutions set out to achieve certain goals, that is, the state of affairs that the society exists to attain or promote, be it to cure the sick, teach children or reform the deviant. We shall depart from Etzioni's scheme, however, to suggest that goals differ not only in kind but also in the perceptions of those individuals who are attached to the institutions and in those of many external observers. Such perceptions change over time and the goal perceptions of different individuals can conflict and compete to an extent which makes this approach far more dynamic than the perspectives suggested by the structural/functionalist school.

Goals also differ in content. Using the concepts of Talcott Parsons, we have found it useful to distinguish three types of goal. Some goals are *instrumental*, in that they are concerned with the transmission of skills and information or with the acquisition of qualifications. Training for a job, teaching an O level, building up physical fitness and dexterity are all examples of instrumental goals. Other goals are *expressive*, in that they are concerned with states of being perceived as worthy in themselves. These will be moral and religious states, or an individual's need for esteem and acceptance. They are concerned with some end state, such as loyalty, tolerance or the creation of a cultivated, sensitive character. Here the concern of the organisation is to inculcate more than the mere acquisition of work skills. An English public school, for example, has both an instrumental and an expressive stress, academic excellence is prized equally with certain moral and social qualities. In contrast, a technical college is more instrumental: students are trained in useful work skills largely irrespective of such considerations as their moral or religious beliefs. Clearly, the achievement of some expressive qualities confers instrumental benefits and vice versa. For example, a person with a strong religious conviction might find employment in child care or social work rewarding but be less integrated in a betting shop. Nevertheless, we believe that this distinction is a useful one to begin our understanding of the sociology of residential institutions.

A third group of goals, which we shall call *organisational goals*, concerns the machinery by which the society continues to operate. Staff and inmates have to be recruited, administration must be efficient and ordered. Organisational goals are therefore concerned with these aspects of maintaining an ongoing organisation and an administrative bureaucracy. An institution's concern with its local public reputation and aspects of its control process can be included in this category. Again, other goals are related to these processes of maintaining an institution's continuity, for many expressive features such as compulsory religious observance or sport serve organisational ends. They keep people occupied or win commitment and enhance the institution's reputation in the locality.

We view institutional goals as existing in some sort of uneasy equilibrium, because goals are in constant conflict with one another and certain goals have a tendency to dominate others. For example, some institutions maintain a pattern whereby instrumental, expressive and organisational aims are equally stressed. A public school is a good example of such an institution. Other institutions have a goal pattern where instrumental and organisational concerns dominate expressive ends; a day school or day-release college provide an illustration of this pattern. There are other possibilities. In progressive primary schools, for example, instrumental and expressive goals dominate the organisational ones, while in organisations such as therapeutic communities in mental hospitals, expressive goals displace both instrumental and organisational concerns. In some institutions the organisational emphasis outruns all else, and continuity, order and reputation become chief concerns. This can give us our fifth goal category, where organisational goals are dominant.

These goal patterns are not static, for they shift over time and are influenced by pressures arising from the functions the organisation fills for society and the constraints imposed by external forces and other para-organisations. This is particularly true for organisational goals, which have an inherent tendency to displace other goals in an almost regular, cyclical pattern. Anyone who has lived or worked in a residential institution knows the cycle of ease and repression in discipline and the regular crises of finance, recruitment and local reputation through which the organisation passes, during which time expressive goals are particularly vulnerable. Over time, therefore, there is a shifting of goal emphasis as these goals conflict and compete.

But goals are not tablets handed down from Mount Ararat, immutable and awful. Every member of the institution, whether staff or inmate, has a perspective on what the place is doing, what it should be doing and what it actually achieves, and these perceptions differ for each individual and among different groups. In a school, for example, an organisational stress on local reputation may alienate older but not younger pupils. Parents and local residents, on the other hand, may say that reputation is very important and should be stressed more. Here, individual perceptions of the school's goals differ considerably and each group will have its own evaluations on what goals are being pursued, should be pursued and are actually achieved. But perceptions are not everything, although phenomenologists sometimes argue as if they were. Because power is differentially distributed in organisations some people's perspectives are more influential than others: the perceptions of those who hold the cash exert a greater influence on what the institution can do than those who peddle ideas or fill the inkwells. The goals which the institution pursues at any time, therefore, will be the outcome of all these conflicting pressures. These pressures will vary in intensity and direction so that at one time instrumental or expressive aims will seem to be prominent in the institution while at another time organisational emphasis will dominate, but over a long period of time there will be a characteristic pattern of goals stressed. These are the implemented goals, the ends to which the resources of the organisations are directed, but a variety of independent factors may defeat their achievement, hence achieved goals will differ from implemented goals. It is one of the tasks of the sociologist in devising his methodology to assess goals and to evaluate the degree to which they are achieved by using independent measures such as success rates of penal establishments or educational attainments in ordinary schools.

Naturally, the degree to which goals are achieved is more easily evaluated in instrumental than in expressive areas. It is simpler to assess the distribution of resources or the quality of examination results than to determine the extent to which values are imbibed. Nevertheless, the problems of measuring implemented goals crystallise some dilemmas inherent in sociological research and should not be ignored. The structural/functionalist approach assumes too readily that the sociologist is nearer to the truth in his assessment of goals than is any other member of the organisation while the phenomenological perspective, in contrast, underestimates the differential power of individuals to influence goals and reduces the importance of the historical and economic constraints that mould the implemented goals of residential institutions.

Other pressures on goals come not only from the perceptions of those in the institution but from external forces such as the functions which the institution fulfils for society. For example, although staff who care for delinquent children may try to implement and speak favourably of certain expressive aims such as fostering warm relationships, the effectiveness of their effort is reduced by the punitive functions that the institution fulfils in taking recalcitrant children away from home. Children tend to see this experience as a punitive one in spite of adult attempts to persuade them otherwise. Certain historical traditions also affect the goals of institutions. For example, those boarding schools which have grown from charity institutions of bygone years still have a somewhat puritan, spartan ethos which stems from the days when they rescued children who were in 'moral danger'. The tradition of the nineteenth-century institution still colours much of the ethos of the institutions for the mentally ill or delinquent and does much to reduce inmates to simple membership roles and to prevent the effective working of regimes which encourage wider participation from staff and patients. The goals of an institution, therefore, not only conflict with each other but are also subject to the differing perceptions of individuals and to the constraints imposed by these external forces.

While this approach to the analysis of the goals in differing institutions in itself explains nothing, it does offer us a framework by which institutions can be compared. All institutions have to develop structures through which their goals can be implemented. This structure is related to the goals we have been discussing but the relationship is more complex than the models of congruence between goals, control and inmate adaptation suggested by Etzioni. If, for example, we examine organisations where expressive goals are dominant, we find many similarities. There is usually some provision for the practice of expressive roles, though the status of those who undertake this will vary. Similarly, institutions which stress expressive goals control members by isolation from outside influences, long stay and the cultivation of a dependency on the institution among inmates. Elements in their structure such as competition and multiple loyalties are designed to fragment and manipulate the informal societies of inmates and there are usually clear formal and informal hierarchies. On the other hand, there is also much variation even among a specific group of organisations such as boarding schools. The degree of federal organisation, controls over privacy, possessions, dress, inter-personal relationships, the role of charismatic individuals and the extent to which the administration is bureaucratised all vary widely.

## The formal social system

This institutional structure which is developed to ensure that certain goals are achieved, we shall call the *formal social system*. One element of this formal social system in institutions is the extent to which the large institution is divided into smaller units such as living quarters, educational groups and administrative departments. Those who run each of these sub-units are given specific roles. When institutions are compared there are wide differences in the degree to which sub-units are autonomous and in the amount of authority which is delegated. In some cases sub-units achieve considerable autonomy, such as in universities or civil service departments. Some of these institutions are very federal, consisting of a scattered constellation of units where staff have considerable power in decision-making, while others are pyramidally structured with power and authority residing in the hands of a few senior staff.

This division into sub-units raises many problems for the organisation, as communication between them can be neglected. Frequently, the areas of responsibility overlap and conflict results. To modify conflict and engender commitment, some hospitals, schools and mental hospitals have attempted to disguise or dismantle the hierarchical distribution of power, and lesser participants in the organisation are expected to contribute to decision-making and to assume new responsibilities. The results of such schemes are variable. Consultation can indeed raise members' commitment but the expression of opinions can be a manipulative device in group discussions. The outcome of quasi-democratic meetings tends to be ultimately constrained by the power structure or by external considerations such as professional authority. In such cases, discussion can lead to considerable frustrations.

Within the sub-units, individuals either are ascribed or achieve certain roles, which can be defined as the behaviour appropriate to a person occupying any given position. The way these roles are linked to the roles of others is known as the *role set*, and as people do not always live up to the expectations of their position, their actual role performance can differ from their formal obligations. Some of an individual's failure in role performance can spring from a tendency for roles to conflict. There are role conflicts confined to the individual—for example, there may be stress between his occupational, family and social roles, or else conflict can arise when his role expectations are incompatible, as in the pastoral and disciplinary role conflicts which are common to teachers. A role player can also experience conflict because of features of organisational structure, such as when two or more people play the same role or where various groups within the organisation have different expectations of the way a person's role should be played. For example, teachers will be aware that pupils may expect entertainment and an easy regime, while headmasters expect sobriety and discipline and boys' parents demand examination successes. These conflicting expectations will influence the way the teacher actually presents himself in the classroom.

In an empirical study of institutions it is not difficult to lay out the areas of role conflict or to identify those members of the institution who will experience this. But conflict is not necessarily detrimental to an institution's effectiveness: such role conflicts may promote change and engender a more flexible and conscious pattern of role performance in staff. The consequences of role conflict for an individual or for the effectiveness of the institution in achieving its goals depend on the extent to which the role player perceives his conflicts and the way in which he then evaluates and solves these conflicts, i.e. the role priorities he adopts. For example, he may rigorously separate his work and domestic roles or give one priority over the other. One of the problems of role analysis is that role conflicts in life are complex and multiple and subject to rapid change. Indeed, while the role played may lay out the broad lines of conduct, within it there will be great differences in the actual behaviour of individuals. Role performance is not the same thing as social behaviour and much of the content of a particular action will stem from forces such as personality and previous socialising experience.

It is the individual's perception of his role relative to the ways in which he views the goal priorities of the institution that is important in determining both his behaviour and his commitment. It may be hypothesized that an institution where individuals' perceptions of their roles coincide with the goals that they consider important will have a higher commitment and be more effective, particularly in expressive areas, than those institutions where this is not the case. Housemasters in boys' approved schools illustrate this situation. They were introduced into existing structures to offer more expressive pastoral oversight and to fulfil certain organisational duties. However, the degree to which housemasters have actually taken up expressive roles varies enormously in different schools and commitment to the goals of schools varies in much the same way. It can also be hypothesized that those occupying newly created positions such as those of housemasters will experience greater role conflict than those who occupy more established roles.

It is important to stress to the reader that this discussion of roles is a very superficial summary of a very complex sociological area and as such has not even raised the question of status and consequently ignores the extent to which all roles are negotiated between participants (Cicourel, 1973).

## Social control

To establish or maintain a consensus on the goals of the institution and to regulate members' role performance, staff and inmates are subject to various forms of social control. The types of social control employed differ greatly in institutions and this is more fully explored elsewhere (Millham *et al.*, 1972). Social control is much more complicated a process than the rewards and punishments with which it is often confused. Young (1971), for example, has shown that the way knowledge is defined acts as a control in educational institutions. Control is also a social process, which exerts pressure on staff and inmates in a variety of ways. In delegation of roles, in the selection and promotion of staff and pupils and in the competition between individuals or sub-units, it is clear that a whole variety of controls are imposed by the institutional structure. There are controls over activity, over relationships, possessions, time, movement and privacy. This we have elsewhere called 'institutional control' and in part it reflects the Goffmanian concept of totality (Goffman, 1961). It is very high in certain types of institution but not in all total institutions.

Inmates and staff are also controlled by the many ways in which institutions seek to orientate their members to certain goals, particularly expressive goals. A whole system of signposts to correct behaviour exists in institutions, in complicated rituals, in competitions, in permitted activities and in the allocation of time and resource. All of these continuously delineate and remind staff and other inmates of the goal priorities of the organisation. For example, approved schools run as therapeutic communities contrast with other schools in that the living quarters are developed at the expense of vocational trade departments and time is allocated to community meetings and to group therapy rather than to education. In one of these organisations boys painted in huge letters the beliefs of the community on the wall and the circle of chairs for the group meeting was left *in situ*.

The reasons why certain types of control mechanism are more effective than others in particular situations are very complex. We have illustrated elsewhere that what is controlled differs considerably across institutions that are ostensibly similar, for example between different schools and different age levels. The extent to which inmates view certain control processes as legitimate will vary with their pre-socialisation and their dependence on the institution to meet a variety of needs. Where inmates are less dependent on the institution, such as in prison, social control can rely less upon expectation and has to employ a system of privileges, sanctions, rewards and institutional control in order to maintain the desired levels of discipline.

## The informal social system

However, there is little point in an organisation prescribing roles for members or elaborating a control process if those for whom they are designed are indifferent to them. Inmate and staff perspectives form what we shall call the 'informal social system'—the values and norms of behaviour which are not prescribed by the goals of the institution. For example, we have examined the ways in which the institution seeks to control its members but we have ignored the control which is imposed by members of the group over one another. This is usually more difficult to avoid than the control exerted by the formal order. Among staff and inmates there will be norms of behaviour which have to be obeyed in order to ensure popularity or acceptance from others. Among staff, those who are too keen or who curry favour with senior staff or who make close relationships with inmates may become unpopular among their colleagues and subject to informal control. On the other hand, certain inmate roles such as the swot, the queer, the bully, the creep may be despised, and unofficial rules which we shall call 'norms' may inhibit such behaviour. Those who defy these unwritten regulations will become unpopular among their peers and will be controlled by ostracism and nicknaming, using slang terms that indicate disapproval by inmates in that institution. Control by physical violence is rare in institutions because the more closed the institution is from the outside world and the more dependent the inmate is on others, the more coercive become pressures such as peer disapproval. This body of values and expected behaviour makes up the informal social system and again all we can offer here is a superficial summary of this concept as it has been more adequately explored elsewhere (Lambert *et al.*, 1973).

In many papers where the informal social system has been accorded considerable importance, it has been suggested that there is a clear relationship between certain structural elements, such as control or presenting culture, and the nature of the informal system of inmates. Our research would suggest that these distinct relationships are not substantiated. One problem of institutional studies is the error that can arise from confirming general hypotheses from limited examples. For example, studies of the informal social system in some prisons or reform schools are frequently used to support general statements of hostility existing between custodians and inmates in total institutions. Similarly, one finds it argued that because lower-grade boys in some secondary schools are alienated from the formal goals of the school, then the processes of streaming and setting are detrimental to much adolescent achievement. In certain schools this is no doubt the case but in others it is much more open to question. Indeed, when a range of institutions are compared, important differences in the nature of informal systems can be observed. In some institutions, the norms which prevail among both staff and inmates reinforce the goals of the institution. For example in a school, informal norms among pupils may put a premium on hard work and so support the academic aims of the school. Obviously, pupil norms may support some goals and reject others. They may approve academic and sporting goals while rejecting organisational and social aims. In other institutions, the informal system of staff and inmates may reject many of the official goals and encourage alternative attitudes and behaviour. These attitudes may vary amongst different groups. David Hargreaves (1967) and Colin Lacey (1970) have illustrated the difference in attitudes of pupil norms to academic progress among different streams in secondary schools. Here, the lower streams rejected official goals and delinquent and anti-social activities were enhanced. The orientation to various goals of the informal system, therefore, will vary for each institution although the majority of norms in any institution will be more concerned with social qualities such as being generous or good-tempered, than with any institutional goals.

Informal systems differ not only in their orientation to institutional goals but also in the strength with which the norms are held and enforced. In some institutions, the informal system is strong, in the sense that group members have to conform or incur sanctions. In other cases, the informal social system can be said to be weak and there is little pressure on members to conform.

The range of attitudes and activities which are controlled by these informal norms also varies. In many residential institutions political attitudes, sexual behaviour, attitudes to staff and personal hygiene are closely controlled by informal norms. In other examples, the norms are less pervasive and control only a few areas such as sycophantic behaviour to staff, the style of inter-personal relationships or social qualities such as being generous or cheerful.

Often these social norms form a curious collection which reflects attitudes held by the wider social class of group members. For example, among engineering apprentices living in a hostel run by an aircraft company we visited, sexual prowess with girls is admired and encouraged, and achieving a pregnancy viewed almost as a badge of courage. However, a hair-style or clothing which is defined as effeminate, such as fancy shoes or flamboyant ties, incurs severe disapproval from fellow-workers. Many other attitudes to the work situation, relationships with foremen, white-collar workers and management are also influenced by the boys' informal system. Some informal systems, therefore, can be pervasive and strong while other examples show an opposite pattern.

Much organisational theory seems to assume that when an inmate informal system is strong it may reject many institutional goals. This assumption stems from some studies of penal institutions. Whatever the justification for such a model in prison settings may be, we found that the informal systems which are cohesive need not necessarily reject institutional goals and that in some cases, such as in progressive schools—that group of boarding schools which set out to offer an education based on the development of an individual's personality free from constraint and external control—the pupils' informal system is not only strong but very supportive of school goals. Similarly, among the eighteen boys' approved schools which we have studied, only three had pupil informal systems that could be said to be both strong and rejecting of most institutional goals.

Other generalisations about informal systems have also been called into question by our studies. For example, the suggestion by Sykes (1958) that one function of the informal system is to meet needs which are not met by the formal society, such as scarce resources in penal institutions, is not entirely borne out when they are studied. He offers us important perspectives on explaining the nature of informal societies but in many cases the situation is very complex. For example, there are many institutions where, despite the deprivations imposed by the formal system, an informal inmate society reinforces rather than soothes the pains of imprisonment. In some boarding schools we visited, a harsh, repressive formal regime was supplemented by a violent and exploitative world that existed among the boys themselves. The pains of imprisonment were intensified rather than moderated.

The factors which influence the nature of informal norms are very complex and an approach which stresses compensations for the pains of imprisonment is only a beginning. For example, in some single-sex, total residential institutions, homosexual behaviour is an important part of the inmate world and there is a well-defined pattern of homosexual activity. Other residential institutions, which are very similar in structure, have informal norms which forbid such behaviour and severely sanction the deviants.

## Relationships between formal and informal social systems

There are, in fact, very few clear relationships between aspects of the formal system, such as levels of institutional control, and the content of informal norms and the nature of the informal system. Much more research is needed to establish clear relationships. One problem is that similar behaviour in different institutions may fulfil very different functions for the inmates. In such situations comparisons become very difficult. In some schools, homosexual liaisons may be primarily pastoral and expressive; in others, may afford physical satisfaction or, elsewhere, be part of a status system. Similarly academic attainment may command high status in some schools and among some groups but have lower status in other schools and in other groups. All these factors have been discussed more fully elsewhere, but generalisations about the nature of the informal societies in any institution must always be treated with great caution.

It would be wrong to assume from these discussions that only the inmates in an institution have an informal world of their own. The norms that operate among staff are equally important although the staff world has received much less emphasis in sociological literature. Naturally, the informal world of staff covers fewer areas of institutional life as staff have access to scarce resources and emotional lives outside the institution, but many staff attitudes are crucial in determining the effectiveness of an institution in achieving its goals. To attempt some explanation of the informal norms of staff many sociological areas would have to be studied: aspects of staff recruitment, training and career prospects, wider background characteristics such as class and education, religious and moral attitudes as well as social and geographical mobility. For example, in most of the boys' approved schools that we have studied, the boys are emotionally deprived and seek attention and support from adults and it is clear, from what children say, that their need for adult support and attention and for pastoral care is greatly in excess of that which they receive. An avoidance of close relationships tends to come more from staff, who resist the children's constant demands. This feature is not confined to approved schools and springs from a variety of causes, of which career insecurity, class background and previous socialising experiences are important.

In other contexts, Hargreaves (1972) has emphasised the influence of the cynicism/mediocrity norm in staff-rooms and shown how staff loyalty to staff as a whole is a cardinal rule. Social acceptance by colleagues is most eagerly sought by new members. The informal world of staff in institutions is an area which is often neglected in research and the ways in which staff are socialised and controlled by their colleagues is an area for fruitful study.

This division between formal and informal systems can be criticised for being too static and artificial. But the distinction is only an analytic concept to aid comparison and it does enable us to formulate some testable hypotheses. In practice, the formal and informal systems do not exist as separate entities but interact with one another. For example, certain aspects of the formal structure may be designed to fragment the informal world of inmates and to prevent the establishment of common norms which could be hostile to formal goals. In a public school, for example, pupils are divided among separate houses; there is intense competition in academic, social, cultural and sporting areas; an elaborate hierarchy of privilege and authority is given to the pupils. All of these disintegrate the consensus and allow formal values to penetrate by shattering the pupils' informal system. This means that most of the pressures for social control in a public school come from the formal system.

The relationships between the formal and informal society, therefore, are dynamic and take varying forms. For example, the formal system, can manipulate the informal by taking advantage of the prevailing norms to achieve certain goals. Staff may give an inmate who has high informal status among his peers the right to control other people and so maintain a tolerable level of order. On the other hand, the formal system may choose to tolerate the presence of the pupil world and ignore it and, except in crisis moments, a blind eye is turned to the norms of the informal society. In other cases, the relationship between the two systems is one of suppression, and any manifestation of informal values such as indiscipline or illicit pleasure is harshly punished. There are even cases where the formal system appears completely ignorant of the informal world and here there is genuine shock and bewilderment on the part of staff when, for example, the police raid the institution and search the inmates for drugs, or a whisky still is discovered in the roof. The formal and informal societies in any institution, therefore, interact and manipulate each other in order to facilitate goal achievement, and much of this activity concentrates in organisational areas where staff and inmates conspire together for a quiet life and maximum gratifications. Such relationships will vary over time and across goal areas. For example, a relationship may change from being manipulative to one of suppression as a result of some manifest inmate misbehaviour. To sit at a meal in an approved school and to witness the spread of a sudden disturbance caused by a fight over food is to see a passive and uncritical informal world suddenly cohere in a way that these anatomical outlines scarcely begin to explain. It is an area we have more fully described elsewhere and although this analytic framework may not provoke much excitement, empirical investigation of its various elements can be highly stimulating.

We have suggested that the organisation sets itself goals and prosecutes them through a series of sub-units of varying autonomy in which participants play many and varied conflicting roles. We have seen that control as a process is exerted not only by the formal order but also by the expectations of staff's and pupils' informal worlds. All these structural elements influence an individual's perception of his social situation and the significance of the relationship between formal and informal orders is clear when the response of inmates to institutional goals is considered.

## Adaptation

It is important at this point to clarify the concept of *adaptation*. The work of Etzioni and the paradigm of responses to social structures offered by Merton (1957) imply that the adaptation of inmates and staff is distinct from the social structure of the institution and such hypotheses suggest that empirical research can reveal the ways in which behaviour is moulded by different structures. For example, much work has been done on pupils' responses to academic pressure in schools, the ways in which different age and ability groups estimate academic goals and the extent to which their informal values mirror those of the formal system.

Such a rigid distinction between structures and behaviour, however, is artificial; many of the concepts we have presented in this chapter, such as perceptions of goals and informal social systems, combine elements of both the institutional structure and the adaptation of members. Goals, as we said, are not concrete entities that elicit patterns of behaviour but individual perceptions of what the institution is doing or should be achieving. Actors' perceptions and the meanings they give to the situations in which they find themselves are a part of the social structure along with more tangible elements such as sub-units or the distribution of power.

This situation raises serious problems for comparative research. While concepts such as goal, role and control guide investigation by defining problem areas and enable the researcher to relate elements of structure to indices of behaviour, such as absconding in approved schools or academic success, we cannot be certain that these classificatory labels are equally valid in all the institutions being studied. For example, the functions fulfilled by absconding in one approved school and the ways it is perceived by inmates and staff may be very different from the patterns in another school. Hence, relating this behaviour to structural features or background characteristics of children across a number of schools still leaves many questions unanswered. This problem is discussed more fully in the chapter by Clarke and Martin and in the illustrations presented in our subsequent chapter. In the same way, homosexual behaviour in residential institutions may fulfil physical, pastoral or status functions and therefore cannot be crudely correlated with structural elements such as totality or the age and single-sex nature of the establishment, as is so frequently done.

The research worker undertaking a comparative study of residential establishments has therefore to choose the approach which will be most useful to his problem. An exercise in overall correlations relating labelled elements of institutional structure to behaviour has proved useful in our own researches but there are frequent ambiguities arising from the process of comparing dissimilar meanings that actors bring to the labels we so readily affix. As we shall see, the framework we have developed is a compromise between these two approaches, but the flexibility we have integrated into the concepts should ensure that labels are not indiscriminately applied to dissimilar circumstances and that the adaptation of staff and inmates is an inherent part of these concepts rather than a determined consequence.

## Change

This completes our exposition of the sociological framework which we have developed in our studies of residential institutions. It is hoped that the concepts discussed are both useful tools of analysis and comparison and are able to incorporate the dynamic aspects of social interaction. We have found that this analysis facilitates comparison of institutions and particularly helps in studies of change in institutions, which must incorporate all the dimensions we have discussed, such as: the external forces which shape institutional goals, the function which the institution serves for society and many of the conflicts and perceptions we have outlined. For example, in 1969 the Children and Young Persons Act brought the approved schools, which cater for persistent juvenile delinquents, into the field of residential care for all children. The Act gave formal recognition to pressures from a variety of external and internal forces to shift the goal stress from the instrumental and organisational concerns inherited from the old industrial and reformatory schools towards a situation where certain expressive goals, such as warm relationships, individuality and pastoral care are given equal priority. The end result has been that many schools have been divided into small house units, and staff whose roles are largely expressive, such as houseparents, have been appointed. But as Heal and Cawson argue elsewhere in this book, more fundamental changes will need to be made to the patterns of authority, communication, and control inherent in the structure of the traditional approved school, before the changes in goals can be properly implemented. We have also discussed elsewhere the structural changes which would be necessary to make the schools co-educational (Millham, *et al.*, 1971). Without the analytic framework to guide us in setting questions to staff and children, the comparative studies we have undertaken of these institutions and the exploration of their effectiveness would have taken longer and been far more difficult to complete.

## Problems of this approach

This approach to the sociology of institutions is of course only one of the many possible starting points and, while any conceptual system can be an intellectual strait-jacket, we believe that this framework is a useful beginning to our understanding of how institutions differ and why they operate in the ways they do. The framework is probably better suited to a comparison of institutions or a study of institutions undergoing change than to a single case study in depth, but it is in the light of these concepts that we can begin to explore the behaviour of individuals in institutions. While this approach is largely sociological, many of the concepts, such as that of role, incorporate the features of both social structure and the personality of individuals. The restrictions imposed by this approach depend largely on the way in which the concepts are defined and applied. Indeed, when one comes to use and test sociological concepts in the field, frequently their level of abstraction and lack of sophistication engender respect for other disciplines such as social psychology or anthropology. In the research situation it is the open mind, the divergent thought-process, that seems to be more fruitful than scrupulous observance of any analytic framework.

It would be unfair to construct this analytical approach to institutions without suggesting some of its considerable deficiencies. As this framework has been constantly revised in the light of empirical research, it represents a working compromise between sociological irreconcilables. It blurs the conflict between the determinist implications of the structural/functionalist approach and phenomenological perspectives. There is no attempt to explore at what point the constraints on behaviour exerted by the social structure give way to the pressures exerted on an individual by his perceptions of his social situation. This is a major deficiency because these pressures will differ among individuals and in varied situations.

Exploration of this area has led Cicourel (1973) to the conclusion that labels such as role, status and norm are inadequate because they ignore the actor's definition of each social situation and the consequent process of negotiation when role players interact. There is also the temptation to allow description to masquerade as explanation, to assume that there is an association between certain structural features and to construct other relationships and hint at causes with little justification. For example, because schools which stress expressive goals emphasise normative control processes and schools with strong instrumental goals use utilitarian rewards and sanctions, it is easy to imply that certain goals are more effectively prosecuted by one control mechanism than by another. A more likely explanation would be that certain social groups are reared differently and that the controls used reflect their expectation of what control should be. There is, for example, a wealth of empirical evidence to suggest that people can be coerced into religious or political devotion, expressive areas in which it is frequently suggested coercive control is ineffective.

Indeed, it may be true that *a priori* considerations determine the extent to which research emphasises similarities and differences between institutions. Those, like Etzioni, who seek to establish generalities may see similarities where none exist, while studies which contrast institutions may ignore fundamental parallels. The work of this research unit has not escaped such considerations. In 1968 the Public Schools Commission was arguing about the integration of independent public schools and the state sector of education, and much writing at that time (Lambert and Millham, 1968; Lambert *et al.*, 1969) emphasised the dissimilarities between public and other schools and the problems of integration. More recent work on approved schools has been undertaken assuming that these schools will be integrated with wider residential provision for children and consequently there has been in our work a greater consideration of similarities.

Again, there is no reason why the sociological factors that we relentlessly explore should be more significant than others which are totally ignored, such as the economic, geographical and even accidental pressures which must act upon institutions. There are also weaknesses in our typology of goals. While the goals that schools prosecute may differ according to the instrumental, organisational and expressive categories we have already laid out, it is unlikely that participants will accord with our perspectives. For example, a bursar may feel that balanced books are things worthy in themselves irrespective of instrumental or organisational considerations: to him the final balance sheet is an expressive fulfilment, to research workers an organisational convenience. Likewise, while goals may seem to differ in kind very radically, in their wider functions they may be very similar. For example, it can be seen that while certain educational institutions such as technical colleges and apprentice-training institutions will stress exclusively work skills which we call instrumental goals, and public schools or colleges for commissioned officers give greater emphasis to the expressive goals of loyalty, obedience, integrity and self-reliance, these different goals have identical features as both enable a given task to be achieved and discourage deviance.

The difficulty in measuring the implemented goals of institutions is another significant weakness, as it is inevitably the sociologists who finally decide what the implemented goals of the institution are and the stresses they are apportioned. For example, in a school we would assume that the headmaster's perspectives on goals would be more important in influencing goals than those of the domestic staff, but this is a subjective judgment and probably not a legitimate assumption for all school goals. We talk of instrumental and organisational goals dominating expressive goals in certain institutions, but problems of measuring the gap between the emphasis in one area and in another are not explored. Thus institutions which we categorise from our goal typology as being very similar may in fact have dissimilar gaps between different goal emphases. It may also be true that the most objective questionnaires on goals may be measuring different features of the goal structure. For example, in a school staff goal perceptions may be an evaluation of long-term implemented goals while pupils' ratings may be influenced by short-term cycles in the implemented goal stress. Differences in the measured ratings may lead the research worker to conclude that there is extensive alienation or commitment among pupils, an observation which may be manifestly untrue over a longer period of time.

There is also the difficulty that in exploring members' attitudes to their institutions we assume that the structural elements we have laid out are the most influential in determining role behaviour. Anyone who has lived for a long time in a residential setting will dispute this simply because the organisation may be fulfilling a number of his other needs, enabling other satisfactions which are quite incidental to the organisation's goal stress or structure to be enjoyed. Personal goals may be very different from institutional goals. Hence a ritualistic or retreatist response in some areas may be complemented by high commitment in others. It could be argued, for example, that those who take up overtly deviant roles in the institution are as dependent on its goals and structure as are those who conform. This could help to explain why both staff and lesser participants remain members of organisations in spite of radical changes in real goals and exhibit largely similar patterns of response. The practice of recruiting new staff when a radical change in goals or regimes is contemplated can prove unsatisfactory as individuals who constantly move jobs are likely to be dissatisfied in any setting, while those who stay can be committed to or tolerant towards a wide range of goals as other of their needs are being met. It is at this point that sociology ceases and social psychology takes over. The discrepancy between structural features and inmate response may be due to individuals sublimating or fulfilling emotional needs through organisational roles. Sociological measures such as the degree of alienation are often poor indicators of actual behaviour and seem to give no accurate prediction of those who will leave the institution and those who will remain in it for years. There are many examples in our research of headmasters whose schools seem structured to fulfil personality needs. One charismatic autocrat withdrew at intervals in order to gain reassurance when his institution dissolved into chaos and he could return to establish order.

Further difficulties in establishing interrelationships between structures and inmate or staff adaptation arise when we consider individuals' previous experiences and reference groups. A total institution which becomes slightly less repressive may have highly committed inmates if they believe that their circumstances are improving even though the organisation might retain many characteristics of total institutions. Similarly, a boy's commitment to the goals of a residential training establishment may stem from the family or from occupational difficulties he would encounter outside, rather than from the particular goals or structure of the institution. Finally, certain sociological categories tend to become ragbags. They sound sophisticated but are used in very unscientific ways. Terms such as 'culture', 'socialisation', 'functional alternatives' can be used to explain away empirical contradictions to theoretical propositions, but although these concepts appear to be precise, they conceal deep theoretical confusion. Indeed, one has reached the point that when a sociologist uses words such as 'presenting culture', 'alienation' and 'socialisation' one suspects that theory and evidence are beginning to part company. Frequently, the tortuous language of sociology serves to obscure rather than define or elucidate issues.

## Summary

What, then, is the use of this approach to the sociology of institutions? We would stress that these interrelated concepts only form a programme theory and therefore must be judged in terms of their usefulness in validating certain hypotheses. In our researches we have found it valuable as it enables us to relate detailed empirical and theoretical preoccupations to each other. While it does little to facilitate a deeper understanding of social interaction, it does at least set the stage for and indicate some of the constraints operating on interaction. Equally, this framework aids the process of objective analysis and comparison of types of institution. Objectivity lies not so much in employing concepts which are value-free but stems eventually from a number of studies each of which refines previous concepts and exposes methodological weaknesses. In other publications we have discussed the concepts of social control and the informal social system in greater detail and these can be read for a fuller awareness of this approach to institutions. However, a brief glance at the use of this framework in tackling the confused concept of socialisation when applied to residential institutions now follows.

## References

BERGER, P., and LUCKMANN, T. (1967) *The Social Construction of Reality*, New York: Doubleday.
BERNSTEIN, B. (1971) 'On the classification and framing of educational knowledge', in Young, M. F. D. (ed.), *Knowledge and Control*, London: Collier-Macmillan.

BURNS, T., and STALKER, G. M. (1961) *The Management of Innovation*, London: Tavistock.

CICOUREL, A. V. (1973) *Cognitive Sociology*, Harmondsworth: Penguin.

ETZIONI, A. (1961) *A Comparative Analysis of Complex Organisations*, Chicago: Free Press.

GOFFMAN, E. (1961) *Asylums: Essays on the Social Situation of Mental Patients and Other Inmates*, New York: Doubleday: Chicago: Aldine.

HARGREAVES, D. (1967) *Social Relations in a Secondary School*, London: Routledge & Kegan Paul.

HARGREAVES, D. (1972) *Interpersonal Relations and Education*, London: Routledge & Kegan Paul.

LACEY, C. (1970) *Hightown Grammar*, Manchester University Press.

LAMBERT, R. J., and MILLHAM, S. L. (1968) *The Hothouse Society*, London: Weidenfeld & Nicolson.

LAMBERT, R. J., HIPKIN, J., and STAGG, S. (1969) *New Wine in Old Bottles*, London: Bell.

LAMBERT, R. J., MILLHAM, S. L., and BULLOCK, R. (1970) *A Manual to the Sociology of the School*, London: Weidenfeld & Nicolson.

LAMBERT, R. J., MILLHAM, S. L., and BULLOCK, R. (1973) 'The informal social system', in Brown, R. K. (ed.), *Knowledge, Education and Cultural Change*, London: Tavistock.

MEAD, G. H. (1934) *Mind, Self and Society*, Chicago University Press.

MERTON, R. K. (1957) *Social Theory and Social Structure*, Chicago: Free Press.

MILLHAM, S. L., BULLOCK, R., and CHERRETT, P. F. (1971) 'Co-education in approved schools', *Child in Care*, *11*, nos. 3 and 4.

MILLHAM, S. L., BULLOCK, R., and CHERRETT, P. F. (1972) 'Social control in organisations', *British Journal of Sociology*, *23*, 406–21.

MILLS, C. W. (1957) *The Power Elite*, New York: Oxford University Press.

PARSONS, T., and SHILS, E. A. (1952) *Toward a General Theory of Action*, Cambridge, Mass.: Harvard University Press.

SILVERMAN, D. (1970) *The Theory of Organisations*, London: Tavistock.

SYKES, G. (1958) *Society of Captives*, Princeton University Press.

WEBER, M. (1947) *The Theory of Social and Economic Organisation*, trans. Parsons, T., Chicago: Free Press.

YOUNG, M. F. D. (ed.) (1971) *Knowledge and Control*, London: Collier-Macmillan.

# 10 Socialisation in residential communities: an illustration of the analytic framework previously presented

Spencer Millham, Roger Bullock and Paul Cherrett

## Introduction

One of the problems of the social sciences is the distance that exists between the ease of formulating theoretical propositions and the difficulties of undertaking empirical research to test them. Theoretical writings tend to have higher esteem than the efforts of those who labour in the field establishing sociological truths, yet the theoretical framework we have presented would be of little use if it failed to formulate hypotheses or to offer meaningful perspectives on the nature of residential institutions. Whether the approach we have presented lives up to these exacting standards is for others to judge and all that we can offer in this short example is one possible way in which the framework can help us to undertake an investigation of one particular aspect of institutions, the socialisation of inmates and staff.

There is a wide variety of institutions that shelter adolescents. Apart from those that seek to heal the sick, they range from those that set out to change or reinforce adolescent values to those that provide shelter or enable other services to be rendered. In our research, we have been concerned with a wide variety of residential provision for adolescents ranging from exclusive boarding schools and service academies to penal establishments. This analytic framework and methodology would no doubt apply to other kinds of institutions such as prisons, hospitals or barracks but there would be a need for modifications which cannot be discussed here.

How would we approach the well-worn concept of socialisation with our previous analytic framework in mind? Initially, it is useful to see the ways in which this concept has been approached by other writers, particularly those studying residential institutions. Then, clearly defining what we understand socialisation to mean, we can contrast the application of the concept in varying institutions. But mindful that this is essentially a descriptive exercise, we seek to relate socialisation approaches to other structural elements and so construct more general theories and interrelationships. This should illustrate to the reader that whatever the deficiencies in the analytic framework, it does allow us to proceed beyond a set of haphazard observations. We shall start by examining the confusion in the way the term 'socialisation' has been used by other writers. We shall then use the framework to guide investigation and subsequently to develop hypotheses of increasing sophistication.

## *The use of the term 'socialisation' by other writers*

When we look at the ways in which this concept has been used by sociologists and psychologists, the term 'socialisation' appears to be accepted uncritically and used with a variety of meanings. In several books where it might be expected that the term 'socialisation' would be employed, the word is not to be found in the index. Polsky (1962), Hargreaves (1967) and Goffman (1961) avoid the term altogether, while books by Bowlby (1951) and Winnicott (1965) with the titles *Child Care and the Growth of Love* and *The Family and Individual Development* fail to include the concept even though the subject-matter is the socialisation of children in the family setting. In contrast, other writers use the term frequently without offering any definition or discussion of the concept. A good example is Lyn Macdonald's *Social Class and Delinquency* (1969), where the term 'socialisation' occurs on ten occasions but remains undefined. The concept used in her study appears to be the same as 'child-rearing' and consequently fruitful comparisons are made between the development of children in middle-class and in working-class families, but later the terms become confused by the epithets 'early' and 'late' socialisation.

The term 'socialisation' is also used in a completely different sense by other writers. Hadfield in *Childhood and Adolescence* (1962) and the classic discussion of Freud's personality theory by Hall and Lindzey (1957) use the term to mean making social relationships with others, a very different usage from Macdonald's.

Some writers have ventured to define the term. Parsons bravely suggests in *The Social System* (1951) that socialisation is 'the acquisition of the requisite orientations for satisfactory functioning in a role' and Musgrave (1967) talks about 'the child having to build up a role map of his society'. Such an approach has been employed to guide fruitful empirical research so that, for example, Cotgrove and Fuller (1972) talk with confidence of the functions of sandwich courses for occupational socialisation and examine the degree to which science students on sandwich courses aspire to careers as academic or industrial chemists.

The application of the concept 'socialisation' to the learning of roles is clearly attractive to sociologists as this incorporates the individual, society and learning theory while remaining a socio-logical perspective. Many writers, however, have been less concerned with roles and more interested in the way beliefs, values and attitudes are fostered. Dowse and Hughes (1971), for example, talk of 'the family, the school and the political socialisation process' in an article which explores the origins of people's political stance. Other writers specifically seem to relate aspects of early upbringing, such as toilet training and types of discipline that children receive, to features of adults' behaviour, their personality and beliefs.

Even attempts to clarify the position in the narrower field of residential institutions fail to specify exactly how socialisation differs from learning, maturation or the mother-baby tie. For example, Edwards (1970) in an article entitled 'Inmate adaptations and socialization in prison', speaks of 'levels of socialization' and although the term remains undefined these turn out to be, at the first level: learning the routines of prison life, at the second level: learning the behaviour necessary to live amicably with fellow-prisoners and, at the third level: a process of institutionalisation or 'prisonation' where the individual's personality disintegrates into a state of neurosis. Carlebach (1970), on the other hand, when discussing socialisation into approved schools, is more concerned with the types of control imposed over new arrivals. Socialisation in the context of the approved schools is viewed by him as initiation. He concentrates on the new arrivals undergoing a process of stripping of values and of role dispossession very similar to those described by Goffman in total institutions.

Inevitably, the *Dictionary of Sociology* (Mitchell, 1968), gives an all-age, universal definition. Munroe writes that 'socialisation is the lifelong process of inculcation whereby the individual learns the principal values and symbols of the social system in which he participates and the expression of those values in the norms comprising the roles he and others enact'. Although this definition suggests that the process is continuous, the perspectives remain strictly sociological and have little in common with the psychological approach which relates a child's socialisation to characteristics of his adult personality. Unfortunately, so all-embracing is the sociological definition of socialisation that the concept ceases to have much value.

Even when we look at the work of those authors who have described socialisation in a very narrow sense, that of breaking a person into the norms of an institution, considerable confusion arises simply because few writers distinguish formal from informal socialisation. The reader will recollect the distinction made in our earlier chapter between the formal system of the organisation and its informal system.

When socialisation in residential institutions has been explored, sociologists have been usually preoccupied with aspects of informal socialisation, the ways in which new members of the institution are assimilated into the inmate world. They have ignored much of the formal apparatus that signposts values and behaviour. Informal socialisation has occupied such writers as Punch (1967), Wheeler (1961), Becker (1961), McCorkle and Korn (1954) and Dornbusch (1955).

This emphasis on socialisation into the informal worlds of inmates has been attractive to sociologists for two reasons. First, such a study is easy in that boundaries are clearly defined and the level of inmate acceptance of informal norms can be measured. Also, informal socialisation is relevant to the effectiveness of the organisation, for it is the inmates' own norms which evaluate the aims of the organisation and determine the success with which goals are achieved. Such studies, therefore, are very relevant to a wider analysis of an organisation's effectiveness.

Formal socialisation in organisations, however, has been neglected and probably there are good reasons for this. One problem is that the width inherent in the definitions of socialisation we have just outlined implies that almost all elements of organisational structure will have implications for the formal socialisation of inmates and staff. It is extremely difficult to define the boundaries of formal socialisation. Hence the socialisation process becomes indistinguishable from other mechanisms of social control.

If these definitions can be criticised for being too wide to be useful, the situation is redeemed by empirical observation which shows quite clearly that individuals are introduced formally to the values and roles in organisations in different ways. It is also clear that inmates' norms and adaptation to institutional goals differ markedly even among a narrow range of institutions such as boarding schools or approved schools. The emphasis on the different areas or values which are stressed in the formal socialisation process varies among organisations and it might be useful, therefore, to explore the reasons for this and to see whether the conceptual framework we laid out earlier can be used to illustrate any of these observations.

### The importance of formal socialisation

Is the concept of formal socialisation particularly significant? We find support in other research findings for the importance of formal socialisation. For example, Clarke and Martin (1971) found that boys who persistently abscond from approved schools tended to begin their running away soon after admission to the school. A later report by Tutt (1971) showed that absconding could be reduced by devising a more exhaustive procedure for the initial formal socialisation of boys on arrival at an approved school. Similarly, it is well known that the transfer of children from primary to secondary schools gives rise to problems of truancy, delinquency and under-achievement. Some educationalists suggest that the change from a child-centred curriculum to subject-based lessons in a large impersonal building largely explains this sudden increase in the problems presented by the children (Millham *et al.*, 1975). There is evidence that more deliberate socialisation to facilitate the transfer to the secondary school can reduce the pressures on children and prevent these problems from arising on such a large scale.

## Our definition of socialisation

It is clear that the literature on the concept we have chosen to illustrate is confusing and that there are many different definitions of the term 'socialisation'. However, if we select from all of these writings the approach suggested by Parsons, we can then concentrate on *the processes by which a new arrival to a residential institution is introduced to the norms and values of his community*. We choose this approach not because this perspective is more valid than any other but because, in the context of research in residential institutions, this approach employs concepts which form part of our framework. If our interests had been in political sociology, for example, we would be less concerned with learning roles and more involved with the ways in which beliefs are transmitted. But, supposing we choose to make a deeper study of formal and informal socialisation in those institutions we have selected, how does the analytical framework and methodology suggest that we go about it?

Let us assume that the research worker has studied the framework and with a full understanding of the concepts embarks on a study of a number of residential institutions, Initially, he might contrast formal socialisation in two residential schools, a boys' preparatory school to which pupils go before being admitted to a public school, and a co-educational, progressive boarding school which is designed to foster the growth of each child's personality in an atmosphere free from any external constraints. If the research worker stays in these schools and undertakes his study using methods of participant observation, questionnaires and interviews, at the end he might summarise the wealth of material in the following way.

## An example from preparatory and progressive schools

At the age of eight most boys intended for the public schools are boarded in preparatory schools. It is here that a boy is introduced to the structural elements of the public schools and to many of their requisite values and attitudes. On his arrival, much of the Goffmanian stripping process takes place in clothes and personal possessions. He is allocated a place and a bed and most of his mental, spiritual and physical functions are supervised by adults and take place in the company of other boys. He learns the school's geography, its forbidden territories, and the esteemed goals evident in chapel, playing-fields and libraries.

He learns which formal goals are esteemed by the school: in instrumental areas, the high status of classics and mathematics, and in expressive areas, the desired religious and moral states. His formal roles are clearly defined with their obligations and privileges, and he is made aware of an elaborate formal hierarchy in which his worthiness for higher office is continually scrutinised. He learns the limits and proper exercise of authority as well as the acceptance of authority from others. He is familiarised with the control process which employs a high level of what we called institutional control in its rules and regulations, duties and privileges, and he accepts that all moments of his working and sleeping life will be regulated by external constraints. His life becomes intensely competitive in almost all goal areas. He is exhorted by moral precept; in social and sporting areas there is a stress on the sublimation of self and on esteem for the corporate good. His social behaviour is carefully regulated: 'Boys will sit with their knees together or will stand whenever a lady enters the room until she is seated. This should also apply to your mother at home'. At all times his behaviour is expected to be adult.

In the informal world of the boys, he finds it fragmented by many of the control processes such as competition, intense loyalty to sub-units and hierarchies, and he is initially surprised that commitment to formal goals is so pervasive and deep on the part of his peers and that any deviance is sanctioned by ostracism and reporting to staff. Because the goal stress of the public schools and their satellite preps maintains an uneasy equilibrium between instrumental, expressive and organisational goals, and because the behaviour of a protestant Christian gentleman encompasses so many areas, a large number of formal socialising devices exist in these schools.

However, the preparation for the public schools contrasts with the socialising procedures adopted by schools which cater for a similar social class but which have rather different goals. The progressive schools which developed in opposition to orthodox educational practice expanded rapidly in the decades following the First World War. Influenced by contemporary psychological theory, particularly that of Freud, and prompted by the desire to contradict much that the public schools held dear, they developed very different socialisation procedures. The new arrival experiences none of the formal stripping devices that we noted in a range of other institutions. He is not isolated from contacts with home, he wears any clothes he wishes and his personal possessions are little restricted. He is accorded privacy, little of his activity is regulated or in groups, he shares bathrooms, toilets and living accommodation with girls. Frequently women dominate the staff and he calls all staff as well as pupils by their Christian names. There are few forbidden territories although the school's esteemed goals are reflected in the buildings in much the same way as in the preparatory schools. However, here there are no chapels but dominant art and craft blocks, potteries and even a school of dance.

While instrumental goals may be stressed, deep commitment on the part of the child is not enforced. It is hardly even expected: there are no grades or marks, no competition, while certain subjects, frequently classics, are not even taught at all. He finds that there is a stress on practical subjects, on handicrafts and metal work, on printing. Individual skills are stressed in art, in music and pottery, all of which have high status, are part of the curriculum and are not relegated, as in the prep schools, to hobby times. In some schools attendance at lessons is not even obligatory. The sub-units of the schools are clearly defined but the roles played within them by staff and pupils are not clearly prescribed as they are in the preparatory schools.

The control process uses group pressures rather than an elaborate set of rules and regulations. Rewards and sanctions are again vested in the esteem of the community but there is a great stress by staff on what is acceptable behaviour, a process that is very similar to that found in the preparatory schools. Considerable power is vested in the community meeting at which all participate in decision-making and, superficially, democratic procedures stress the rights of individuals and their obligations.

While the formal system provides few formal guides to the behaviour of the children in progressive schools, far fewer than we found in the preparatory schools, it can safely leave the informal world of the pupils to exact conformity in a wide range of areas. Unlike our prep schools, the pupils' informal order in progressive schools is cohesive and pervasive and its values are deeply held. The child entrant soon learns what are the acceptable norms of behaviour among his peers and is greatly influenced by the example of the leading crowd at the top of the school. In fact, conformity is exacted in non-conformity so that bare feet and jeans almost become the unofficial uniform and short hair a sign of deviance. Social qualities, individual spontaneous expression and child-like values are at a premium—noise, display, self before others. While the child may appear to be more free in that institutional controls are very low, the control exercised by peers can be just as severe as any set of regulations and its values less open to manipulation by staff. Escape from such control or opposition to it is much more difficult and incurs much more severe group sanctions than does deviance in our preparatory schools.

There is rarely conflict with staff, all of whom are deeply imbued with the progressive child-centred philosophy and in fact subscribe to the children's values. Unlike the prep schools, the adult values of sobriety, responsibility and industry are very much at a discount, and child-like values are prized. Naturally, the children are intensely committed to their schools, and the problem is raised of over-conformity and deep dependence on unreal, inward-looking institutions. Indeed, by an entirely different approach, the effect can be quite as claustrophobic as in any traditional prep school. What is important, is that the progressive schools quite clearly adopt a different approach to socialising the new arrival. They leave much of the inculcation of values and large areas of control to the pupils' own world. However, both types of institution are characterised by isolation from the local community and long periods of residential stay, features frequently adopted by communities stressing expressive goals. Indeed, there could be no better contrast between the two approaches than that shown in Table 10.1, an extract from the sets of regulations governing the sleeping hours of the young in these different schools.

We cannot illustrate in this short chapter all of the types of evidence which demonstrate the differing processes of formal and informal socialisation in schools. Nevertheless, it may be of interest to examine examples of children's replies to questionnaires, as these not only show the effects of differing techniques of formal socialisation but also explain how abstract ideas can be manifested in clear empirical realities.

While Bernstein (1971) has demonstrated the importance of perceiving educational knowledge as a social construction, this difficult concept becomes a reality when we analyse the replies of ten-year-old boys in preparatory and progressive schools to the question: 'To have a worthwhile, successful career, in which subjects do you think it necessary to excel?' The replies are given in Table 10.2.

This shows quite clearly the effectiveness of formal socialisation techniques in each of the schools as the choices of children reflect the patterns of implemented goals. With the exception of the classics, the ratings from the prep schools are closely correlated to those from the progressive and grammar schools, while the results from the secondary modern school are related only to those from the primary school. This would suggest that despite variations in one or two items making up the curriculum, those schools whose functions for society and implemented goals are concerned with maintaining or promoting social mobility show similar effectiveness

TABLE 10.1

| Prep. school | Progressive school |
|---|---|
| Boys must be in bed by 8 o'clock and have passed Matron's inspection | Please remember another girl or boy may be sleeping next door. Don't disturb them and try to be in bed by 8 o'clock when your Housemother will be round to say goodnight |
| No boy is allowed to leave his bed without permission of the Dorm Monitor | |
| Boys must not talk and may read only those books approved by the Housemaster until lights out | |
| Beds must be kept 5 feet apart, stripped each morning and lockers kept tidy for inspection | |
| Only boys with medical reasons may have drinks or pills by their bedside | |
| Prayers both in the morning and evening will be taken by the Dorm Monitor | |

TABLE 10.2　*Rank orders of pupils' replies*

| | Prep. | Prog. | State Primary | Grammar Jnr | Sec. Mod. Snr |
|---|---|---|---|---|---|
| Mathematics | 2 | 4 | 1 | 1 | 1 |
| English | 3 | 1 | 2 | 3 | 5 |
| Science | 5 | 3 | 3 | 2 | 2 |
| Humanities/Geography/History | 6 | 7 | 7 | 6 | 6 |
| Art, Music, Drama | 7 | 5 | 8 | 7 | 8 |
| Craft, Metalwork, Woodwork, Printing | 9 | 6 | 5 | 9 | 3 |
| Engineering | 8 | 8 | 4 | 5 | 4 |
| Latin, Greek, Ancient History | 1 | 9 | 9 | 8 | 9 |
| Modern Languages | 4 | 2 | 6 | 4 | 7 |

in their patterns of formal socialisation. Schools where mobility goals are less pronounced, the primary and secondary modern, have different implemented goals and the socialisation of new pupils therefore is reflected in choices of subject which contrast with those obtained from the other schools. Many of the implications of this for the sociology of knowledge have been explored by Bernstein (1971) and others.

In another question about friendship, we asked groups of 10-year-old children in a preparatory, progressive and day primary school to choose a friend to help them with certain tasks. These tasks were: to help with my arithmetic, to bat in my cricket team, to lend me money, to play a musical instrument, to cheer me up and to look after my pets. Boys in the preparatory school tended to choose a different boy for each of the tasks, saying that their choice was the best at that particular thing. In contrast, boys in the progressive and primary schools nearly always chose the same friend for everything, saying that the boy they chose was also their best friend. Such a clear distinction in the replies tells us much about the effectiveness of formal and informal socialisation in these institutions and demonstrates that at an early age the collective orientation of the pupil world and the social evaluation of others so deeply stressed in prep schools are clearly implanted in the pupils' value system.

Other more statistical approaches are possible and we have found that the process of correlating early experiences of life in residential institutions with other behaviour is both simple and profitable. In a large, boys' public school, for example, we were able to correlate the levels of homesickness when first leaving home for a boarding school with later behaviour such as academic performance, informal status among peers, attitudes to home environment and participation in the many activities offered in a public school. A group of sixty-seven new arrivals who had never boarded before were assessed for the degree of homesickness they experienced by means of replies to questionnaires set to staff and boys. Three years later, when the boys were aged about sixteen, a further questionnaire was administered to the sixty-two boys who stayed, to explore their satisfaction with school life, their participation in activities, their friendship choices and their academic progress.

Correlations between initial homesickness and behaviour assessed in the later questionnaire show clearly that boys who were the most homesick on arrival tend to achieve less academically, have fewer friends, participate less in school activities and enjoy school less than boys who were not homesick. These product moment correlations are sufficiently large as to be unlikely to have occurred by chance, as Table 10.3 shows.

TABLE 10.3    *Correlations between degrees of homesickness and later behaviour*

| | |
|---|---|
| Number of O levels passed | $-0.28*$ |
| Number of CSE subjects passed | $-0.09$ |
| Number of A levels being studied | $-0.36†$ |
| Number of close school friends | $-0.32*$ |
| Rating by staff as informal leader of age group | $-0.52†$ |
| Participation in sports | $-0.18$ |
| Participation in societies | $+0.05$ |
| Score of positions of formal status held | $-0.31*$ |
| Girl friend at home | $-0.42†$ |
| Score for involvement with home neighbourhood | $+0.08$ |
| Enjoyment of time at school | $-0.29*$ |
| Satisfaction with school life | $-0.17$ |

$N = 62$    * $p < 0.05$    † $p < 0.01$

Such correlations have to be interpreted with caution as other factors such as intelligence or family background may be intervening in these relationships. Nevertheless, this exercise shows clearly the importance of early experiences in residential institutions for subsequent behaviour of many kinds. The process of correlating these factors offers us opportunities to explore the relative importance of factors in predicting behaviour and provides practitioners with an instrument for identifying groups that may pose problems for the institution, such as early leavers or low achievers.

Despite this sophistication, however, this exercise still fails to answer many important questions. It is very difficult, for instance, to establish any factors which identify the homesick group from the remainder. Correlations between boys' background and homesickness are generally insignificant, with the exception of intelligence, showing that at the time of admission the homesick boys have no distinct features. Other research has encountered this problem. In our research into 1,150 boys in approved schools we were not able to establish any clear relationship between background and commitment to school, neither could Street *et al.* (1966) in their American study. Similarly, Clarke and Martin (1971) found difficulty in establishing the particular personality characteristics of persistent absconders from approved schools although they were able to show that absconding correlates with a failure of training.

This correlation exercise also denies the human emotions inherent in a phenomenon such as homesickness. We gain little insight from statistical measures into the nature of the problem or the ways it is experienced by individual children. Terror, sickness, depression and bewilderment are absent from such perspectives and we consequently learn little about the experience as an emotional response or the process of socialisation as a whole with its complex web of roles, rituals and controls.

Much sociological investigation has followed the path just suggested of validating hypotheses by increasingly sophisticated measurement and definition of important structural elements. Our researches are characterised by such approaches, but it is interesting how few key relationships appear and how much that is intuitive and vivid can be lost in the process. For example, the following contrasting accounts (from diaries written for us by pupils) of returning to school, one by the public school head of house and the other by children returning to the progressive school, strongly contrasts both the formal and the informal socialisation experience of new arrivals. Such material can supplement and enlarge the information gained by statistical approaches.

First our public school boy complains:

Coming back a day early is hardly exhilarating, especially to act as maiden aunt to the new boys. I hate the house when it's empty. I said goodbye to my father, dumped my gear and paid dutiful calls on Matron and neatly avoided the Chaplain, then a long chat with Mr Johnson (Housemaster) who gives me lots of breakdown on each new man—prep, family, academic and games ability—and I have their old school reports to go through when (if) I have time. Then see Grimshaw (groundsman), the pitches seem in good shape in spite of last term's bashing.
. . . My talk to the new boys seemed OK, one or two are quite perky, not quite last year's crowd of wets. However they didn't seem to grasp much and I will have to do most of it again in a week's time. I explained who people were, took the boys round the house and school to show them where things were, told them the notice board should be scanned every morning and lunch time. I dealt with fagging, making prep available, games, etc., and stressed that they should not be afraid to ask the prefects or me if they get worried. People won't be too hard on them in the first few weeks. Then I emphasised the right things to do: not to crowd people, push or hog the scene, be friendly and decent but not too keen to be everyone's ideal man. Then I left them to get to know each other.
Go back to my study which has lost its curtains—some wretched woman's inefficiency, that my fag can sort out. I make out the duty lists and read the house book—fascinating, didn't

know that Nigel had a soft spot for me! That's probably why
I'm sitting here! Then I walk down to the new boys' dormitory
and as everything seemed quiet I called on Mr Johnson for
some coffee and got a glass of beer instead—things are looking
up!

One sees here not only the formal system embodied in the house
captain orienting new boys towards orthodox goals but also guidance
towards acceptable informal behaviour, distanced relationships, concealed enthusiasms. It is also evident how successfully the interplay
between formal and informal socialisation has influenced him. Note
*Mr* Johnson for his housemaster, Grimshaw for the groundsman,
and role names for marginal figures matron and chaplain. Other
interesting features are the low emotional key and the surprise that
a previous head of house writing comments in the sacrosanct house
book should have noticed him years previously. Above all, this
extract from a boy's diary reflects a sense of care and responsibility
of boy for boy which, as we shall see, has no parallel in our progressive's arrival:

Christ, tired old trees and that field again, green and drippy,
bog roll still fluttering in the hedge from last term's final rave-
up. Citroen grounded, give Ma a hug and leave her to unpack
my junk from the back, f—k, I've left my tennis racket
behind—throw a fit in the hope I'll get a new one.
Then into school. Everyone's back! Rachel gives me a hug
and says a crowd is in her room, smell of booze, din of records.
Chris (housefather) comes in full of his India trip, transcendental
meditation is in, three hours staring at your navel, would rather
stare at Clarissa's—I couldn't stand it. Rachel's sister's there,
she's new, says nothing, which is a good thing—it takes ages to
get accepted here. Call on Hermione (housemother), she has
a crowd of new kids there, so I flee. Some prep school boy
still wearing a tie and a baby face asks me when's the first
school meeting of term. I don't know, or care, it will only
discuss what time we should go to bed, no-one will agree or
observe it.
Oh the first day back is marvellous and crazy. I don't ever
want to leave.

Such material is useful in illustrating and enlarging perspectives
gained by more systematic approaches.
One of the uses of our framework is to guide observations and to
select those topics which are relevant to a sociological comparison.
Criteria for the contrast between the two schools can be developed

so that differences in roles, goals and informal systems illuminate
the formal and informal socialisation processes in each institution.
More important, the cultural context in which socialisation takes
place is considered so the research worker can learn the values and
activities that are important in the school and can explore these
more deeply.

## Other methods useful for the study of socialisation

Of course, participant observation and questionnaires are not the
only research methods available to the sociologist. There remain
many areas relevant to socialisation into roles that cannot be
examined in depth by any of the methods we have so far outlined.
Certain areas are more complex and can best be examined by personal
discussion or interviews. Problems of change, power and conflict
are best explored in this way and such interviews add depth to the
insights gleaned from questionnaires, for example the difficulties of
role performance and negotiation. Interviewing is, of course, a
technique of its own, especially when emotive issues are being
discussed, so the situation has to be carefully planned. It is possible
to use interview material in a statistical way, but the exercise is
open to greater methodological criticisms than are questionnaire
replies.

It is also useful to construct scales which can give a greater
objectivity to the comparison of structural elements across schools,
for example in aspects of the control process, restrictions on privacy,
relationships, contact with the outside world, dress, etc., all lend
themselves to cross-school comparisons of a more objective sort.
Similarly, scales can be constructed on the provision of formal
socialisation devices which would facilitate comparison across a
range of institutions.

While this discussion of methods must remain superficial, it
provides some glimpse of the ways in which socialisation might be
explored. Yet this is still little more than sophisticated description
and much valid criticism of such sociological evidence implies that
novelists can do this far better. Iris Murdoch (1957) and Dean
Farrar (1858) lay out the role conflicts found in public schools in a
deeper way than the more abstract analysis of Gross et al. (1958)
and Banton (1965). Our analytic framework can be justified only
if it facilitates conceptualisation at a higher level, to produce more
than mere description. For example, we may ask of the prep school
we discussed earlier whether the elitist goals of preparatory and
public schools are related in any way to the distance maintained
between dormitory beds or the spiritual role of the dorm monitor,

or the distanced pastoral care of the house captain just illustrated. It is hypotheses of this kind that the framework helps us to posit and explore by research.

## The development of middle-range theory

It is impossible to understand formal and informal socialisation processes and the relationship between them unless one appreciates the wider social system of which the institution is a part. For example, much of the formal socialisation into the preparatory school appears absurd unless the wider functions and aims of the schools are understood. They view themselves as fashioning an executive and administrative class. Without knowledge of the qualities thought necessary for such a ruling élite in society—the concealed emotion, dependency on the group, a flourishing of the public self and the atrophy of the private self, the display of stability and rationality— much of the formal socialisation in preparatory schools appears extraordinary. The need for the stripping of privacy, public living and scrutiny, expressive rewards and an awareness of your own and others' authority can be understood only when the wider functions and aims of the schools are considered. Similarly, it is only when we understand the high commitment of prep-school boys to their schools' goals that many of the informal socialisation devices, such as the rigorous use of surnames, can be viewed as complementary to formal socialisation devices rather than as absurd or quaint survivals. Because state boarding schools and approved schools have not such elevated functions, it can then be seen why such elaborate procedures have not developed in these institutions.

The socialisation of new arrivals will vary, depending on the aims and functions of the institution, and one use of this analytic framework is to enable us to move from a descriptive, empirical level to an awareness of the relationships between structural elements. This is to construct what Robert Merton (1957) calls 'middle-range' theories.

But the comparative perspective is essential, and the framework does enable us to compare like with like across a range of institutions. There is indeed a danger when middle-range theory is developed from single-case studies. In the study of prisons, for example, Sykes (1958) and Giallombardo (1966) both explain the nature of the inmates' informal social system, after studying one prison, as compensating for the pain of imprisonment. A study of the informal system in a second prison might have uncovered a different state of affairs which would invalidate the earlier conclusion. It is by testing hypotheses in comparative studies, therefore, that sophistication can be built into middle-range theories.

Naturally, the approaches given in our example of preparatory and progressive schools could be much extended if we looked at a large number of other institutions, and here the analytic approach is similarly rewarding. We would find in the approved schools, for example, that much of the socialisation is allowed to take place through the informal system, particularly in social areas. But in those areas that are considered particularly important, such as the instrumental areas, many formal socialisation devices are employed. We find that approved schools also rely much more on formal control mechanisms and less upon the expectations of the informal system. Similarly, if we look at the approach of the armed forces, we find that non-commissioned entry involves isolation in reception units, the obligatory wearing of uniform and even a ritualistic return home of civilian clothes, much of which is reminiscent of the stripping process elaborated by Goffman. Often, special supervisory staff are appointed and rules and regulations suspended for new arrivals, who are kept away from other recruits.

Yet it is quite clear that goals considered significant by the authorities are either emphasised by elaborate formal socialisation procedures or achieved through manipulations of the informal system of recruits. In the Services, the expressive areas that receive greatest stress are loyalty, obedience and group solidarity, all of which depend on an informal inmate system which is granted considerable licence in the process of engendering group commitment and enforcing conformity. It is interesting that many of the feuds between various sub-units, barrack rags and raids, riotous runs ashore and initiation procedures are connived or winked at by the formal system. Unlike many schools and establishments training commissioned officers, large areas of non-commissioned behaviour are unapproached by formal socialisation procedures for recruits. Attitudes in moral and spiritual areas are less manipulated. Indeed, anyone generously endowed with moral qualities would probably reject many of the real goals of any fighting force. Hence in a Naval NAAFI, condoms happily jostle with the tins of Nescafé displayed for sale and might even be viewed as a signpost directing an esteemed social activity. Such contraceptive devices would hardly grace the tuckshop of a public school and would at least appear in plain envelopes amid the honey and yoghourt breakfasts at progressive schools. Yet if formal socialisation devices ignore the moral and spiritual ideas of Service recruits, in the area of real goals—the fashioning of an obedient, disciplined, unquestioning fighting force— the signposts employed by the formal organisation are considerable and familiar.

The different styles of residential institutions, the way in which they employ signposts to guide the new entrant and the various formal socialisation procedures can be explored more fully, but at least we have illustrated something of the theoretical use of our previous classification. This development of middle-range theory in our approach to socialisation therefore leads us to pose the following kinds of question. Do processes of socialisation vary in institutions with differing goal stresses? How far do the strength and orientation to goals of the staff's and inmates' informal systems determine the nature and effectiveness of socialisation processes? Is socialisation related to other aspects of the institutional structure, such as the role system and mechanisms of social control? In fact, can we employ this analytic framework to posit and explore more sophisticated hypotheses? When we try to establish theoretical propositions empirically, at least two paradoxes at once stand out as problematic.

Primarily, formal socialisation does not seem to be related to the stated goals of institutions, a situation which can cause the observer some surprise. It is interesting, for example, that those institutions which have to reform deviant adolescents employ fewer formal socialisation devices and give fewer signposts to behaviour than do other institutions that have a far simpler task. Public schools merely reinforce attitudes and behaviour already stressed by children's families and peer group. Yet they employ a whole range of formal socialisation devices to emphasise official goals. In the armed services, where self-selection is operating and where in the early years several formal declarations of commitment are explicit in signing for engagements, many similar formal socialisation procedures are evident. It seems that those organisations which need formal socialisation procedures least, in that they have a group of members who are familiar with and committed to a whole range of their institutional goals, employ formal socialisation procedures the most. It is where formal socialisation processes might seem most relevant, in organisations that have to resocialise deviants or involve the hostile and indifferent, that they are employed the least. It is only when one undertakes an analysis of the implemented goals of the institution that the paradox is resolved, for in approved schools reform is usually incidental to the achievement of short-term instrumental and organisational objectives. Prisons are less concerned with reform and rehabilitation than they are with good work output and a quiet life. In these cherished areas formal and informal socialisation devices are more in evidence.

A second paradox is that formal socialisation procedures can be irrelevant in influencing a new arrival's values because of the expectations operating in the world of his associates. New arrivals, both staff and inmates, in many institutions are assimilated into this informal world and soon learn the behaviour that will make them popular or unpopular with their colleagues. The pressures to conform to these informal norms may be very strong, as in the so-called progressive boarding schools where pupils' norms dictate fashions of dress despite the absence of any formal edict on uniforms. Clearly, problems will arise when the values of the formal order are not esteemed by the informal inmate world. There would, for example, be little point in the Service rituals of parades commemorating historic victories or of awarding medals and stripes if the informal values of cadets put a premium on conciliatory, non-violent behaviour. In this situation the values stressed by the informal world would conflict with formal goals and diminish organisational effectiveness.

The relationships that can exist between formal and informal worlds are very varied and in some institutions will be supportive, in others manipulative, hostile or rejecting. In many schools where the boys support a wide range of formal goals, their informal socialisation devices closely reflect those socialisation processes extensively employed by their schools' authorities. For example, public-school boys have more informal regulations governing dress, relationships and territory and more informal rituals than could ever be devised by staff organising formal socialisation devices. Indeed, the theoretical distinction that we made between formal and informal socialisation begins to dissolve when the informal values of the inmate world fully approve the school's implemented goals. Many of the formal procedures of socialisation become indistinguishable from the informal, and the more overt processes of formal socialisation that we noted in our prep-school example disappear. Here, the formal system provides opportunities for the new members to watch and then imitate the behaviour of those already socialised. In many sixth-form colleges or at senior levels in public schools, house meetings, meal-times and extra-curricular activities all provide opportunities controlled by school authorities for much of this learning to take place. At more adult levels, particularly in Oxbridge colleges and professional training establishments, the provision of an endless round of social activity achieves exactly the same thing. The stand-up gin and chatter parties of almost all middle-class institutions provide the opportunity for younger members to witness and imitate the acceptable behaviour and values of others.

Thus our analytic framework enables us to move towards and validate more sophisticated hypotheses. When the informal system of those being socialised supports formal goals there will be mirroring of formal and informal methods of socialisation and the two will become empirically indistinct. Elaborate formal socialisation will be reflected by equally elaborate informal mechanisms.

In contrast, where the informal society of inmates rejects many institutional goals, it is not possible to predict the pattern. In some of the residential institutions we have studied there will be a strict process of socialisation into an informal world which is hostile to official values and aims. In other cases this does not occur. Indeed, the inmate world does not automatically compensate for deficiencies in regimes, for repressive and cruel regimes in total institutions are often reflected by equally violent and unpleasant informal inmate societies. Far from moderating the pains of imprisonment informal societies can intensify them.

Before seeing how the framework helps us to explain further the relationship between socialisation procedures and elements of the organisational structure, it is important to stress that many of these formal socialisation procedures are functional in other ways for goal attainment in the organisation. For example, they allow the members to see clearly and to learn many of the complex roles they are expected to play in the organisation. Such processes also moderate the pains of deferred gratification by constantly reminding inmates of the inevitable rewards that finally come to committed and loyal members. Many of these devices of formal socialisation also help to split the informal world of inmates, keeping it from cohering and challenging important formal goals.

## Explanations in terms of factors other than social structures

At this point, the acute reader may suggest that we are hastening towards the trap we laid out in our earlier chapter. There is no reason why the observed paradoxes must be explained solely in terms of other structural elements. For example, it could be suggested that deviance in expressive areas is more likely than in other goal areas, as such areas involve the deeper needs of human beings such as their relationships, their need for achievement and other personal values. Hence more effort must be made by the formal system to signpost correct behaviour, both formally and by manipulation of the informal system. This is true not only of residential institutions but also of those expressive organisations which are physically fragmented, such as the clergy, craft unions or political groups. If adherence to the faith or brotherhood is to be pursued, there is a need to weld these diverse groups together by constant reminders and by many devices of formal socialisation. As the areas in which deviance is possible are wide, social control is exercised by continuously orienting members to central beliefs and by reminding them of their membership of an extensive and committed group. This is very clear in the case of minority religions or political groups. When expressive goals are associated with particular expressive roles, such as that of a school chaplain, constant formal socialisation devices are employed to counteract any opportunities that the role might provide for deviant behaviour. Interestingly, where a high degree of technical skill (an instrumental role) is combined with an expressive role, processes of formal socialisation abound, for example in teaching, in medicine and in public service. We would suggest that the more organisations become federal and expressive, the more they require extensive formal socialisation devices.

Similarly it may be equally fruitful to explore other areas for an explanation of the paradoxes we observed in the different provision of formal socialisation across institutions. It need not be related to institutional goals even in the indirect ways we have previously suggested. It will be remembered that we stressed in our theoretical introduction the constraints which are exercised on many organisations by external forces, for example by their wider functions for society or by tradition. It may be true that some of the socialising procedures found in institutions where membership is now voluntary are relics of past days when their entrants were far less willing and the institutions' functions rather different. Do some of the formal socialisation devices that survive in institutions continue to serve a purpose or are they relics of the past, when such devices may have been necessary? Do the socialisation devices that abound in the armed forces or the public schools survive from a period when the clientele was very different from that found today, unwilling, unmotivated and uncouth? The fact that the rapid disappearance of many formal socialisation techniques has not led to a reduction in the commitment of inmates, both in the Services and in schools, would support such a suggestion.

Some of the contradictions between what we might expect of formal socialisation procedures and what we find in practice may also stem from the degree of dependency of inmates on the institution. This term 'dependency' must not be confused with institutionalisation, which implies a breakdown of personality or a neurotic condition. Dependency is the degree to which the individual relies on the institution to fulfil a variety of physical, emotional, spiritual or educational needs.

Some organisations such as boarding schools and mental hospitals will try to meet all these needs in one building, while others will delegate responsibilities to other social agencies such as the family. The degree of dependency will be determined by the individual's definition of his needs and the number he sees the organisation as fulfilling. Of course it is quite possible to be more dependent on a diffuse expressive organisation such as a religious or political group than on the total institutions just mentioned. We have suggested elsewhere that the more dependent the individual, the less the need for a system of utilitarian rewards and sanctions or for institutional controls (Millham *et al.*, 1972). Individuals who are dependent respond more readily to formal socialisation, especially of the manipulative kind, than those who are not. The effectiveness of different types of control depends on many factors, one of which is the degree of dependency of the staff and inmates on the institution. Indeed, at this point the concept of socialisation can be viewed as one aspect of the whole process of social control.

There are of course many other reasons why socialisation procedures may not be related to stated goals but we cannot explore them fully here. For example, the background and training of staff may mean that those running residential institutions are unaware of many devices of socialisation that might be meaningfully employed. Alternatively, the desire on the part of staff for a quiet life in a smooth-running establishment may mean that a child's rapid acceptance by the inmate group, whatever its values, is actively encouraged. Some other organisations, such as children's homes, may model their approach on the family and, as families do not employ formal socialisation techniques, the use of such procedures is rejected. Each of these hypotheses provides an interesting and valuable area for research. But at least the reader should be aware of how far we have come, in formulating hypotheses and testing them empirically. from the simple description that opened the chapter. The usefulness of the analytic framework we presented earlier can now be seen.

## Conclusion

This paper has attempted to lay out the chief processes of socialisation evident in a wide variety of residential institutions and so to illustrate how the framework enables the concepts discussed in the previous paper to be interrelated. We would suggest that the devices used to introduce and orientate new arrivals do not differ from procedures used in less total environments. But it is clear that the extent to which residential institutions use formal socialisation devices depends largely on the goals they seek to emphasise. Expressive goals stressed in organisations which have a highly supportive long-staying membership lend themselves to prosecution by, and are dignified through, these formal socialisation procedures. Some of these processes are a clearly defined programme of initiation while others can be seen more as an interplay between the formal and informal social systems. On the other hand, organisations which stress instrumental goals that are characterised by short stay and calculative attitudes among members have few well-defined processes for formal socialisation. Their goal settings are often custodial or sheltering need cases and their membership is mostly involuntary. All this inhibits the development of the elaborate procedures found in other institutions.

However, to repeat a question asked earlier, does this middle-range theory tell us much? One of the problems is that socialisation as a sociological concept seems virtually meaningless because it embraces an introduction and response to all aspects of society. Much that happens in residential institutions is irrelevant when compared with socialisation into the wider society. Putting on a school cap is an insignificant socialising device compared with learning to read. Control by a prefect is far less awesome than the expectations of one's family. Indeed, to concentrate solely on the way in which an individual is familiarised with institutional goals leads finally to error, simply because what seems to be so contrasting at a certain theoretical level may be very similar at another. For example, progressive and public schools differ clearly in their formal and informal socialisation procedures and in their goal stresses within the institution. But while they are clearly different in such a narrow comparative context, in their wider functions for society they are identical, both fashioning for different but equally elitist positions in our society, the one bureaucratic and administrative, the other creative and expressive. While state boarding schools and even some approved schools come closer to public schools in their provision of formal socialisation devices, in their functions for society they are very different, largely fulfilling an administrative/sheltering role. A senior nautical approved school may mirror in its structure and informal socialisation devices much that would be familiar in a naval college training officers. However, the future role performance of the two groups of recruits is likely to be very different. We have therefore to decide which is the more important exercise, to view these institutions in the context of wider society or to devote ourselves to the comparative/descriptive middle-range approach that our analytic framework facilitates.

Whatever the empirical details of the socialisation a new entrant undergoes, therefore, the forces of the wider society will determine to a large extent the roles he will take up. Like all individuals, he is constrained by the pressures of the social system in which he moves. The analytic framework we have presented takes account of the external forces acting on goals such as the demands of employers, the expectations of inmates' families and economic pressures, and acknowledges the constraints imposed by the functions that institutions fulfil in the wider society. These perspectives may overwhelm the relevance of observed differences in socialisation procedures.

The approach we have offered in the previous chapter and in this brief examination of socialisation in residential institutions, therefore, enshrines all the problems of sociological theory. At one level, the concepts add sophistication to a cosy, fact-gathering empiricism while allowing at another level interrelationships to be drawn between components of the social structure. As institutions function in a wider society, however, it is also inevitable that the goals and structure of the institutions will reflect pressures imposed by other elements in the social system, and that the socialisation process will consequently be influenced by the functions and aims of the institution.

Whatever the defects, this discussion of socialisation has tried to illustrate the uses that the static concepts laid out in our first chapter can afford in research situations and the ways in which the framework can be employed at various levels of theoretical abstraction, ranging from the ordering of data to the construction of middle-range theories and generalisations about whole societies. We stressed in the first chapter that this approach was a compromise between sociological irreconcilables yet, in the research situation, such an eclectic flexibility may be its principal strength.

## References

BANTON, M. (1965) *Roles—An Introduction to the Study of Social Relations*, London: Tavistock.

BECKER, H. S. (1961) *The Boys in White: Student Culture in Medical School*, Chicago University Press.

BERNSTEIN, B. (1971) 'On the classification and framing of educational knowledge', in Young, M. F. D. (ed.), *Knowledge and Control*, London: Collier-Macmillan.

BOWLBY, J. (1951) *Maternal Care and Mental Health*, Geneva: World Health Organisation.

CARLEBACH, J. (1970) *Caring for Children in Trouble*, London: Routledge & Kegan Paul.

CLARKE, R. V. G., and MARTIN, D. N. (1971) *Absconding from Approved Schools*, London: HMSO.

COLEMAN, J. (1961) *The Adolescent Society*, Chicago: Free Press.

COTGROVE, S., and FULLER, M. (1972) 'Occupational socialization and choice: the effects of sandwich courses', *Sociology*, 6, 59–70.

248    *Spencer Millham, Roger Bullock and Paul Cherrett*

DORNBUSCH, S. (1955) 'The military academy as an assimilating unit', *Social Forces*, *33*, 316–21.

DOWSE, R. E., and HUGHES, J. (1971) 'The family, the school and the political socialization process', *Sociology*, *5*, 21–46.

EDWARDS, A. R. (1970) 'Inmate adaptations and socialization in prison', *Sociology*, *4*, 213–26.

ETZIONI, A. (1961) *A Comparative Analysis of Complex Organisations*, Chicago: Free Press.

FARRAR, D. (1858) *Eric; or, Little by Little*, Longman.

GIALLOMBARDO, R. (1966) *Society of Women*, New York: Wiley.

GOFFMAN, E. (1961) *Asylums: Essays on the Social Situation of Mental Patients and Other Inmates*, New York: Doubleday; Chicago: Aldine.

GROSS, N., MASON, W. S., and MACEACHERN, A. W. (1958) *Explorations in Role Analysis*, New York: Wiley.

HADFIELD, J. (1962) *Childhood and Adolescence*, Harmondsworth: Penguin.

HALL, C. S., and LINDZEY, G. (1957) *Theories of Personality*, New York: Wiley.

HARGREAVES, D. (1967) *Social Relations in a Secondary School*, London: Routledge & Kegan Paul.

MCCORKLE, L. W., and KORN, R. R. (1954) 'Resocialization within walls', *Annals of the American Academy of Political and Social Science*, *293*, 88–98.

MACDONALD, L. (1969) *Social Class and Delinquency*, London: Faber & Faber.

MERTON, R. K. (1957) *Social Theory and Social Structure*, Chicago: Free Press.

MILLHAM, S. L., BULLOCK, R., and CHERRETT, P. F. (1972) 'Social control in organisations', *British Journal of Sociology*, *23*, 406–21.

MILLHAM, S. L., BULLOCK, R., and CHERRETT, P. F. (1975) *After Grace— Teeth, A Comparative Study of the Residential Experience of Boys in Appoved Schools*, London: Chaucer Publishing Company.

MITCHELL, G. D. (ed.) (1968) *A Dictionary of Sociology*, London: Routledge & Kegan Paul.

MURDOCH, I. (1957) *The Sandcastle*, London: Chatto and Windus.

MUSGRAVE, P. W. (1967) 'Towards a sociological theory of occupational choice', *Sociological Review*, *15*, 32–46.

PARSONS, T. (1951) *The Social System*, Chicago: Free Press.

POLSKY, H. W. (1962) *Cottage Six, the Social System of Delinquent Boys in Residential Treatment*, New York: Russell Sage Foundation.

PUNCH, M. (1967) 'The student ritual', *New Society*, 7 December 1967.

STREET, D., VINTER, R. D., and PERROW, C. (1966), *Organisation for Treatment*, New York: Free Press.

SYKES, G. (1958) *Society of Captives*, Princeton University Press.

TUTT, N. S. (1971) 'Towards reducing absconding', *Community Schools Gazette*, *65*, 65–8.

WHEELER, S. (1961) 'Socialization in correctional communities', *American Sociological Review*, *26*, 697–712.

WINNICOTT, D. W. (1965) *The Family and Individual Development*, London: Tavistock.

# 11 A study of absconding and its implications for the residential treatment of delinquents

R. V. G. Clarke and D. N. Martin

## Introduction

In this chapter we describe some research into the problem of absconding from approved schools. The technical aspects of the work and its immediate practical applications have been dealt with elsewhere (Clarke and Martin, 1971) and the emphasis here is on the way the research developed and on its wider implications. Our approach to the problem, which was governed by assumptions of the 'internal causality' of behaviour, resulted from our training as clinical psychologists and from the prevailing ethos of the schools in which we were employed. As the research progressed we gradually abandoned this initial approach in favour of what might be called an 'environmental/learning theory' view of the problem. This came about principally because we found that variations in absconding behaviour were more a function of the nature of the school regime than of the characteristics of residents.

An important implication of our altered view, especially when set within the wider context of current theory about personality and its relation to behaviour, is that relatively short-term residential care (e.g. in approved schools) cannot be expected to achieve more than very limited success in treating delinquency. The use of residential care for the purpose of the treatment of delinquency (among the other purposes served by such care) may be unavoidable, however, at least until effective community-based treatments can be developed. At another level, the research draws attention to the value of correlational studies of school regimes and also to the difficulties as well as the advantages of being employed by the institutions which are being studied.[1]

## Approved schools and the internal causality of behaviour

Consequent upon the implementation of the Children and Young Persons Act, 1969, approved schools as a separate legal category no longer exist. They have been assimilated into a system of 'community homes', along with children's homes, reception centres, remand homes, and some other establishments formerly administered by local authorities or voluntary bodies. We shall briefly here describe the position as it existed during the period covered by the research.

At that time, the approved school order (now abolished in favour of a care order to the local authority) was the main disposal open to the courts for offenders aged between 10 and 17 (and for some children subject to civil proceedings) who were thought to need residential training. The schools provided some 9,000 places in a total of 121 establishments—88 for boys and 33 for girls. Of the boys' schools, four were regional 'classifying schools' where boys spent a few weeks after commital before being sent to an appropriate 'training school'. A number of remand homes/classifying centres performed a similar assessment and allocation service for girls.

Training schools, where children normally stayed for between one and two years, were graded according to the age of the children accommodated. Some of the schools were in modern, purpose-built house-unit accommodation, others occupied old mansions or institutional blocks. They might be located in or near large towns or cities, or deep in the heart of the country. The schools were all 'open' establishments except for three small special units for persistent absconders and very difficult boys. They varied greatly in philosophy and regime, placing different degrees of emphasis, for example, on trade-training, formal education and religious observance. Some retained a highly structured regime while others experimented with group therapy and resident self-government. Many operated some form of individualised psychiatric intervention; some attempted to make therapy continuous as part of the general milieu and routine of the school.

Nevertheless, we believe that there was a general trend for the system as a whole to operate increasingly according to a medical model of delinquency and its treatment: though the analogy does not always fit exactly (for example, the managers of approved schools did not have the freedom to select their charges that is often enjoyed by hospital consultants) the steps taken by the approved schools to treat delinquents were like those which a hospital takes in relation to its patients. The child was referred by the court (now by the social work agency), removed from his home environment and admitted. He was observed by house unit staff in the classifying school, and psychologists, psychiatrists, social workers, teachers and doctors gave their specialist opinions. A treatment plan was formulated and the child was moved to an appropriate training school. The staff of this treatment centre attempted to alleviate personality and emotional problems and develop social, educational and occupational skills. As treatment progressed, the child was gradually exposed to outside school influences. This convalescence culminated in his rehabilitation under compulsory after-care. A relapse in the shape of further offences could lead to readmission for further treatment. If, after a suitable period, the child was free from symptoms of continuing delinquency, treatment was considered to be successfully completed. While the child underwent treatment, his parents were advised by social workers who attempted to maintain family ties.

The central assumption underlying this procedure was that delinquent behaviour is a symptom or derivative of an abnormality in the child which may be innate or acquired early in life and which will tend to manifest itself whatever his circumstances. This is what Sarbin and Miller (1970) describe as an 'internal causality' theory. They trace the lineage of such theories to medieval demonism and argue that the belief that those who engage in criminal activity are driven or possessed by internal entities, forces, demons, humours, id-impulses, and so forth, has 'long been an integral part of the Judeo-Christian philosophy and tradition'. The administrators of approved schools did not believe in demons, but they did as a rule believe in personality, and the 'illness' which approved schools sought to treat was generally identified as a disturbance of personality.

Theories of personality attempt to account for the observation (which we will later question) that the behaviour of an individual is largely consistent over time and across varied situations, but different from the behaviour of other individuals. Some individuals, for instance, appear usually to behave aggressively (and attract the label 'aggressive') while others appear usually to behave timidly (and attract the label 'submissive'). Interpersonal differences and intra-personal consistencies of these kinds may be accounted for in different ways. According to *trait* theorists for example, and putting it crudely, personality is made up of a number of discrete dimensions, such as extraversion or neuroticism. An individual's personality may be described, with appropriate techniques of measurement, by locating his position in this multi-dimensional matrix. Some psychologists regard traits simply as convenient constructs, others as corresponding to real physiological variables. Psychodynamic theorists, on the other hand, believe that personality is a *state* in which psychic forces are balanced in a particular way, giving rise to characteristic patterns of motivation. The balance of forces depends on the manner of progression through a series of early developmental crises, and on the extent to which conflicts are resolved and basic needs met.

Whatever their preferred theory of personality, the staff of approved schools generally sought to explain a child's behaviour in terms of his particular personal characteristics rather than in terms of his immediate environment. Treatment, which took place in one environment so that behaviour and adjustment might be improved in another, was directed at the modification of the important personal characteristics. As newly qualified clinical psychologists we were perhaps likely to fall in with these ideas, particularly as the classifying school in which we worked allotted a central place in the assessment process to the psychologist. He was seen to be qualified to make the 'objective' assessments of personality without which no reliable treatment plans or prognoses could be formulated.

## The problem of absconding

It was against this background that absconding was proposed to us as a field for research. As approved schools were 'open' institutions, absconding had always occurred, though its frequency had been increasing steadily over a number of years.[2] It posed a problem to the schools not just because it disrupted discipline and because the staff felt it to be a rejection of themselves and the care they offered, but also because its consequences could be very serious for the boys and girls involved. Many absconders returned to their home areas where they might be harboured by relatives or friends, but others steered well clear of places where they might be recognised. This exposed them to the danger of sexual and other kinds of exploitation. The reappearance in the courts of its boys and girls for offences committed whilst absconding did little to help a school's reputation; in particular, the theft in the vicinity of the school of food, money, or transport prejudiced good relations with the local community and police—something that was clearly not in the child's interests. There was also a general belief in the schools that absconding disrupted the treatment of the child concerned ('How can you treat someone you have not got?'), though the rationalisation that absconding could be good for a child ('It enables him to work through his problems') was gaining currency, perhaps as the situation grew worse. It is undeniably true, however, that absconding was the main factor in the transfer or recommittal of boys and girls to other approved schools or to borstals. In addition, although this was not well known when the research began, there was an association between absconding during the training period and reconviction following release.

Absconding was an attractive topic for research because it was unambiguously defined and routinely recorded (thus making it possible to undertake retrospective studies) and because a great deal was known or might (in theory) be discovered about the boys and girls involved. A further advantage was that the school environment is relatively finite and its main features might be studied with relative ease. Since absconding is prohibited behaviour it seemed to have much in common with delinquency in general and therefore the research might have wide application. As we were employees of an approved school we wished to do research which could readily be seen to be of practical use and, further, we agree with the view expressed by Tizard (1972) that 'it is through a proper consideration of practical issues that social science is most likely to make theoretical advances in the present century.'

## Individual differences and absconding

Given the medical model of delinquency treatment current in approved schools, the assessment function of the classifying school in which we were employed[3] and the traditional interests of our discipline, it was not surprising that we embarked on the research hoping to identify the special personality and other distinguishing characteristics of the absconder which would enable us to predict and explain his behaviour. In the light of a proper understanding of his special problems, new measures could be taken to treat him more effectively and thereby reduce the likelihood of further absconding.

It was certainly believed by most of those whom we talked to who worked in approved schools that the absconder was of a different personality-type from other boys. This was also the dominant theme of the admittedly sparse literature, although there was remarkably little agreement as to exactly how he differed. (It was only later in the research that we began to pay more attention to another theme in the literature—that absconding is a symptom of low morale in the school and a product of its general environment.)

Concentration upon the absconder himself seemed to be justified by the early discovery that the distribution of abscondings amongst approved school boys was not random: curve-fitting techniques were employed at several stages in the research, and in the case of every sample of children to which it was applied, a *Poisson* distribution proved a poor fit to the observed frequency distribution of abscondings. Similar results in the field of accident research have given credence to the concept of accident proneness, and we regarded our results as evidence of 'absconding proneness' amongst some boys. It was also found that boys who abscond from one establishment are likely to abscond from others and that the more often they have absconded before, the more likely they are to abscond in the future. The conclusion that absconding was consistent behaviour amongst a sub-group of approved school boys was an essential condition for an explanation in terms of individual differences.

The next step was to identify the particular individual characteristics associated with absconding and we began by looking at 'hard' facts recorded in the assessment reports. Included in the studies we undertook, or in studies undertaken by others whose results were available to us, were a very large number of variables related to the boy's personal characteristics (e.g. age, height, weight, intelligence, reading age), his home background (broken home, area of residence, type of accommodation, number of siblings, criminality or mental illness in family, etc.), delinquency history (number of previous court appearances, age at first court appearance, type of current offence, previous court disposals), psychiatric history (e.g. enuresis, referral to child guidance clinic, psychiatric diagnosis), and school and work record (truancy, number of jobs held, type and number of schools attended, etc.).

Remarkably few differences were consistently found between boys who absconded and those who did not. The absconders proved to be of similar intelligence (slightly below average), to have comparable educational attainments (two to three years retarded), and to be of similar build to the non-absconders. There were no differences in home backgrounds, psychiatric histories, or school and work records. The main differences to emerge, and these were not at all marked, were that absconders tended to have appeared in court for the first time at an earlier age, and to have had more court appearances at shorter intervals of time—in other words, absconders seemed to be a little more delinquent than other boys. It was also found that older absconders ran away more frequently, although absconders on the whole were no older than other boys. As mentioned above it was already known that absconders tended to have a history of running away from some other residential placement. These findings enabled us to say with some confidence that the best (though still not good) predictors of further absconding would be details of previous absconding. The main effect of the research done so far was, however, to discount a large number of the hypotheses which could be advanced to explain why some boys in particular were likely to abscond.

Although by this time our faith in the importance of individual differences was a little shaken, we thought that the background variables studied may have been the wrong ones, though it was difficult to think of any likely ones which had been left out of account. The possibility also remained that the personal characteristics involved were independent of background factors and that a direct investigation of personality with standardised tests would be more sensitive.

Personality differences between absconders and non-absconders had been found in a number of previous studies using rating methods. In all cases, however, these could have resulted from the bias of raters who may have known which of the boys they were assessing had absconded. We decided to compare the performance of absconders and non-absconders on a number of paper-and-pencil tests which were broad in their coverage of personality variables, theoretically relevant to absconding (i.e. they were likely to be able to distinguish between more and less delinquent boys), and could be used with the population. These were the Junior Maudsley Personality Inventory, Gibson's Spiral Maze, the Jesness Inventory, Cattell's HSPQ and a version of Osgood's Semantic Differential. No differences were found on any of the tests between absconders and non-absconders. Two further studies were carried out, one (with the Junior Eysenck Personality Inventory) to see if boys of particular personality types ran away from particular schools, the other (with the Spiral Maze) to see if it made any difference if boys were tested in the training school rather than in the classifying school. The results were negative and merely confirmed the general conclusion that absconders and non-absconders were remarkably similar groups in nearly every respect but absconding behaviour itself, and that this would be very difficult to predict.

### The importance of school environment

During the course of this somewhat discouraging work on personality we had begun to examine variations in the classifying school's absconding rate to see if they could throw light on the problem. This work was greatly helped by the absconding records that this school, in common with most other approved schools, had kept for many years. The records served as a basis for the absconding and bound-breaking returns made routinely to the Home Office,[4] and included details of time of absconding, names of confederates, offences committed, date of return, place recovered, and action taken.

We soon found that there was a seasonal variation in the classifying school's absconding rate during the five years studied (1960–4), with a peak in the autumn months and a trough in the summer months. The effect was consistent and very marked and could not be explained by different kinds or different numbers of boys being in the school at different times. (There were no holiday periods at the school, and because of the pressure for places it was more or less full throughout the period studied.) It transpired that the absconding rate closely paralleled hours of darkness except during December, January and February when it dipped a little, perhaps because of very cold weather. We thought that the main reason for the association between absconding and hours of darkness was that darkness provided greater *opportunities* for boys to abscond and we have since come across numerous other examples in the literature of the significance of opportunity factors in absconding.

This was an important finding for it helped us to understand the power of the environment in producing absconding—there was about *two and a half times* as much absconding from the school in November as in June—and it made us look more carefully at what had been written about absconding and the effect of the school and wider environment. This did not amount to a great deal; the only well-supported generalisations being that the rate of absconding from training schools is high in the first few weeks after admission and is also high after holiday periods. Commentators believe that this results from the 'admission crisis', a period of unhappiness and anxiety experienced by boys recently removed, or removed once again, from their familiar home environments.

The school's routine absconding records were used again in a study of the effect of caning boys for absconding. We were asked to look at this by the senior staff in the school because of disagreement about its value. At the time caning was commonly used by the classifying school, just as by most other approved schools, as a punishment for absconding. Many staff defended its use, but a growing number were beginning to regard it as an infringement of a boy's rights and as psychologically damaging. They also felt that it did nothing to remedy the 'basic problem' responsible for absconding.

We set out to discover, first, whether boys who were caned for absconding were less likely to run away again than boys who were not and, second, whether there was less absconding from the school by *other* boys following a caning than when an absconder had not been caned. We found that boys who were not caned were more likely to run away again than boys who had been caned, but this may have been because the headmaster was less likely to cane boys who he thought would run away again anyway. The findings concerning the effect on other boys were more interesting; there was strong evidence that caning a boy for absconding reduced absconding by other boys, particularly for the older age group.

The significance we attached to these findings had not so much so do with the pros and cons of caning: many considerations other than preventing misbehaviour are relevant to a judgment about whether corporal punishment should be used. (It is interesting that despite our findings, which we believe were accepted as valid, the use of the cane in the classifying school decreased, as it did in most other approved schools.) The findings were significant because they showed that absconding can be affected by the way the school is run and because they raised the possibility that many other variables of school regime and practice might be related to absconding. Indeed, together with the findings concerning opportunity, they suggested that the school and wider environment might be much more important in absconding than the personal characteristics of the boys and girls themselves. This perspective was developed more fully after we had examined the effects of some other environmental variables.

Before going on to describe these studies, however, it should be mentioned that the findings concerning opportunity and corporal punishment have caused us considerable embarrassment. Some people working in approved schools or associated with them have criticised what they assume to be the implications, namely that we are advocating greater security and restrictiveness on the one hand, and more severe punishment on the other. This, as we hope to show later in the paper, is not the way we think the problem should be tackled.

Because of limited resources we were only able to examine the role of the environment in single schools; first in the classifying school and later in a training school for intermediate-age boys. We had also to be content with only those variables that could be quantified easily and abstracted from existing records. In spite of these limitations, a number of factors of the school and the wider environment were found to be related to absconding. In many cases we were only able to make guesses at the reasons for the relationship, and these explanations could be classified crudely into two main groups: first, there were factors which seemed to be related to absconding through their effect on the happiness and contentedness of the boys in the school and, second, there were those which seemed to mediate opportunities for absconding. It is often difficult to make this classification work, but here we are not so much concerned with the precise reason for the relationship in particular cases as with illustrating the general theoretical framework that we had begun to develop in an attempt to understand absconding.

During the investigation of seasonal variations we found a complex association between absconding and hours of bright sunshine. In months which had been either unusually sunny or dull for the time of the year, for instance when there had been a particularly sunny March or particularly dull August, absconding rates were high. We thought this could be because very dull weather might make confinement depressing, whereas very sunny weather might make the outside world and freedom especially tempting.

Boys who had not been visited recently by parents or by relatives were more likely to abscond, and it seemed reasonable to suppose that this was because they became anxious about what was going on at home, or about their own relationship with their parents. When house-units were particularly full or when unusually large numbers of boys had been recently admitted, absconding rates were disproportionately high. This might have been because housemasters were under greater pressure at these times and might not have noticed the boy who was anxious or miserable, or have had the time to help a new boy settle in the school.

On the other hand it could be that there was more absconding at these times simply because the housemasters and other staff members were not able to give adequate supervision to the boys, who consequently had more opportunities to abscond. The marked variation between days of the week in absconding (with, as we found out later, different schools having different high risk days) was difficult to explain other than in terms of daily variations in routine and practice, with corresponding variations in opportunity. Boys admitted to a school close in time to, or in the company of, a boy with a history of absconding from other institutions were more likely to abscond themselves. We thought that this was because newly-admitted boys spend time together and are thus likely to take cues from each other about how to behave.; exposure to the influence or example of a confirmed absconder is another way in which opportunity can play a part in absconding.

The importance of school environment in absconding was finally demonstrated by a study of variations in absconding rates between schools. This study was made possible by the discovery that tables of abscondings from individual schools were produced on a routine half-yearly basis for internal Home Office use, and that these could be made available to us. All approved schools which were operating under the regional allocation scheme whereby they received their intake from a comparatively local catchment area were included in the study. Junior, intermediate and senior schools were examined separately because, as we had found previously, the frequency of absconding is related to age. The range of absconding rates proved to be very considerable, some schools having rates *five or six times* greater than others catering for the same age groups. These variations between schools were relatively stable in that schools with high rates at one time were more likely to have high rates at another (see page 272). The differences could not be attributed to the characteristics of the children going to different schools; regional allocation provided a crude 'built-in' control.

Had we been employed throughout by a central organisation such as the Home Office Research Unit, it is probable that our first step would have been to examine national rates and between-school variations. Sinclair (1971) did this in his study of absconding from probation hostels, avoided detailed and unproductive studies of the residents' personalities and quickly recognised the importance of the hostel's environment. Comparisons undertaken between large numbers of institutions of the same general type have considerable methodological advantages. They make it possible, as Sinclair has shown, to study the relationship between particular treatment variables and measures of effectiveness (for example, reconviction or absconding) while holding intake constant through the use of partial correlation or regression methods.

We should have liked at this stage to have undertaken a cross-institutional study of approved school environments in relation to absconding. In particular we should have liked to have studied the effects of differing styles of management, differing treatment philosophies and corresponding variations in routine and staff-child interaction. Research of this kind might well have produced results of considerable practical value, but it was at the time beyond our resources. It became possible later to use this kind of design in clarifying the relationship between absconding and reconviction after release (Sinclair and Clarke, 1973).

## The contribution of learning

It was now becoming necessary to reconcile the view that absconding is largely under the control of school environment with our earlier findings that not all boys in a school are equally likely to abscond and that boys who run away from one residential establishment are likely to run away from others. Although these findings had been interpreted as evidence of the existence of a personality factor in absconding, they might equally have reflected a learning process. Thus it might be argued that certain boys, initially not much different from others (i.e. at the time of their first placement in a residential institution), happen to abscond in particular situations and as a result of their experiences become more likely to abscond again when they later find themselves in similar situations. In short, absconding becomes a habit.

To summarise the theory that had so far evolved: we believe that the main reason why boys (and girls) feel impelled to run away from the school is that they have met or been placed in a situation that makes them unhappy or anxious, and absconding is a way of dealing with these feelings.[5] There are a great many situations in which a boy could be made anxious; it may be because he has been bullied, because he is in trouble with the staff, because a friend has left the school, because his parents have not visited, because he has wet his bed, because he is being made to play games he is not good at, because his girl friend has broken off their relationship, or because of any one of dozens of other situations and circumstances that residential staff could well enumerate. In a school that is administered with sensitivity and skill many of these situations can be prevented, and the harmful effects of those outside the control of the school can be cushioned by action on the part of the staff.

Even in the best-run schools, however, all boys will from time to time encounter situations that make them unhappy. But not all boys run away and this is because absconding is only one of a number of competing responses to feelings of misery and anxiety. For example, a boy who is miserable may deal with his feelings by picking a fight with another boy; he may masturbate or engage in some other form of sexual activity; he may withdraw to a distant part of the grounds to cry or have a smoke; more constructively, he may share his feelings with another boy or a member of staff. Which of these competing responses he makes will depend on the variety of internal and environmental cues he experiences at the time. Important internal cues will be his experience of, or beliefs about, the consequences of the actions available to him. If he has not experienced directly comparable situations, the most influential cues may be external, and of these, the opportunities open to him to abscond (or perform a competing response) will probably be the most significant—if it is easy to run away on an occasion when he is unhappy, he will be more likely to run away than if it is difficult.

As most boys have no relevant previous experience the likelihood that they will become absconders could depend on what they happen to experience in the school. The experiences consequent upon absconding, if it occurs, will help to determine whether or not the boy will abscond again when placed in a similar position. Because previous absconding predicts more rather than less absconding, it seems likely that absconding is more often reinforced than punished. The simple relief of getting away from an anxiety-provoking situation in the school might be a sufficiently powerful reinforcement in some cases, but there are other ways in which a boy could find absconding rewarding. He may initially be welcomed at home, he may enjoy himself while away from the school, and on his return he might have some brief prestige among the other boys. The probability of repeating the behaviour could be lowered through being caught quickly, having a miserable time on the run, or even, perhaps, through being caned on return to the school. It is clear that, according to this account, some boys could through an accidental combination of circumstances develop a strong abscond ing habit while others never get to practise the behaviour at all.

In order to distinguish it from the 'internal causality' theory that we started out with, we have termed this approach to absconding an 'environmental/learning' theory. It allows for boys' heterogeneity in terms of observed absconding behaviour and for its persistence in some cases. It also allows for the unpredictability of absconding until it has occurred and requires no special reference to personality or other variables to do with an individual and his background, except for his previous experience of highly specific and relevant situations.

Although the theory fitted the facts as known and had interesting implications it could not be held confidently without testing it with fresh data. For the sake of an economical theory, we wanted to show not only that learning takes place, but also that what the boy brings to the school in terms of personality can to all intents and purposes be left out of account in considering absconding. Although we had found that the extent of previous delinquency relates to absconding, this might only be because absconders from approved schools include in their number more of those with a record of absconding from a previous placement and who are therefore likely to be among the more delinquent.[6] We saw the chance of serving two purposes in a single study by showing, through an analysis of the distribution of abscondings in the population, that boys' heterogeneity in terms of absconding reflects a continuous process of differentiation (i.e. learning), and *not* the operation of some inner predisposition (i.e. personality). If this could not be achieved, it was hoped to show in a further study that learning, or some other process, does take place whether or not individual differences also play a part.

The attempt to realise the former aim involved difficult technical problems similar to those experienced by accident researchers, and outlined in the context of criminology by Carr-Hill (1970). The object was to compare the observed frequency distribution of abscondings with theoretical distributions predicted from each of two models: the first (learning) model assumes that all boys start off with the same probability of absconding,[7] but that the probability increases as a function of the number of actual occurrences; the second (individual differences) model assumes that boys start off with varying probabilities of absconding and that the differentiation is constant and unaffected by practice. The learning model predicted a *negative binomial* distribution and the observed distribution of abscondings proved indeed also to be of this form. This was highly satisfactory except that the second model predicted an identical distribution. Various existing and some new methods for distinguishing between the two possible explanations were tried but without success (Green and Martin, 1973).

The alternative aim of showing that learning *at least* took place, was realised more successfully with a different methodology. Two groups of persistent absconders, one of 84 girls in six schools and the other of 85 boys in five schools, were studied. All subjects had absconded at least six times and the principal data were the time intervals between these abscondings; we predicted that the more frequently a boy or girl had absconded, the shorter would be the interval between recovery and the next absconding. This expectation derived from two basic laws of learning theory: that learning would increase the *probability* of absconding in a particular situation and that, through *stimulus generalisation*, absconding would occur in response to an increasingly wide range of stimuli. The operation of either law or both together should result in intervals between abscondings becoming shorter and, in fact, intervals were found to decrease as anticipated. Most learning appeared to take place as a result of earlier rather than later abscondings, the decline in intervals fitting a typical exponential 'learning' curve. No decline in intervals was evident, however, for certain sub-groups; boys and girls aged over $14\frac{1}{2}$, and those with previous absconding experience, tended to abscond at a steady but high rate. These findings were consistent with those already mentioned in relation to the effects of age and previous absconding experience, and it was argued that the learning curves of these children were being sampled closer to their asymptote and that learning had taken place elsewhere. In addition, the intervals between absconding for boys and girls at certain schools did not show a decrease, but this was anticipated on the grounds that learning (and absconding) are largely under the influence of environmental conditions, and that schools are known to provide widely differing environments. In other words, the environment in some schools brought absconding, and the reinforcements attendant on absconding, under control.

The findings of this study show that some process of continuous differentiation of absconders from non-absconders does occur, though it is not certain that it is a result of learning. It was a particularly satisfying study because valid predictions were made from theory that were not directly implied by any previously known facts about absconding. Indeed, on the grounds that absconding is generally at a peak after admission, it could have been anticipated that intervals would *increase* as function of time, whatever they did as a function of practice. It was satisfying also because we are not aware of many other successful attempts to demonstrate the utility of learning theory principles using naturalistic data of the kind available to us.

## Absconding and reconviction following release

Before going on to describe what we see as the implications of our research, we should draw attention to the findings of one final study which underlines the need to bring about a reduction in absconding. This arose out of some work undertaken by Wilkins and, like his, is concerned with the relationship between absconding and the success of approved school training. There was already ample evidence that absconding, and the offending that so often goes with it, afforded the main grounds for removing boys and girls from their approved schools and placing them in other schools or in borstals. Wilkins's evidence suggested that there was, in addition, a relationship between absconding from approved school and re-offending *after* a normal release from the school. In his unpublished prediction study of the success/failure of approved school training he found that he could not derive a satisfactory predictor of outcome by using only information available about boys before they began their period of training. But he was able to predict outcome if he included information about boys' absconding behaviour during the period they spent in the schools. Although he does not develop the argument in this fashion, and indeed may not wish to, we thought that in view of the relative dependence of absconding on school environment this fact suggested a dependent relationship of some kind between absconding and further reconviction after release. The argument is that if absconding, which is mainly a function of school environment, is associated with reconviction, then absconding itself, or something associated with it, must affect the boy so as to make him more likely to re-offend.

At the time our main report was published this was the only evidence we had that absconding increases the chances of later reconviction. Subsequently, however, one of us has had the opportunity, while working in the Home Office Research Unit, of undertaking a further study on the topic (Sinclair and Clarke, 1973). The absconding rates of sixty-six boys' schools were correlated (separately for junior, intermediate, and senior schools) with their success rates, while holding constant certain intake factors associated with success (the mean intelligence and previous court appearances of boys admitted to each school). It was found, as expected, that schools with high absconding rates also had low success rates.

This was interpreted as further evidence that absconding in some way increases the likelihood of failure after release.

A possible explanation is that many absconders commit offences while absent, which increases the subsequent probability of their offending after release, and we will return later in the chapter to this argument. One other point that should be made about the study is that although we have stated above, and believe it to be true, that the findings underline the necessity for reducing absconding, it should be recognised that the relationship between absconding and later offending is not all that powerful: if absconding from approved schools ceased forthwith it is unlikely that success rates would improve dramatically as a result; for example, absconding accounted for only about 10 per cent of the variance in the success rates of senior approved schools. It may not have been possible to demonstrate the relationship at all had we been unable to include information from so many schools in a single study.

## Strategies for reducing absconding

We had undertaken the research in the hope that it would be possible to make practical suggestions about how absconding should be reduced and in this respect we took the findings to be grounds for optimism.[8] Had it been found that absconding was deeply rooted in personality, rather than the product of school environment, it might have been difficult to make useful recommendations: we might have suggested that psychiatric services should be intensified, but psychiatrists working in the schools (e.g. Walker, 1968) as well as others, have expressed considerable doubts about the practicability of undertaking psychotherapy with the boys. Efforts made to modify the school environment to reduce absconding might meet with more success than attempts to alter boys' 'personalities'. The other side of the coin is, of course, that the schools and the staff working in them are now faced squarely with the responsibility for absconding. In our view it is no longer credible to blame high levels of absconding on the 'disturbed' personalities of the boys admitted.

We considered separately measures for reducing occasional or casual absconding and those for the management of persistent absconding. In dealing with the former, we urged schools to consider ways of reducing the often fortuitous stresses and anxieties that lead boys and girls to want to run away, and it was here that we most felt the lack of comparative studies of approved school environments.[9] We were able to make some specific suggestions for smoothing the admission crisis, for making holidays fit the needs of the boys rather than those of the institution, and for helping parents keep in contact with their children. But we were in no position to make general statements about the kind of regimes that seemed to be associated with low rates of absconding or about the ways in which staff could best manage and relate to the boys and girls in their care. Sinclair (1971) has shown that absconding from probation hostels is largely determined by the way the warden manages the boys. Wardens who were kind but strict in their dealings with the boys, and who were in agreement with their wives about the way the hostel should be run, had the lowest absconding rates. Findings such as these, which underline the importance of staff behaviour, can inform those responsible for training and for making appointments.

A further taste of the kind of information we might have been able to produce had it been possible to undertake comparative studies has been given by the work of Anne Dunlop (1975). She examined the regimes in eight intermediate approved schools and found that the schools which appeared to the boys to emphasise trade-training and responsible behaviour tended to have low absconding and high success rates.

Apart from reducing the motivation to abscond, we thought it important for schools to consider carefully what opportunities their routines afford for absconding: a great deal of casual, but nevertheless harmful, absconding could be prevented if only schools became more security-conscious. In our experience, such suggestions are strongly resisted by staff who take pride in the open traditions of the schools. We believe, however, that measures such as the locking of some strategic doors at night, the reduction of exit points from the school grounds, and the proper supervision of boys when the risk of absconding is high (as on dark autumn evenings) could do much to reduce absconding without prejudicing the essentially open character of the schools.

The main strategy for dealing with persistent or, as we prefer it, 'habitual' absconding in the approved school system was to remove the boy concerned to one of the three special (closed) units, which provided a total of 80 places (enough for about 1 per cent of the population). This measure was usually delayed until the boy had shown himself unable to adjust to at least two open training schools. Such a procedure would be justifiable in terms of an 'internal causality' model of absconding, on the grounds that a boy is no more of a persistent absconder at this stage than he ever was but having been identified as such, he can be given the 'intensive care' he has always needed.

We would argue, on the basis of the environmental/learning model of absconding, that the intervention was coming too late and that the child had been allowed to become a serious problem when this might have been avoided. Although special units have been successful in containing boys they do not appear to have had much effect on their behaviour after release. This is not surprising if the experience of absconding has in some way already raised the chances of a boy behaving delinquently in the future. Where children are progressively acquiring a behaviour pattern which is undesirable, early intervention in the way of prevention is a better strategy than a belated attempt at 'cure'. Security should be used with children who are beginning to acquire the absconding habit, or who can be identified as potential absconders on the grounds of previous absconding from other establishments. (It was established in our research that boys who absconded more than once at the assessment stage were quite likely to abscond persistently from training schools.) Early experience of security could encourage the selection and reinforcement of more constructive responses to stress, such as confiding in staff, and could prevent absconding during the period of high risk which follows admission.

In the technical report of the research, we advocated the progression of children through secure to open conditions and the gradation of security in some ordinary training schools. A great deal of money is presently spent on special units for children who have failed to respond elsewhere, and any further sums might be better spent in supporting the less specialised establishments.

## An alternative view of behaviour

The research set out to find solutions to an operational problem within the approved school system, but the results raise wider questions about the appropriateness of attempting to 'treat' delinquency on a residential basis and, in this sense, the results do not generate quite as much optimism. If absconding is largely under the control of the school environment, rather than a sign of underlying personality structure, could this not apply to other aspects of behaviour in the schools? Is behaviour in general, and delinquent behaviour in particular, more under the control of the environment in which it occurs than much current psychological (in contrast to sociological) theory would hold? If so, is it appropriate to deal with delinquency on the basis of a medical model which assumes that behaviour which occurs in one environment can be successfully treated in another?

Mischel (1968) took up where Vernon (1964) left off and, in an extensive review of research, roundly attacked the 'trait/state' approach to personality. According to traditional personality theory, behaviour should generally be consistent across situations and stable over time. He claims that there is very little evidence that it is either, and that dynamic theorists have not argued a convincing case that superficial inconsistencies in behaviour may conceal underlying motivational consistency. Low but significant coefficients of situational consistency and temporal stability are usually interpreted as evidence of enduring dispositions, but Mischel argues that the important thing about such coefficients is that they account for only a tiny proportion of behavioural variance and are thus evidence of the relative unimportance of generalised personality variables. Low correlations in personality research are often attributed to errors of measurement; Mischel argues that this is accounting for instability with instability and that as measurement has developed, so the grounds for questioning the existence of enduring traits and states has become firmer.

He suggests that beliefs about the consistency of personality may be maintained in part by physical consistencies in the person's appearance, speech and movements, and by regularity in his environmental contexts. The clinician perseveres in making unrealistic claims for his insight or tests because clients congratulate him on his perceptiveness whatever he tells them about themselves (Ulrick, Stachnick and Stainton, 1963). Mischel concludes that 'with the possible exception of intelligence, highly generalised behavioural consistencies have not been demonstrated and the concept of personality traits as broad response predispositions is thus untenable'. Vernon earlier reached a similar conclusion: 'the real trouble is that (the trait/factor approach) has not worked well enough, and despite the huge volume of research it has stimulated it seems to lead to a dead end'.

Mischel offers a social learning account of behaviour as an alternative and shows that it can accommodate the findings from research. Social learning theory differs fundamentally from 'trait' and 'state' theory in its view of the determinants of behaviour. Trait and state theories look for stable response predispositions in individuals as the generalised and enduring causes of their behaviour. Social learning theory seeks the determinants of behaviour in the environmental conditions that co-vary with the occurrence, maintenance and change of the behaviour. While trait and state theories search for lawfulness in the shape of consistency of behaviour across situations, social learning theory seeks order and regularity in the form of general propositions which relate environmental changes to behaviour changes; the new question is how experience changes and regulates behaviour. In attempting to deal with this, Mischel describes three social learning paradigms: observational learning, classical conditioning and response-contingent reinforcement. He shows how the laws of contiguity, generalisation, discrimination and reinforcement lead to an account of behaviour which is consistent with its non-generality; behaviour is seen to depend on the exact stimulus conditions in the evoking situation and on the individual's previous experience of similar situations.

Social learning theory leads to a quite different approach to assessment and behaviour change. Assessment requires measurement of the conditions which give rise to and maintain a person's behaviour rather than the making of inferences about his attributes. Treatment aims to modify the consequences of behaviour and the emotion-arousing properties of stimuli rather than attempting to change the responding individual himself. Just as efficiency in prediction is greatest when the predictive behaviour is most similar to the criterion behaviour, so 'therapeutic transfer is best when the treatment situation most closely overlaps with the life situation in which change is desired'.

The validity of this has been shown in an important series of researches into the effectiveness of hospitalisation in the treatment of mental illness (Fairweather, see p. 290, Mischel). The patients who remained out of hospital longest were those who had the greatest support in the community. Post-discharge behaviour could not be predicted from adjustment to the demands of work and ward-living within the hospital, but correlated well with variables in the outside environment. Treatment worked well within the hospital but the arm of the doctor was short: when the environment changed, so did behaviour.

## The effectiveness of approved schools

Fairweather's findings and Mischel's critique give a good deal of substance to our own misgivings about the 'treatment' role of approved schools. If the school can so readily, as the research on absconding suggests, condition the behaviour of the resident, and if any enduring personality characteristics have such a limited effect, it would seem reasonable to expect that the environment to which the child is released will have an equally ready impact. According to the theory of response and stimulus generalisation, this impact is only likely to begin to be challenged if the actual behaviours requiring modification are treated directly in the schools, and if the treatment environment can be made to resemble in important respects the environment in which the newly acquired behaviours are to be practised and enacted.

In common with other similar treatments, there is in fact little evidence that approved schools did influence the delinquency of children after they left (and delinquency is pretty well the only post-release behaviour that has been studied). In *The Sentence of the Court* (Home Office, 1969) the success rates of various measures open to the courts were compared with predicted rates calculated on the basis of intake variables which are known to be important. Approved schools show no gain over other measures and even fall short of expectation. The best predictor of post-treatment behaviour in general is pre-treatment behaviour, and not the type of treatment applied. Our findings of an association between absconding and later reconviction, and those of Dunlop who found that schools with an emphasis on trade training and responsible behaviour were those with higher success are, we believe, the only reasonably sound evidence of some lasting (though perhaps not very powerful) behavioural effect of approved school training.

The most probable explanation of our finding of a relationship between absconding and reconviction is that boys frequently commit offences while absent from the school. Because these are offences committed in the community, the conditions for response and stimulus generalisation are met: if an offence committed during an absconding is positively reinforced so the chances of re-offending after release are increased. Figure 11.1 illustrates the way in which we think absconding arises and how it raises the probability of re-offending after release.

This explanation of an apparent effect of approved school training may also apply to Dunlop's results because, apart from being more successful in terms of reconviction rates, schools with an emphasis on trade training and responsible behaviour tended also to produce less absconding. One difficulty with this position is that Sinclair (1971) has found that lads who abscond from probation hostels and who are not known to have committed offences, are no less likely to be reconvicted subsequently than those who absconded and did commit offences. If the lads in Sinclair's sample who were not known to have committed offences really *did* commit fewer offences while absconding, and if similar evidence were forthcoming for approved school boys, then this could create real difficulties for our position. It would then be necessary to argue that absconding is functionally equivalent to other forms of delinquency for the boys and that the performance of one behaviour raises the probability of the other. We hope this will not prove necessary since it would involve postulating a highly generalised predisposition to behave in a delinquent fashion, which is the kind of concept we have not found useful in our own research and which, on a broader front, has been rejected by Mischel.

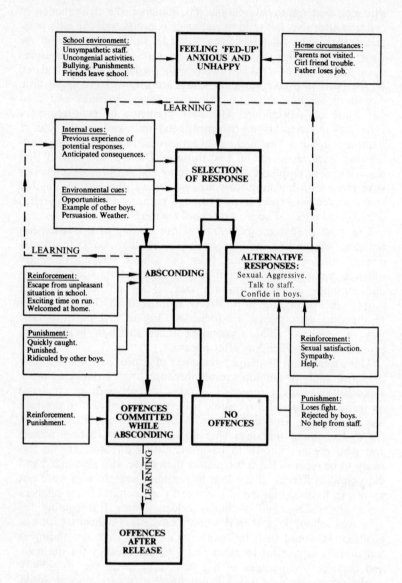

FIGURE 11.1    *The development of absconding and its relationship with offending after release (an environmental/learning theory)*

## The future of institutional treatment

Our analysis of the way in which absconding contributes to reconviction, if correct, underlines the principle that schools, and other agencies with similar treatment aims, must operate directly on those behaviours (or their closest analogues) that they wish to change. Trying to stop a boy being delinquent by changing his personality or his attitudes will not succeed if his delinquent behaviour is unchecked or unmodified. But it is not possible to deal directly with most forms of delinquency in an institutional setting, simply because they cannot manifest themselves—they depend for their occurrence upon unrestricted movement in the environment of daily life.

For this reason we believe that in dealing with delinquency the emphasis should be shifted to the modification of the social and economic conditions in the community which establish and maintain delinquent behaviour, or at least to more intensive work in the families, schools, and work-places of offenders. The focus of action should be shifted from the individual to his environment. We thus seem to have reached a position, by a somewhat different route, that is held by many deviancy sociologists, and one that is also in tune with much official thinking: paragraph 189 of the Seebohm Committee report expresses the conviction that 'children must ... be helped in the contexts of their families (if they have them), the communities in which they live and to which they will return, and the schools they attend'. Jehu *et al.* (1972) has provided some pointers to the way in which social workers might help the delinquent using methods based on social learning theory, and a recent publication edited by Stumphauzer (1973) reports recent American attempts to apply behaviour therapy to delinquents in the community.

How consistent is this analysis of the kind of treatment role appropriate for approved schools with what is likely to happen? The schools have recently become part of the community homes system. Although at one time they were seen as being likely to integrate completely, in that their role in the new system would be indistinguishable from that of the former children's homes, it now seems that in most regions of the country they will retain a particular identity. They will still be seen as providing the most appropriate environment for children who come into care because of serious behaviour problems.

Undeniably the schools can serve a valuable *caring and containment* role for such children, particularly when at the present time the measures that we favour for direct intervention with children in their home environments are a long way from being implemented on the necessary scale. Moreover, such measures may not always be relevant to a child's particular problems. Also it should not be

TABLE 11.1  Absconding rates* during 1964 and 1966 for all boys' training schools operating under regional allocation

| Senior schools | Absconding rate 1964 | Absconding rate 1966 | Intermediate schools | Absconding rate 1964 | Absconding rate 1966 | Junior schools | Absconding rate 1964 | Absconding rate 1966 |
|---|---|---|---|---|---|---|---|---|
| School | 1964 | 1966 | School | 1964 | 1966 | School | 1964 | 1966 |
| 1 | 10 | 10 | 1 | 3 | 10 | 1 | 0 | 0 |
| 2 | 13 | 38 | 2 | 4 | 8 | 2 | 0 | 4 |
| 3 | 14 | 14 | 3 | 7 | 10 | 3 | 0 | 4 |
| 4 | 21 | 18 | 4 | 10 | 9 | 4 | 0 | 5 |
| 5 | 21 | 23 | 5 | 11 | 17 | 5 | 1 | 22 |
| 6 | 22 | 14 | 6 | 11 | 25 | 6 | 2 | 1 |
| 7 | 22 | 21 | 7 | 12 | 11 | 7 | 2 | 3 |
| 8 | 24 | 29 | 8 | 12 | 13 | 8 | 2 | 5 |
| 9 | 25 | 33 | 9 | 16 | 36 | 9 | 9 | 5 |
| 10 | 26 | 37 | 10 | 16 | 47 | 10 | 9 | 11 |
| 11 | 27 | 25 | 11 | 19 | 18 | 11 | 11 | 15 |
| 12 | 28 | 47 | 12 | 19 | 23 | 12 | 12 | 18 |
| 13 | 29 | 45 | 13 | 22 | 50 | 13 | 12 | 44 |
| 14 | 32 | 43 | 14 | 23 | 21 | 14 | 16 | 25 |
| 15 | 34 | 26 | 15 | 23 | 22 | 15 | 17 | 4 |
| 16 | 46 | 27 | 16 | 24 | 28 | 16 | 19 | 2 |
| 17 | 75 | 59 | 17 | 26 | 14 | 17 | 20 | 22 |
|  |  |  | 18 | 32 | 21 | 18 | 24 | 15 |
|  |  |  | 19 | 32 | 37 | 19 | 29 | 5 |
|  |  |  | 20 | 34 | 39 | 20 | 36 | 18 |
|  |  |  | 21 | 35 | 30 |  |  |  |
|  |  |  | 22 | 47 | 17 |  |  |  |
| Average | 27·6 | 29·9 | Average | 19·9 | 23·0 | Average | 11·1 | 11·4 |

Correlations (Spearman's coefficient) between 1964 and 1966 rates:
Senior schools = 0·65 (p < 0·01)     Intermediate schools = 0·56 (p < 0·01)     Junior schools = 0·43 (p < 0·10 > 0·05)

* Number of boys absconding in each year expressed as a proportion of the daily average population.

forgotten that in most cases when a child is removed from home, a range of less drastic measures will already have been tried and failed with him. Removal of a difficult child from his home can in some cases make the family's other intractable problems more capable of a solution. Placing him in a former approved school may ensure that he obtains the basic education and training in work habits that he might otherwise never receive. It can also afford the community some relief from the delinquencies of children at an age when they are most active and, most importantly in our view, it can protect the children, especially the girls, from the often serious consequences of their own behaviour. This could be better done, however, if absconding from the schools were to be reduced and, as far as other matters are concerned, the benefits of a spell in a former approved school would sometimes be better capitalised upon if there were more intensive and active after-care.

How far the schools will still be seen, or will continue to see themselves, as having a longer-term *treatment* function is not yet known. If there were greater recognition of the limited part residential measures can play in the treatment of delinquency, or of other maladaptive social behaviours, perhaps fewer children would be made subject to them. It is probable, however, that most schools will retain treatment ambitions (cf. May, 1971) though a less central position will be allocated to the 'symptom' of delinquency (cf. Home Office, 1970). Instead, there will be more talk of helping boys and girls to develop into contented, fulfilled citizens and sensitive, sympathetic parents—though how this is to be achieved without dealing directly with delinquency is not clear. What is certain is that a great deal more thought needs to be given to the objectives served by residential child care and how best to meet them.

# References

CARR-HILL, R. (1970) 'Victims of our typologies', in *The Violent Offender, Reality or Illusion?*, Oxford Penal Research Unit.

CLARKE, R. V. G., and MARTIN, D. N. (1971) *Absconding from Approved Schools*, London: HMSO.

DUNLOP, A. B. (1975) *The Approved School Experience*, London: HMSO.

GREEN, J. R., and MARTIN, D. N. (1973) 'Absconding from approved schools as learned behaviour: a statistical study', *Journal of Research in Crime and Delinquency*, 10, 73–86.

HOME OFFICE (1969) *The Sentence of the Court*, London: HMSO.

HOME OFFICE (1970) *Care and Treatment in a Planned Environment*, London: HMSO.

JEHU, D., *et al.* (1972) *Behaviour Modification in Social Work*, London: Wiley–Interscience.

MAY, D. (1971) 'Delinquency control and the treatment model: some implications of recent legislation', *British Journal of Criminology*, *11*, 359–70.

MISCHEL, W. (1968) *Personality and Assessment*, New York: Wiley.

SARBIN, T. R., and MILLER, J. E. (1970) 'Demonism revisited: the XYY chromosomal anomaly', *Issues in Criminology*, *5*, 195–207.

SINCLAIR, I. A. C. (1971) *Hostels for Probationers*, London: HMSO.

SINCLAIR, I. A. C., and CLARKE, R. V. G. (1973) 'Acting-out and its significance for the residential treatment of delinquents', *Journal of Child Psychology and Psychiatry*, *14*, 283–91.

STUMPHAUZER, J. S. (ed.) (1973) *Behaviour Therapy with Delinquents*, Springfield, Ill: Chas. C. Thomas.

TIZARD, J. (1972) 'Research into services for the mentally handicapped: science and policy issues', President's Address to the Midland Society for the Study of Mental Subnormality.

ULRICK, R. E., STACHNICK, T. J., and STAINTON, S. R. (1963) 'Student acceptance of generalised personality interpretations', *Psychological Reports*, *13*, 831–34.

VERNON, P. E. (1964) *Personality Assessment: A Critical Survey*, New York: Wiley.

WALKER, L. W. (1968) 'The limits of therapeutic methods in Approved Schools', in Sparks, R. F., and Hood, R. G. (eds), *The Residential Treatment of Disturbed and Delinquent Boys*, Institute of Criminology, Cambridge.

# Notes

## Chapter 2   Residential care of children—a general view

1 In 1967, 15 per cent of boarders at recognised independent schools and 40 per cent of boarders at direct grant schools received financial assistance towards the costs from public funds, 51 per cent and 40 per cent of these respectively being helped by local authorities, the rest being helped directly from central government (these figures exclude handicapped children maintained by education authorities at independent schools wholly or mainly for handicapped pupils). Local authorities give help because parents live abroad or are liable to frequent moves; because a child has a special aptitude; or because home conditions are 'seriously prejudicial to the normal development of the child'. Central government normally gives help to parents who are employees living abroad. Thus, apart from potentially rather unsettling home circumstances, few children receiving assistance at non-maintained boarding schools are liable to be either deprived or impaired (Public Schools Commission, 1968a).

2 E.g. the effects of the 1969 Children and Young Persons Act on regional planning, and the greater involvement of voluntary bodies in this process; the establishment of social service departments which has brought local authority mental handicap provision under the same umbrella as child care provision; and the government White Paper *Better Services for the Mentally Handicapped* which calls for collaboration between local authorities and regional hospital boards in developing plans for their areas.

3 For instance a strong case has been made out for the greater involvement of boarding education in the care of 'deprived' children at present in the care of social service departments in children's homes and foster homes (Woolfe, 1968).

4 These twelve categories are not comprehensive. Among the types of provision not covered in the remainder of this chapter are: non-psychiatric hospitals; mental illness hospitals and units; junior detention centres; and mother-and-baby homes.

5 Non-responding units, direct grant and independent schools and hospital provision for mentally handicapped children are not included in the census information described below unless specifically mentioned.

6 This figure is in fact a considerable underestimate, since it does not include the hundreds of trusts, private proprietors, religious orders, etc., responsible for the 973 independent schools for non-handicapped pupils.

7 What size constitutes a community in these terms is a moot point and clearly no one population figure will be applicable to all areas. Following the guidelines in the Seebohm Report (1968), social service departments which aim to be community-based often take

50,000 as a minimum basis for area offices. But even this may be too large, and an area of about 10,000 similar to that served by a local secondary school, is probably more relevant to most people. Taking a national average, a catchment area of 50,000 would need to supply about 100 beds just to cover existing provision, excluding independent schools for non-handicapped children and non-psychiatric hospitals.

8 These regions are those used for establishing regional planning committees under the provisions of the 1969 Children and Young Persons Act, i.e. North; Yorkshire; North West; West Midlands; East Midlands; East Anglia; Home Counties (North); London; South East; Wessex; South West. The overall figures include direct grant schools, hospital provision for mentally handicapped children and non-responding census units, but exclude independent schools.

9 Provision in independent schools for non-handicapped people is not included in all these examples; if it had been included, it would have mostly tended to accentuate the differences.

10 The study included direct grant schools, hospital provision for mentally handicapped children and non-responding census units, but not independent schools for non-handicapped children.

11 The bed and children data are not wholly compatible for children's homes and mental handicap provision. For children's homes, supply covers all local authority and voluntary units, but demand does not include some 5,000 children in voluntary agency care as opposed to local authority care. For mental handicap provision, supply covers local authority, voluntary, private and hospital provision and need includes only children in hospital board care who constitute approximately 85 per cent of the total in mental handicap provision.

12 The inclusion of mental subnormality hospitals, direct grant schools and independent schools for this item would have made these proportions very much higher. This would also have been the case had units for which no census returns were received been included, since the lowest response rates were for various categories of residential schools.

13 This excludes senior staff with the declaration of recognition of experience.

## Chapter 3    Quality of residential care for retarded children

1 It is, however, not simply the gravity of the handicaps which makes this likely: the poor quality and the inadequacy of much of our provision for retarded children who live at home and for their families adds greatly to the families' difficulty in coping with them. Moreover, the fact that society legitimises the placing of handicapped children in institutional care by calling the institutions 'hospitals'—though there is no long-term treatment in a medical sense for most

of the handicaps the children suffer from—weakens the parents' natural resolve not to part with their children: except for their own good of course.

2 These findings have, however, been disputed by Kushlick who argues that the mental subnormality hospitals were in fact much worse off for staff than the hostels. Kushlick's criticisms have been answered—to our satisfaction though not to Kushlick's—by King (1973).

3 As mentioned below the terms *accept* and *reject* were operationally defined and could be reliably measured.

## Chapter 4  Organisation and change in children's institutions

1 'Senior staff' were headmasters and deputies. Senior assistants were not included in this category, as they also fulfil teaching or 'house' duties which give them a different order of contact with the boys. The term 'lower level' staff in this paper refers to teachers, instructors and 'house' staff.

## Chapter 5  Varieties of residential nursery experience

1 This study is now available, Tizard and Rees (1975).

## Chapter 6  The influence of wardens and matrons on probation hostels: a study of a quasi-family institution

1 A point of interest is the persistence of these differences. About 50 per cent of the successes (boys who left because their period of residence had expired) were reconvicted within two years of leaving. With the exception of one regime there were no differences among these 'old boy' reconviction rates. Boys entering high failure rate regimes, however, had a much higher chance of reconviction within three years of arrival in the hostel, since so many of them were reconvicted in the first year. An example may make this clear. If 100 boys enter a regime with a first-year reconviction rate of 60 per cent, 60 of them would be reconvicted in that year, and 20 (50 per cent of the remaining 40) in the following two years, giving a three-year reconviction rate of 80 per cent. The comparable figures for a regime reconviction rate of 20 per cent would be 20, 40, and 60 per cent. In one sense, therefore the differences are persistent, in another sense not.

2 This is a point of some importance to the study of delinquency in general. The effect of the warden on his charges cannot be explained in terms of heredity or his early handling of them, nor are differences in delinquency rates between hostels attributable to differences in police practice. This makes it unlikely that similar explanations could account for all the associations between unsatisfactory families and delinquency.

3 A regime was included if the expected number was $\geqslant 5$ in each

cell of a 2 × 2 table. Fourteen of the forty-six regimes did not meet this condition.

4 For a rather similar analysis of hostels for ex-prisoners see Sinclair and Snow (1971).

5 A particular problem here is that those who make good front-line residential staff would not necessarily be efficient higher in the hierarchy. This factor tends to produce low turnover. Most techniques for increasing recruitment are likely to result in the appointment of more ambitious men, whose turnover will be greater. In this way, efforts to control the small family institution will tend inevitably to bureaucratise it and turn it into something else. This dilemma applies to other suggested solutions.

### Chapter 7    Measurement of treatment potential: its rationale, method and some results in Canada

1 Mr Grossman was the first recipient of the honorary doctorate in criminology, conferred on him in 1971 by the University of Ottawa for his support of research and for his outstanding contribution to social policy based on research.

### Chapter 8    The measurement of staff-child interaction in three units for autistic children

1 A profound and general failure to develop interpersonal relationships, a delay in language development together with abnormal usage when speech develops, and the presence of ritualistic or compulsive phenomena.

2 We are most grateful for the assistance of Drs L. Bartlet and S. Wolkind in assessing inter-rater reliability.

### Chapter 11    A study of absconding and its implications for the residential treatment of delinquents

1 We were both employed by Kingswood Classifying School, an approved school, at the outset of the research—R. Clarke as research worker, D. Martin as educational psychologist.

2 The official statistics distinguished between unauthorised absences which resulted in the boy or girl being returned to the school before midnight on the day of running away, which were known as 'boundbreakings', and those which did not, which were known as 'abscondings'. In fact most of those who ran away were returned to their schools within a day or two and we did not follow official practice but called all unauthorised absences 'abscondings'. Following our usage, there were 2,682 abscondings from boys approved schools in 1956 (when records were first kept), 5,066 in 1965 (when the research began), and 11,557 in 1971 (the latest year for which, at the time of writing, figures were available). The number of boys accommodated in the schools has been relatively constant over this time. At the time of the research about 40 per cent of boys and

60 per cent of girls absconded at least once from approved schools. We estimated on the basis of various criteria that it would be legitimate to regard about 5 per cent of boys and 10 per cent of girls as persistent absconders.

3 If we had not been employed in the schools we may not so readily have fallen in with the assumptions on which they operated; it was certainly easier to extricate ourselves from this perspective once we had left their employment. In spite of this, we feel there were real advantages to undertaking research as a member of staff. It makes it easier to gain acceptance and help from other staff and, as indicated in the text, it also imposes the valuable discipline of having constantly to justify the research in terms of its practical payoff.

4 It seems unlikely that community homes will keep absconding records as a matter of practice, which from the point of view of research at least will be a serious loss.

5 When asked why he has run away a boy will very often say that it was because he was 'fed up' or 'chokka' or whatever other synonym is current for expressing feelings of disgruntlement. Some commentators believe that absconding can be motivated by a desire for excitement. There may be something in this, but quite often excitement is desired in order to displace some pressing anxiety.

6 We are not especially anxious, except in the interests of parsimony, to discount the possibility that some personality correlates of absconding from approved schools will be found. Indeed, as we show, it might be necessary to postulate the existence of a generalised disposition to behave in a delinquent fashion in order to account for the relation between absconding and later offending. We believe, however, that the relationship of any such variables to absconding will be weak compared with the strength of the relationships between absconding and many environmental factors.

7 Boys with a previous record of absconding were not included in this study. It was in the course of the study that the effects, which are discussed in the text, of rate of admission on absconding and of being admitted in the company of a known absconder, came to light.

8 The suggestions are no less relevant now that the approved schools have been assimilated into the community homes system; absconding will still be a problem.

9 As mentioned in the text, however, most residential staff know very well the kinds of circumstances and incidents that result in boys and girls becoming miserable and anxious.

# Index

staff stability—*cont.*
 in probation hostels 124
 in residential nurseries 108, 109,
  115
staff support 77, 85–6, 94–5
staff talk in residential nurseries
 111
staff training 2, 11, 12, 13, 62–3,
 67, 109, 113, 138–9
 effect of on patterns of care
  63–4
 in mental subnormality units
  62–4, 67
 in probation hostels 138–9
 relationship to role performance 63–4
 in residential nurseries 109, 113
staffing patterns 5, 10–13, 40–3;
 *see also* staff/child ratios
status of inmates 217
steampress model 3, 4, 5, 10, 11,
 12
stimulation levels 103
stress (in staff) 138–40
subnormal children
 behaviour of 65–6
 in hospitals 6, 25, 52–68; *see
  also* subnormality hospitals
 in hostels 6, 38, 52–68; *see also*
  subnormality hostels
 institutional care of 52–68
 numbers in institutional care 6,
  27, 53, 54
 places for in GLC area 30
 quality of care for 52–68
subnormality hospitals 7, 10, 11,
 52–68
 numbers of children in 53, 54
subnormality hostels 7, 11, 52–68
 numbers of children in 53, 54
subnormality institutions 6, 7, 10,
 11, 13, 17, 25, 27, 30, 38, 52–68
 autonomy in 61–2
 child management practices in
  56–8, 178
 child orientation in 56, 58
 comparisons between 52–68
 effects of care on children 64

institution orientation in 56, 58
organisational structure of 52,
 55, 65–6
patterns of care in 56–8
staff activities in 57–62
staff/child interaction in 56, 57,
 59
staff ratios in 58–9
staff roles in 52, 59–61, 62–4
staff training in 62–4, 67

teacher/pupil interaction 73–4,
 175–80; *see also* staff/child
 interaction, staff/inmate interdependence
teacher/pupil interaction assessment techniques 175–80
teachers' roles *see* staff roles
teaching goals, assessment of
 175–6
teaching skills, assessment of
 175–6
time sampling 179
toileting 181
total institutions 3, 39–40, 56, 88,
 122, 203, 211, 222, 227, 243
 Goffman's definition of 4
trade training 265, 269
training centres 141–70; *see also*
 borstals
 behaviour ratings in 143, 144,
  147–50, 162, 165
 measurement of treatment
  potential in 141–70
 recidivism in 154, 156–8
 social adjustment of inmates
  154–6
 sociometric status in 144, 145,
  162, 166
 staff/inmate interaction in
  142–3, 151–2
 staff/pupil ratios in 161
training schools 141–70; *see also*
 approved schools
 behaviour ratings in 143, 144,
  147–50, 162, 165